French-Canadian Theater

Twayne's World Authors Series
French-Canadian Literature

David O'Connell, Editor
University of Illinois

TWAS 774

French-Canadian Theater

By Jonathan M. Weiss

Colby College

Twayne Publishers • Boston

French-Canadian Theater

Jonathan M. Weiss

Copyright © 1986 by G. K. Hall & Co.
All Rights Reserved
Published by Twayne Publishers
A Division of G. K. Hall & Co.
70 Lincoln Street
Boston, Massachusetts 02111

Copyediting supervised by Lewis DeSimone
Book production by Elizabeth Todesco
Book design by Barbara Anderson

Typeset in 11 pt. Garamond
by Modern Graphics, Inc., Weymouth, Massachusetts

Printed on permanent/durable acid-free paper
and bound in the United States of America.

Library of Congress Cataloging in Publication Data

Weiss, Jonathan M.
　French-Canadian theater.

　(Twayne's world authors series; TWAS 774.
French-Canadian literature)
　Bibliography: p. 173
　Includes index.
　1. French-Canadian drama—History and criticism.
　2. Theater—Québec (Province)—History.　I. Title.
　II. Series: Twayne's world authors series; TWAS 774.
　III. Series: Twayne's world authors series. French-Canadian literature.
PQ3911.W45　1986　　842'.009'9714　　85-27215
ISBN 0-8057-6625-1

For my mother and father

Contents

About the Author

Jonathan M. Weiss is associate professor of French and chairman of the modern foreign languages department at Colby College. He took his B.A. degree at Columbia and his Ph.D. at Yale, and, before coming to Colby, taught for two years at the University of Warwick in England. He has contributed articles to *The American Review of Canadian Studies*, *Voix et images*, and *Etudes françaises*, most recently on the novels of Victor-Lévy Beaulieu and Jacques Poulin. He is on the editorial board of *Quebec Studies* and the *Journal of Canadian Culture* and on the executive board of the Association for Canadian Studies in the United States. With his wife and three sons, he resides in Sidney, Maine.

Preface

This book is an introduction to the theater of Quebec. Some familiarity with European (especially French) theater is assumed on the part of the reader, as is some acquaintance with the basic history and politics of French Canada. A reading knowledge of French will be helpful for the reader who wishes to delve further into the subject and to read the texts in the original; for those unfamiliar with French, I have translated all translatable titles and quotations.

I have chosen to concentrate on dramatic literature rather than on performance; the reader outside Quebec has easier access to text than to live theater. Hence a good deal of nonpublished theater, and theater difficult to read in text form (such as Sauvageau's *Wouf-wouf*), is not studied here. Similarly I have touched only lightly on the recent phenomenon of women's theater, much of it unpublished and, increasingly, the subject of articles and books on feminism in Quebec. What I have emphasized are what I believe to be the enduring literary texts of the dramaturgy of Quebec.

If this book exists at all it is thanks to the help, wisdom, warmth, and encouragement of Laurent Mailhot and Elyane Roy. Without them I would have been lost; under their guidance I got to know and admire Quebec, its people, and its culture.

I also owe thanks to Benoît Melançon, to Jean-Cléo Godin, and to the Centre d'Etudes Québécoises of the Université de Montréal, as well as to Pierre Lavoie, Raymond Laquerre, and Paul Lefebvre. Gaston Miron, Ronald Sutherland, and Jacques Allard gave me important (if divergent) insights into Quebec and, like so many Quebecois too numerous to mention, showed me very generous hospitality.

Much of this book was researched in Montreal thanks to grants from the United States Office of Education (Fulbright-Hays Program), the Government of Quebec, and Colby College. Their generosity is much appreciated.

Jonathan M. Weiss

Colby College

Chronology

Dates refer to first performances of plays, not to their publication.

1608   Samuel de Champlain founds Quebec City.

1694   Monseigneur de Saint-Vallier prohibits Molière's *Tartuffe* in New France.

1759   Wolfe defeats Montcalm on the Plains of Abraham.

1774   Treaty of Paris; Quebec, along with most of North America, is under British rule.

1791   Quebec Act passed; the right of French Canadians to their language and religion is recognized.

1837   Rebellion (crushed by British troops) of the Patriotes.

1844   Antoine Gérin–Lajoie, *Le Jeune Latour*.

1865   Pierre Petitclair, *Une partie de campagne*.

1867   British North America Act; creation of Canadian confederation.

1885   Félix–Gabriel Marchand, *Les Faux brillants*.

1898–1914   Increase in number of French theaters in Montreal.

1917   Conscription crisis; riots in Quebec in reaction to forced military service in World War I.

1937–1952   Les Compagnons de Saint Laurent, under the direction of Emile Légault, bring European stage techniques to Quebec theater.

1937–1946   Gratien Gélinas, *Les Fridolinades*.

1942   Conscription crisis: in a plebiscite 72 percent of Quebec's voters oppose military service in Europe; 80 percent of English Canadians favor it.

1948   *Refus global* (Global Refusal) manifesto signed by sixteen artists and authors in Quebec.

1949   Gratien Gélinas, *Tit-Coq*.

1952   Théâtre du Nouveau Monde founded in Montreal.

1953   Marcel Dubé, *Zone.*

1955   Riots in Montreal following suspension of hockey player Maurice Richard.

1960   Victory of Liberal Party in Quebec; beginning of Quiet Revolution.

1961   Creation of a Ministry of Cultural Affairs in Quebec.

1963   First wave of terrorist bombings by the F.L.Q. (Quebec Liberation Front).

1964   Public school system and Ministry of Education created in Quebec.

1964   Théâtre de Quat'sous founded in Montreal.

1965   Centre d'Essai des Auteurs Dramatiques (Experimental Center For Dramatic Authors) founded in Montreal.

1967   General Charles de Gaulle says "Vive le Québec libre" from the balcony of the city hall in Montreal.

1968   Parti Québécois founded. Jacques Ferron, *Les Grands soleils.* Michel Tremblay, *Les Belles-soeurs.* Robert Gurik, *Hamlet, prince du Québec.*

1969   Le Théâtre d'Aujourd'hui founded in Montreal by Jean-Claude Germain. Françoise Loranger and Claude Levac, *Le chemin du Roy.*

1970   Imposition of War Measures Act (October crisis). Françoise Loranger, *Médium saignant.*

1971   Antonine Maillet, *La Sagouine.* Jean Barbeau, *Ben-Ur.*

1972   Robert Gurik, *Le Procès de Jean-Baptiste M.*

1973   Michel Garneau, *Quatre à quatre.*

1974   Michel Garneau, *Strauss et Pesant (et Rosa).*

1976   Victory of Parti Québécois in provincial elections. Réjean Ducharme, *Inès Pérée et Inat Tendu.* Antonine Maillet, *Evangéline Deusse.* Jean-Claude Germain: *Un Pays dont la devise est je m'oublie. La Nef des sorcières.* Michel Tremblay, *Sainte Carmen de la Main.*

1977   Michel Tremblay, *Damnée Manon sacrée Sandra.*

1978   Denise Boucher, *Les Fées ont soif.*

1980   Quebec voters defeat referendum on sovereignty-association.

1981   Jean-Pierre Ronfard, *Vie et mort du roi boiteux*. Jovette Marchessault, *La Saga des poules mouillées*. Marie Laberge, *C'était avant la guerre à l'Anse à Gilles*. Normand Chaurette, *Provincetown Playhouse, Juillet 1919, j'avais 19 ans*.

1982   Constitution Act passed; 1867 constitution replaced.

1984   René-Daniel Dubois, *Ne blâmez jamais les Bédouins*.

Chapter One
Birth of a Theater

Theater gives us an insight into the values and myths of any society. Unlike poetry and prose, theater depends on the public for its existence as an art form; the *poète maudit* may take solace in being rejected by a society that does not understand him, but the playwright must, if he is to accomplish anything more than the writing of the skeleton which is the text, find some element in society that is sympathetic to his message and his style. Hence the reciprocal relationship that the theater has with its public, a relationship which presupposes a group experience and is linked to the historical, social, and political conditions surrounding the presentation.[1]

The relationship between theater and society has been a rough one in French Canada, and the development of French-Canadian theater took place after poetry and prose were well established in Quebec. The reasons for this tardy development will be explored presently; although original works of drama were written and produced in Quebec since the mid-nineteenth century, it is only since the late 1960s that theater has become an important national art form in Quebec.

The coincidence of the birth of Quebec theater and the rise of contemporary Quebec nationalism is significant. If the Quiet Revolution of the early 1960s provided the conditions for the development of theater in Quebec (government subsidies, reduced influence of the Church, a growing middle class), separatism gave it inspiration. Not that every play produced since 1968 was politically inspired; on the contrary, as the various chapters of this book will show, political theater is only one of the many kinds of drama that have flourished in Quebec in the past fifteen years. But it is a characteristic of Quebec literature in general that nationalism as an inspirational force produces far more than political statements. Nor is nationalism always seen in political terms; national self-determination has and continues to be related to personal freedom, to self-knowledge, to love, to discovery of the land, and to a host of other literary themes.

1

But to speak of nationalism as a theme is somewhat inaccurate, because it is in the act of creation itself that the national dilemma of Quebec—a French "nation" within an essentially English-speaking political entity—is most important. On the one hand is the strong feeling among numerous Quebec intellectuals that the act of aesthetic creation presupposes cultural and political autonomy, and that Quebec literature or art would have no meaning in an English-dominated society. It is such a sentiment that inspired the poet Jean-Guy Pilon to write in 1969:

If, sooner or later, we're condemned to disappear, that is, to speak English, to live in English (even if, in the evening by candlelight, we still whisper a few French words), the efforts going on today at every level of creation and of intellectual activity are useless and of no avail.[2]

On the other hand, and perhaps more important, is the idea that the act of artistic creation in French in Quebec is of itself an assertion of independence from English Canada. A most influential book of the early 1970s, *Le Canadien français et son double* [The French Canadian and his double] by Jean Bouthillette put the problem succinctly and brutally: contemporary Quebecers relive the conquest of 1759 every day, within themselves, as they struggle to find their identity. In other words, the conquest has lost any meaning as a military or political humiliation and has become the loss of self-confidence, even of a sense of self. "Wherever we look," writes Bouthillette, "inevitably we meet the eyes of the Other—in this instance the English [Canadian]—whose gaze troubles our own."[3]

Now, as we shall see, French-Canadian theater existed in Quebec well before 1960. The very forces that kept Quebec apart from English Canada encouraged a cultural intimacy that allowed theater to become, in many instances, popular entertainment, village *fêtes,* and, later (thanks to radio and television) drama and melodrama that often expressed the pressing concerns of average French Canadians. But it was only when Quebec felt certain of itself politically and culturally that this popular and populist strain in its theater could appear openly to the rest of the world and take shape with the drama of Michel Tremblay and others.

Similarly, it was only when the political climate in Quebec became sympathetic to nationalism that playwrights could express openly their identity not as Canadians but as themselves, as Quebecois. In fact, by the middle of the 1960s, the term *French-Canadian* had been largely replaced, in Quebec, by the term *Québécois,* and one spoke, unofficially at least, of the state (rather than the province) of Quebec. None of this necessarily presupposed political separatism; by the time the Parti Québécois had become a major political influence (1973), Quebec's artists and intellectuals were well on their way to achieving a new cultural identity as Quebecois. Nor will the results of the 1980 referendum or the electoral fortunes of the Parti Québécois do much to affect what is essentially an inner, personal process of self-affirmation. Whether Quebec remains in Canada or not, it has profoundly changed in the past twenty-five years. Freed from the shackles of pan-Canadianism and from the darkness of inward-looking conservative nationalism, Quebec's intellectuals continue to create a culture that is universal while being particular, that is diverse while being interconnected. Theater is only one element of that new culture, but it is the most vibrant, the most exciting, and, given Quebec's past, the most unexpected.

1650–1935

Traditionally, theater has had a difficult and problematic existence in Quebec. "One cannot," writes the critic Max Dorsinville, "study Quebec drama without first reflecting on the close interrelationship between the early predominance of classical European drama and the clergy's role in fostering it."[4] In fact, from the very beginning of New France the Catholic clergy, realizing the power of theater to influence the minds of those colonists who had few other distractions, made sure that the only plays people saw were those of which it approved. When, in 1694, a group of actors proposed to present Molière's *Tartuffe,* the archbishop of Quebec, Monseigneur de Saint-Vallier, reacted with a severity out of all proportion to the attitudes of his fellow clergy in France (where the play had been presented since 1669). Saint-Vallier had the play's director, Mareuil, put in prison for blasphemy, and he threatened to excommunicate any Catholic who might think of attending the play's performances. In fact, Saint-Vallier had more than one reason to fear Molière's satirical wit: the archbishop had just forbidden women to wear dresses that showed too much shoulder or bust, and the famous scene in *Tartuffe* where the hypocrite tells Dorine to cover her breasts hit too close to home. But Saint-Vallier went much further than the censure of one specific play. In his *Instructions for the Enlightenment of Conscienses Regarding Comedies,* issued in January 1694, he characterized all comedies as "a criminal or dangerous thing, a sin, or an invitation to sin."[5]

The *Tartuffe* affair, as it came to be known, was settled amicably when Frontenac (governor of New France) having been offered 100 *pistoles* by the bishop, agreed to have the play withdrawn,[6] but Saint-Vallier's actions had a damping effect on all theater in the colony. "It was . . . a terrible blow for theater in general and, except for occasional spectacles presented in institutions of learning, the well of culture or of amusement through dramatic art went dry throughout the rest of the French regime."[7]

The situation of French theater did not improve much after the conquest; the British were only too content to entrust the governance of the culture of Quebec to the Roman Catholic clergy, and so, from the end of the eighteenth century to the middle of the nineteenth, just about the only theater of note was that produced in *collèges* (under the control of the Church) and that of a few amateur troupes that were allowed to present plays as long as the Church approved of them and as long as no women appeared on stage. Some exceptions exist, however, for the French-Canadian public was not very pleased with the Church's attitude and witnessed, undoubtedly with some envy, the growth of English theater in Montreal and the establishment, in 1825 by John Molson, of the Theatre Royal. In 1790 Joseph Quesnel, a Breton who had been in Canada since 1779, managed to have his operetta, *Colas et Colinette,* produced on the stage of the Théâtre de Société, an amateur association which Quesnel and associates had founded in 1789. The play concerns a young woman courted by a peasant boy and a bailiff; the role of Colinette was played by a disguised male actor, but even this adherence to the strictures of the Church did not exempt the play from the criticism of the clergy.[8] Quesnel's theater closed after two years, and by 1839, when Lord Durham issued his *Report on the Affairs of British North America,* he could write with a degree of exactness that "though descended from the people in the world that most generally love, and have most successfully cultivated the drama, . . . the French population of Lower Canada, cut off from every people that speaks its own language, can support no national stage."[9]

Toward the middle of the nineteenth century some changes take place. Most important, there begins to appear a new breed of writer, the French-Canadian dramatist, whose subjects concern the life and history of his own province. Antoine Gérin-Lajoie, well known for his successful novel *Jean Rivard* (1864), also wrote a tragedy entitled *Le Jeune Latour* (1844).[10] Written in rhymed alexandrine verse, Gérin-Lajoie's play takes up the same theme as his novels: fidelity to the "race," to the land. It is a period piece without much dramatic merit, his characters mouthpieces for a Canadian nationalism that had recently flared up in the revolts of 1837.[11] The same can be said for Louis Fréchette's play *Félix Poutré*, performed in 1862.[12]

A more enduring, if less well known play, is *Une Partie de campagne* by Pierre Petitclair (1865). Here the plot has some complexity. The situation of a pretentious but naive French Canadian who apes the mannerisms of the more powerful English is analyzed psychologically rather than politically, with the result that the play's main character becomes valid in his own right, and the play gives us some idea of the ambiguities of French-Canadian life in mid-nineteenth century.

As the century progressed, theater became increasingly popular in Quebec, but continued to encounter substantial problems. A French actor, Alfred Maugard, came to Quebec in 1871 and tried to found a permanent theater there. A year later Maugard had succeeded in attracting the support of Félix-Gabriel Marchand, a member of the provincial parliament and later premier, and presented the first of this politician's popular plays, *Erreur n'est pas compte* (A mistake can always be corrected), which shared the stage with Rodolphe Tanguay's *L'Intendant Bigot,* two French-Canadian plays in a single evening. Tanguay is largely forgotten now, but Marchand is not, especially since the contemporary Quebec playwright Jean-Claude Germain rehabilitated him by presenting, in 1977, a "paraphrase" of Marchand's best work, a vaudeville called *Les Faux-brillants* (All that glitters). Marchand's play was first performed in 1885, twelve years before the playwright was to become Quebec's premier, the last true liberal until 1960, asserts Germain.[13] In fact, it is true that Marchand's pet project, the establishment of a Quebec ministry of education, was seen (correctly) by the Church as an attempt to wrest control of schools from ecclesiastical authorities and was not to take place until 1964; it is also true that Marchand was an honest politician in a day when corruption and bribery were commonplace. But a great playwright Marchand was not, despite his erudition (he was educated in Quebec and in Paris), and *Les Faux-brillants* is a farce, in rhymed verse, poking fun at the pretensions of a Quebec middle-class paterfamilias ready to sacrifice the happiness of his family to gain the favors of a false Italian baron intent on seizing the family fortune. The father's exaggerated admiration for social rank and the affected European mannerisms of the false baron remind one of Molière's Orgon in *Tartuffe,* but the play's style and plot (all is saved by the intervention of a long-lost nephew, a kind of *canadien errant*) owes more to the farces of Georges Feydeau than to the mordant satire of Molière. Germain's "paraphrase" is more full of life, more authentic than Marchand's original, and takes full advantage of the use of joual (Montreal slang) to show the contrast between the admirers of Europe and those Quebecois who are happy with their own way of life. It is doubtful that Marchand's theater could have survived without Germain.

Despite the popularity of Marchand's play, Alfred Maugard's theater shortly fell on bad times. In particular, it found itself the object of the special venom that the Church reserved for dramatic art. On 7 November 1873 the archbishop of Quebec, Monseigneur Taschereau, issued a letter to be read in all the churches of the province forbidding Catholics from attending Maugard's theater; the theater closed. A similar fate befell the French actor Achille Fay-Génot who arrived in Montreal with a theater company in 1874. The bishop of Montreal, Monseigneur Bourget, issued a letter condemning "the most shameful and humiliating outrage" that foreign actors have perpetrated on "a Catholic city which still respects itself."[14] Monseigneur Bourget had a particularly virulent dislike of theater; in 1868 he had, in a pastoral letter, warned those who frequent theaters that they "play with the devil" and "as a consequence renounce the happiness promised by Jesus Christ" and he labeled the art of the theater "the most detestable school of vice even in the eyes of honest pagans and respectable Protestants."[15] A similar admonishment was issued in 1885 by Bourget following the first of Sarah Bernhardt's three tours of Quebec.

Yet, despite the open hostility of the Church, people continued to disobey the clergy and go to the theater. The popular Parisian repertory of light comedy and moralizing dramas (such as Dumas Fils's *La Dame aux camélias*) was often played by visiting French troupes, a phenomenon that reflected the continuing development of a French-Canadian urban middle class (professionals and small businessmen) for whom theater was a legitimate form of amusement.

The Church, however, continued to insist that theater, if it had any value at all, must be "a school of morals, of language, and of ideas."[16] So in 1894 the Church-affiliated Société St-Jean Baptiste inaugurated the theater of the Monument National which allowed troupes of amateurs to present "family evenings" and to be trained in elocution and acting techniques. The director of the Monument National, Elzéar Roy, did not hide the didactic purpose of the enterprise: "The public . . . will forget, we hope, the ways of certain English theaters where art is replaced by immorality and which recruit their clientele in large part among French Canadians."[17] Ironically, of course, it was because of the Church's traditionally short-sighted attitude that Quebecers were obliged to frequent English-language theaters. Nevertheless, as the nineteenth century came to a close, the position of theater in Quebec society decidedly improved, so much so that the critic and literary historian John Hare has called the years 1898–1914 the "golden age" of theater in Montreal.[18]

It was inevitable that the amateur productions of the mid-nineteenth century would lead to professional French-Canadian theaters; at the same time, the impressions created by visiting actors from France, especially by Sarah Bernhardt, would encourage French Canadians to pursue careers in the theater. By 1902 there were three important professional theaters presenting French plays in Montreal: the Théâtre des Variétés, the Théâtre National, and the Théâtre des Nouveautés. Of these the latter two presented "serious" plays (Molière and a classical French repertory) while the other concentrated on vaudeville and melodramas. Another "serious" theater was the Conservatoire d'Art Dramatique Canadien which a Frenchman, Eugène Lasalle, opened in 1907. Despite its name, this conservatory never gave birth to a national theater, a phenomenon which did not arise until the late 1960s.

Theater in Quebec in the early days of this century was not without its problems. The Church's censors were somnolent, but not completely asleep, and when the Théâtre des Nouveautés presented a work by the French playwright Henri Bernstein in 1907, Monseigneur Bruchesi forbade Catholics to attend.[19] In fact, if the Church could no longer order theaters to close, it still claimed the right to preview plays, often changing words and cutting text that was felt to be immoral. A more lasting challenge to theater than the Church was the newly born cinema; in 1906 Ernest Ouimet opened Montreal's first movie house, and this form of entertainment became increasingly popular after 1910.

In the main, the first third of the twentieth century did not see the production of any French-Canadian plays of quality; most of what was presented in Montreal, as late as the 1930s, had been written in France. Montreal theater in its heyday was anything but intellectual; the plays that attracted the public were those that produced emotional reactions (Dumas Fils's *La Dame aux camélias* or Edmond Rostrand's *L'Aiglon*); even then, the audiences often laughed in the wrong places and seemed to the newspaper critics incredibly naive.[20] The French-Canadian plays that were produced were complacent retellings of popular myths (*La Veillée de Noël* [Christmas Eve] by Camille Duguay, *Jeanne d'Arc* by Madame A.-B Lacerte, or *Les Ames héroïques* [Heroic souls] by Brother Romulaud-François).[21]

World War I put an end to the "golden age" of this type of theater; actors were mobilized to serve in the armed forces, and money was scarce. Once the war was over, actors and directors tried to assert themselves once more, but the public, now quite used to cinema, was hard to attract and the only formula that seemed to work was the sketch or humorous revue. When the Théâtre National tried to present a serious play, *L'Avocat* by the naturalist French playwright Eugène Brieux in 1923, the result was so disastrous that the theater could no longer pay its debts and had to close.[22] The only hope on the horizon was the Stella Theater which was open from 1930 to 1935 and directed by two famous Montreal actors, Fred Barry and Albert Duquesne. The Stella, in a small house (443 seats), put on plays by Somerset Maugham, Marcel Pagnol, and other serious dramatists.

1935–1968

By the mid-1930s the theater in Quebec was beginning to divide itself in two very distinct directions. Both of these directions have their origins in the period we have just reviewed, and both would have an influence on the new Quebec theater when it came into being in 1968.

Popular Theater. As we have noticed, a type of theater that gained popularity after World War I was the sketch or humorous revue. This was a form of theater that addressed itself for the most part to the common man and woman of the working and middle classes of the francophone population; it was a reflection of popular (as opposed to elite) culture, and in Quebec this meant that its subject matter and language were rooted in French-Canadian (as opposed to European) life.

The origins of this "popular" theater are uncertain, although Jean-Cléo Godin has hypothesized that "the review develops in the wake of boulevard and vaudeville theater, and undoubtedly corresponds to a desire to counter the influence of a newly born cinema."[23] In any case, by 1912 a theater called the Théâtre Gayety opened its doors in Montreal (it would stay open until 1950) and presented a varied repertory of plays in the tradition of the American burlesque theater; these are revues and sketches whose purpose is unabashedly to amuse the audience. Theater critics habitually turned up their noses at this type of theater, and few texts of the sketches are to be found, but, as Godin remarks, the titles would indicate a certain affinity with the slapstick humor of the Three Stooges or the Marx Brothers (*Allons-y, tape dans l'tas, pif! paf!* [Give em Hell, Bam! Bam!] or *Cocorico* [Cock-a-doodle-doo]).[24]

The revues and sketches of the 1920s, 1930s, and 1940s were an amalgam of dance, songs, and dialogue; gestures often were more important in getting the audience to laugh then the text itself. These plays filled a very specific role in Quebec society, providing an outlet for criticism of government, Church, and society at a time when criticism was rarely aired publicly. Revues appealed to male audiences particularly (who often came to see a popular woman storyteller, La Poune), serving as a social gathering center, while women usually met one another in the home.[25]

The most famous, enduring, and influential of these revues began in 1937 on the Montreal radio station CKAC and moved, a year later, to the stage. It was called *Les Fridolinades,* played until 1946, and was written and directed by Gratien Gélinas. Gélinas created, in the context of the traditional revue, a character (Fridolin)[26] who was to develop with the years and become "the king's fool, the people's fool,"[27] an individualist whose comic antics revealed a very serious criticism of society as it was and a wistful glance at what it could have been. Fridolin aims his wit at the Church, at the economic system, at the political situation; Gélinas's text, in the idiom of east-end Montreal, is full of revealing ambiguities and double meanings, and there are intertextual references that refer the public back to the nationalism of Groulx or the agriculturalism of Paul-Henri Grignon.[28] *Les Fridolinades* is the epitome of the popular revue form but its content has implications that go beyond that of other revues and constitute an important point of departure for the theater of the 1970s.

Two sketches stand out as thematically important. The first of these, presented in 1945, was called "La Vie édifiante de Jean-Baptiste Laframboise" (The edifying life of Jean-Baptiste Laframboise) and it is a series of tableaux presenting various stages in the life of a French-Canadian poet manqué. The irony in the title was immediately evident to the audience; Jean-Baptiste's life is edifying in its anti-Catholicism, for, from birth on (the choice of a name depended on the life of a saint) this young French Canadian will find his future blocked by the Church. In an attempt to be educated he attends a seminary but is expelled for reading Baudelaire; in an attempt to find support he confesses to a priest that he wants to be a poet, only to be told "take care that it isn't the devil that's tempting you with the sin of pride."[29] He becomes a *notaire,* marries a supremely uninteresting woman, dies after an uneventful life. In fact, his life becomes interesting only after he dies; as Laurent Mailhot notes, "the death of the *notaire* Laframboise announces the birth of Quebec literature."[30] It is only after his death that Jean-Baptiste, in a circle of light on a darkened stage, realizes that the real obstacle to his self-fulfillment was not the Church but himself: "I would have never thought that it [becoming a poet] could happen to a [French] Canadian," he laments.[31] This is a collective as well as personal tragedy, says Laframboise, and it is at the heart of the dilemma faced by Quebec culture in the 1940s:

The great misfortune of our people is that they do not have confidence in themselves. . . . Every time someone with talent comes along they won't admire him until he's gone abroad and has been called great by foreigners.[32]

When one realizes the coincidence between this declaration and the exile of such artists as Paul-Emile Borduas or poets such as François Hertel, the importance of Gélinas's impatience is evident. The mid 1940's mark a turning point in Quebec literature; it was a time of new ideas, of a questioning of conservative Catholic values; it was also a time of frustration. Gélinas's sketch not only reflects this situation, it helps to create it.

Another sketch in the 1946 Fridolinades is important because it provides the groundwork of one of the most successful of all French-Canadian plays, *Tit-Coq* (542 performances from 1949 to 1981).[33] *Le Retour du conscrit* (The return of the conscript) is more of a monologue than a play: the conscript, having served in the European theater of combat in World War II, returns home to find his fiancée already married. He confronts her, learns that she still loves him, but he is obliged to accept her (never satisfactorily explained) decision. The short dialogue between these two figures is relatively uninteresting, but the conscript's lines contain resonances that could not fail to be noticed after the war when, despite its opposition to the idea and despite promises made by Prime Minister MacKenzie King, Quebec saw its sons drafted and sent to fight in Europe. The conscript's disappointment and bitterness take on a political tone when he tells the audience: "If you've got nothing better to do, think of me from time to time on November 11th. . . . And if you need me for the next war, be my guest!"[34]

When, two years after *Le Retour du conscrit, Tit-Coq* appeared on the stage of Montreal's Monument National (with the same leading cast as the revue), Gélinas had worked some changes into the text that effectively transformed the original sketch into a play combining some elements of the revue with a remarkable amount of dramatic depth. The political and social criticism of *Les Fridolinades* reappears but it is no longer essential to the play: in *Tit-Coq* there is a dramatic tension caused by conflicts within the characters themselves. The unidimensional conscript of 1946 is replaced by a complex character whose bastard origins become symbolic of Quebec itself,[35] symbolic of a shared alienation. Herein lies the dilemma for Tit-Coq, the returning soldier. He searches for legitimacy and security by falling in love with the image of the perfect family; when this dream falls apart, he is led to rebel against those very values that he so sought to find. Like Tit-Coq, the fiancée (Marie-Ange) is a prisoner of a way of life and thought that only admits love within the context of the family, the one element that is permanently missing in Tit-Coq's life. Her reasons for breaking her promise to him are no more precise in this play than in *Le Retour du conscrit,* but it is in Marie-Ange's own inability to understand her actions that we realize how powerful is the impulse to obey the accepted social order, and how comforting it is for her to abandon a dream of anarchistic, passionate love for the security of a family life with a man she does not love.

Tit-Coq is contemporary with Gabrielle Roy's novel *Bonheur d'occasion* *(The Tin Flute)* and Marie-Ange's fate is not that different from Florentine Lacasse's (although Roy's novel presents a richness of feminine characterization absent in Gélinas's play). Both works share a vision of the family as both an imprisoning and a comforting institution in Quebec society, and of the protagonist as a "pathetic hero, victim of a fatality."[36]

Tit-Coq's dilemma is also one of language, and in his portrayal of the working-class protagonist Gélinas shows us how language creates the expression of thoughts and emotions. Early in the play Tit-Coq complains to the army chaplain that he can't "find the words" to express his emotions for Marie-Ange whom he has just met;[37] this problem becomes a fatal flaw later in the play when, while in Europe, Tit-Coq can express himself to Marie-Ange only by the language of the letters he sends:

Guys who've had education talk about the moon, the stars, the clouds . . . and everything they touch turns to phrases of love. But when I write: "I'm crazy about you, I love you, you're always on my mind," when I've written that, I'm done, I've got nothing left.[38]

In the end Tit-Coq's writing arm will be broken, and he'll have to ask Marie-Ange's brother to lend feelings to his words. But it is too late, and Tit-Coq's failure in love is made even more bitter by this poverty of language, a poverty Gélinas conveys very well in an era before joual (Montreal slang) could be admitted on stage.

When *Tit-Coq* appeared it was lauded as the "explosive beginning of Quebec theater."[39] It is clear now that this was not the case. Gélinas's play has the merit of having brought the working class onto the stage of the "serious" theater and of having created a dramatic situation whose significance went beyond the realm of theater. But *Tit-Coq* does nothing with theater itself, and despite one critic's attempt to show that the play is one of the first in Quebec to make full use of the possibilities of the stage,[40] Gélinas in truth does little to break out of conventional realism; the plot unfolds through dialogues some of which are easily predictable, and, aside from the play's hero, Gélinas's characters have little to make them memorable. The social reality of Quebec has changed considerably since 1948, and the play's value now is that of showing us a state of mind that existed just as Quebec was beginning the process of change that was to culminate in the Quiet Revolution of 1960. Gélinas has continued to be interested in social reality, and in the two plays he has written since *Tit-Coq* he has observed the transition of Quebec society from the alienation of Tit-Coq to the pointed separatism of the late 1960s. *Hier les enfants dansaient* (Yesterday the children were dancing), first presented in 1966, is a play about a political family, one which spans both sides of the separatist issue. The plot is somewhat contrived: the federalist father, having been offered a position in the cabinet, confronts his separatist son who intends to make his mark on politics by dynamiting symbols of English-Canadian domination. In the end both father and son are searching for personal autonomy, but it is the political situation rather than internal conflicts that interests the author here.

The flatness of the dialogue and the complacency of the political formulas make the play rather uninteresting dramatically. A little more depth went into Gélinas's earlier play, *Bousille et les justes* *(Bousille and the Just)*, first performed in 1955. Here the tradition of *Les Fridolinades* is still apparent; the play is an indictment of the Duplessis government, of the Catholic church, and of the system of justice. Bousille is like Tit-Coq, an orphan, victim of a society that seems to have no merits whatever: honesty is replaced by the fear of scandal, justice by self-interest, and awareness of reality by blind obedience to Catholic ritual. At the same time that *Bousille* was performed, Pierre-Elliott Trudeau was writing about the Asbestos strike,[41] and there is a similar sense of outrage at social injustice in Gélinas's play. One of the characters says: "Don't waste your time, you won't find anyone more rotten than us;"[42] indeed, the play is exceedingly pessimistic, and if there is a glimmer of hope at the end of *Tit-Coq* (stage directions indicate that Tit-Coq "begins a long voyage"),[43] in *Bousille* the play ends with the suicide of Bousille himself, a gesture that has no impact on the other characters who can think of nothing except the scandal the suicide will bring on the family. But in *Bousille* the blackness and pessimism never go beyond the social criticism, and Bousille's death, indeed his entire existence, is interesting only in what it shows us about the seamy side of Quebec society on the eve of the Quiet Revolution.

Gélinas's theater is not the only example of the influence of the revue and music hall on Quebec drama. The monologist Yvon Deschamps, one of Quebec's most popular showmen, owes much to

Fridolin as he straddles the light humor of the vaudeville and a darker, pessimistic criticism of Quebec society. Later on, dramatists of the 1970s such as Jean-Claude Germain, Le Grand Cirque Ordinaire, or Yves Sauvageau in *Wouf wouf* will incorporate elements of the revue into their theaters.

Another playwright whose career began in the 1950s presents certain similarities with Gélinas. He is Marcel Dubé, and although he does not share the vaudeville origins of the author of *Les Fridolinades,* he does go through a similar evolution from plays dealing with the problems of the working class to plays about Quebec's upper classes and political families. And like Gélinas, Dubé is a conservative playwright who prefers the traditional well-made play to the experiments of the avant-garde.

Dubé's dramatic career began in 1953 when his third play, *Zone,* won the first prize in the Western Quebec Regional Festival and later at a national festival in Victoria, B.C. *Zone* is certainly one of the most popular plays of the 1950s, second only to *Tit-Coq,* and it is easy to see why. The play is set in an area of Montreal similar to the St. Henri district depicted in Roy's *Bonheur d'occasion;* it is the "place in society where human happiness is almost impossible."[44] Like the French film of 1952, *Les Jeux interdits (Forbidden Games)* children (here, adolescents) are caught up in a world that accords them no happiness and where a shadow of danger and death hovers over their lives. In *Zone* the "game" they play is the smuggling of American cigarettes to Canada, not to buy alcohol or drugs but rather to help the family pay its bills and to save for an education. And as in *Tit-Coq,* the hero of *Zone* is a lost soul named Tarzan, an orphan looking for an attachment that will justify his existence.

There is no doubt, then, that *Zone* struck a responsive chord in the Quebec society of the 1950s not only through its "text full of humanity"[45] but equally through what were perceived to be "true resonances, . . . authentic human beings."[46] In retrospect, it is not the play's realism that makes it important (in fact, Dubé takes pains to stylize the decor) but the deeper, tragic resonances that Dubé manages to put into a familiar setting. The play's structure is reminiscent of classical tragedy: three moments in time are presented ("The Game," "The Trial," "Death"), each of which is the culmination of a series of events and leads to the inevitable end. In fact, the event that provokes the tragedy (Tarzan has killed a U.S.

customs officer) occurs before the play has begun. The action is thus complete before the drama begins.

Zone evokes, as Jean-Cléo Godin points out, the legend of Tristan and Iseult, "the mythic expression of impossible love,"[47] in the relationship between Tarzan and the sixteen-year-old Ciboulette (her name, like his, is a nickname designed to hide their identities) which is rendered eternal by the death of the hero. The play also makes use of the mataphor of Christ's death, an image which Dubé evokes in the decor (the clotheslines on stage are attached to "a poor, thin cross with neither thief nor Christ on it")[48] and which he sustains throughout the plot. Although Tarzan on one level is guilty of manslaughter and has none of the innocence of Jesus, on another level Tarzan is profoundly innocent because he is a child, uncorrupted in his heart which is capable of love, and because he is betrayed by a Judas whom he forgives just before his death. The tragedy of *Zone* is that of a generation of young Quebecers betrayed by their elders, but, at the same time, it is the tragedy of all youth forced by social conditions to become old before their time.

In its pure, classical respect of the conventions of tragedy, in its expressionistic decor, in its use of metaphor, *Zone* seemed to forecast the beginning of a new Quebec theater, with Dubé one of its most celebrated playwrights. This did not happen for two principal reasons. The first of these concerns language: in the second version of *Zone* (1954) Dubé rewrote the dialogue to make it approximate the language of Montreal's working class, but in the third and final version (1954) the author went back to a more grammatically correct French. This indecision with regard to the ways in which characters express themselves reveals a weakness in Dubé's theater; as Godin points out, the accumulation of inconsistencies in the dialogue "destroys the charm of the play and breaks up its harmoniousness."[49] Dubé flatly refuses to do what Tremblay, Germain, and other post-1960 playwrights knew they had to do: invent a medium of expression appropriate to the Quebec stage. Dubé confuses correctness of language with levels of discourse, and, in the late 1950s, opts for "a new orientation": "I became suddenly conscious of the importance of the French language as a primordial, determining, indissociable condition of our survival."[50] His subsequent plays abandon the working-class milieu and use an international brand of French, not identifiable with the idiom of Quebec. The fact is that language as a system of signifiers does not interest Dubé: "what is important for me," he says, "is to succeed in emotionally moving people."[51]

The second reason why the promise of *Zone* was unfulfilled has to do with the subject matter of Dubé's plays. As his theater evolved, and particularly by the 1960s, his plays, now situated in the salons of the upper-middle class, became increasingly preoccupied with the political situation. This new interest could have proved fruitful had Dubé tried to construct a specifically political theater, but instead he used (and continues to use) politics as a backdrop to what are essentially static, melodramatic plots.

An example of what Dubé's theater has become is *Au retour des oies blanches* (When the white geese come home). It was first presented in 1966 and concerns a subject that preoccupies Dubé and that is closely linked to his interpretation of politics: the generation gap. Here it is an aging politician of the Duplessis era, convicted of corruption, who represents the past: he is desperately trying to clear his name now that the (formerly Duplessiste) Union Nationale party is in power again, but finds that even his old cronies have adjusted to the new political reality of the Quiet Revolution and will support him no longer. The young generation is represented by his daughter, a tormented soul who confronts the family with a sort of game of truth, the revelations of which are devastating. It is not the father's political opinions that are behind the problem but rather a deep-seated flaw in the human character that prevents people from attaining their ideal of happiness. Here the impossibility of the situation (the daughter falls in love with a man who is revealed to be her natural father) and its dark Freudian overtones would seem to lead to tragedy, but the play never achieves a high enough level of language and sentiment for that. "Are we in a Greek tragedy or in a vaudeville drama?" asks one of the characters in the play, to which another answers: "We're in life, I believe. And in life these are two genres that are often confused."[52] Dubé has indeed confused the genres in this play, and neither the setting nor the characters themselves lead one to see in the daughter's suicide the tragedy one could easily see in *Zone*.

Dubé's theater, in the end, has become popular melodrama, often written for and presented on television. Like the theater of Gélinas, it is significant for the content of its plots rather than for any clear conception of theater as an art form. It has some importance in tracing middle-class reaction to Quebec's political changes, but it cannot be said to herald a new era of theater.

Avant-garde Theater. The second important direction Quebec theater took in the 1940s and 1950s was that of the avant-garde. Unlike the popular theaters of Gélinas and Dubé, which depend (in Gélinas) on American forms and (in Gélinas and in Dubé) on North American contexts and situations, the avant-garde in Quebec turned to Europe for its inspiration. In the theater this European orientation affected staging techniques as well as the written plays themselves.

It is Emile Legault, a Holy Cross priest, who in effect brought a European concept of theater production to Quebec from 1937 to 1952 with his troupe called Les Compagnons de Saint Laurent. In 1938, a year after having founded his theater, Legault went to Europe. He was accompanied by his most important spiritual influence, the French Catholic dramatist Henri Ghéon whose plays Legault frequently performed in Quebec. What Legault saw in Europe was to set the standard for Quebec's avant-garde: the austere stage and skeletal decor of Michel Saint-Denis; the close study of classical texts to be presented in new ways of Dullin, Baty, and Pitoëff (members of the "Cartel des Quatre"); the renovation of the architecture of the stage and a redefinition of the role of the director in the theater of Jacques Copeau. Legault also spent time observing the theater of Henri Brochet, a Catholic dramatic art center in Paris whose purpose it was to create, on a medieval model, a religious theater for a large, popular audience.[53]

What Legault brought back to Quebec was a sense of theater as an autonomous form of art whose possibilities should not be determined by conventions of the past, particularly by realism. "Theater is not," says Legault, "the minute and realistic re-edition of everyday life but a transposition, an interpretation of all that is human."[54] Like the French reformers from André Antoine to Jean-Louis Barrault, Legault refused "overblown acting and expensive stars,"[55] insisted on a varied repertory, and asserted the "superiority of poetry" in dramatic discourse.[56] Between 1939 and 1952 Legault insisted on the anonymity of his actors and actresses, on imaginative and pared-down scenery, and on a repertory that included works by Molière, Anouilh, Obey, Giraudoux, Claudel, T. S. Eliot, and Cocteau, among others. His was the only French theater in Montreal to present a classical and serious modern selection of plays during the 1950s, but Legault had another purpose that went beyond the

selection and interpretation of texts. True to the model of Jacques
Copeau whose influence Legault calls "my bread and honey,"[57] Legault tried to make his theater a center for the cultural and spiritual
education of the public. In 1948 Legault founded the Centre Dramatique des Compagnons in Montreal which was to become the
Ecole des Compagnons for the formation of a new breed of actors
and a new public for whom respect of theater as art was to be the
credo. A "complicity of the hearts"[58] was what Legault wanted
between audience, actors, and the text, and this notion had a spiritual dimension as well, for Legault saw in his audience "a sort of
spiritual family"[59] united by faith in Christianity. In the Quebec
of the 1940s and early 1950s, when reform movements (such as La
Relève and La Jeunesse Etudiante Catholique) had strong Catholic
roots, this religious orientation was easy for Quebec intellectuals to
accept. Today it would be well outside the mainstream of Quebec's
cultural life, and here we see the limits of Legault's theater which
did not separate religion from culture. Another limit can be found
in Legault's choice of an almost exclusively European and U.S.
repertory (in thirteen years he produced only four French-Canadian
plays, and only one of these—*Maluron* by Félix Leclerc—was not
a religious work).[60] Despite Legault's assertion that "if you want to
rediscover all the nobility of theatrical art, you must see it as as-
sembling an entire people around its national soul,"[61] it is clear
that the experiment of the Compagnons de Saint Laurent did not
have as its purpose the creation of a French-Canadian dramaturgy.

When the Compagnons gave their last performance in 1952 (too
many actors had left the company, many to go to France) they had
opened up a wide variety of dramatic possibilities that playwrights
would later use in developing a specifically Quebec theater. Legault's
work, as one critic has remarked, was that of "clearing the woods."[62]
Many of his actors went on to found the Théâtre du Nouveau Monde
which was to be instrumental in the creation of Quebec theater.
Above all, Legault gave those who came after him standards of
anticommercialism, of aesthetics, and of production techniques to
aim for.

Just as Legault was bringing European production techniques to
Quebec, a group of writers and artists were constituting a movement
that was to have important effects on the theater. Inspired by European surrealism and the automatic writing of Breton, the Quebec
automatistes, painters and writers,[63] began a long journey of ques-

tioning authority, even (and especially) the authority of the *logos,* of the word. In 1948, as Legault was presenting Anouilh's *Antigone,* the painter Paul-Emile Borduas and fifteen other avant-garde painters and writers signed a manifesto entitled *Refus global* (Global Refusal). This is one of the most influential documents in Quebec literature, and it puts into question the history, politics, and culture of French Canada. It is a call to liberation—political and cultural—but especially of thought. "The society born in faith will perish by the weapon of reason: intention," the manifesto claims,[64] and proposes that the subconscious, magic, "objective mystery," love, and a reading of "real poets" such as Sade, Lautréamont, and the surrealists replace the rational, classical culture of the past.[65]

One of those who signed *Refus global* was a poet and playwright, Claude Gauvreau, whose career was to end prematurely with his suicide in 1971. Gauvreau was a giant of Quebec letters, a figure who is just beginning to receive the critical attention he deserves; he is as much a myth as the author of texts whose hermetic quality often prevents any immediate analysis. His influence is substantial on the poetry and theater of Quebec. One of the most important theater troupes of the 1960s, for example, called itself the *Egrégore,* a word Gauvreau had coined in his play *Les Oranges sont vertes* (The oranges are green), which means "passionate exteriorization, . . . delirious abstraction and the feeling-up of the earth without regret, . . . birth with endless roots of new harmony."[66] An important director of the 1970s, Jean-Pierre Ronfard (who produced *Les Oranges sont vertes* in 1972) says that his own, and all of Quebec theater's, debt to Gauvreau is to have shown that "theater is a place of choice to exorcise collective fear, to shamelessly insist upon dignity, to stir up the sleeping wealth of the subconscious, to celebrate the word and to call for liberation."[67]

Les Oranges sont vertes is probably Gauvreau's best-known play, and it dramatizes some of the principal theories in *Refus global.* The *Égrégore* is at the heart of the play: it is the sublime moment of poetic creation which a group of *exploréens* (another coined word) are in the process of enjoying through automatic writing and probing into the subconscious in visual art. Yvernig, the supreme artist, is surrounded by other *exploréens* who appreciate his theory that poetry can come only from "needs that surge forward volcanically, without preconceived ideas,"[68] and his openly erotic sense of sexuality. But society is lying in wait for the *exploréens* who threaten not only its sense of order but equally its concept of the imagination. The wealthy, the friends of art, introduce into the group of *exploréens* an artist, Paprikouce, who says "we should all remain open to experimentation"[69] but whose real purpose is to recuperate the unnameable, categorize it, make it the new artistic order. Yvernig becomes increasingly quiet; he can hardly spit out a few syllables but manages to write a testament in which he attacks all those who have betrayed him as the "propagandists of a vegetative life without adventure or risk . . . enemies of all that troubles the spirit."[70]

There is certainly a romantic element in this theme of the *poète maudit,* but it is the way in which the theme is presented that is interesting theatrically. As the play progresses, the level of aggressiveness increases—aggressiveness against Yvernig (who is killed with blows and with words, thrown as objects), and also against the audience. For, as the play ends, a figure for whom all have been waiting since the beginning, Batlam (historically, a romantic hero of the battle over Hugo's *Hernani*)[71] comes on stage accompanied by eight armed companions who "fire simultaneously and gun down the assassins of Yvernig and the whole audience."[72] The long-awaited savior, the figure who, in the tradition of seventeenth-century drama, would establish order, has turned out to be a destroyer. As one critic has remarked, "the mysterious Batlam has no meaning other than to be himself: the result is a feeling of intense fear."[73]

Yvernig's revolt was total and unconditional: even as a priest tries to administer the last rites he finds the force literally to spit out his anger and his refusal of "all that enslaves."[74] A more accessible text on a similar subject was the short radio play, which was presented on station CBF in 1952 (and won the Canadian Radio Award), entitled *Le Coureur de marathon* (The marathon runner). It exists on two levels: there is the story of the runner, a champion who has fallen upon bad times and has been warned by his doctor that the race he is presently running will surely be his last. Marvaux, the runner, is on one level an ordinary hero fighting to remain autonomous ("it is particularly unpleasant for me," he tells his notary, "not to be able to control myself freely")[75] in a world where the only real autonomy can be achieved through wealth, and where financial need determines what one does. Like Yvernig, Marvaux is betrayed by those who see in his art of running their own profit.

The second level of *Le Coureur de marathon* is a vertical line running through the play, in contrast to the linear, horizontal line of the main plot. It is Marvaux's subconscious, represented by another voice called Marvaux II. Marvaux II opens up a new vision for the listener's imagination; he appears just as Marvaux is losing strength and urges him on even though such advice is clearly going to lead to Marvaux's death. In fact, death here is the one liberating experience; as Marvaux had hinted at the beginning of the race, "it's comforting to no longer want to be a body . . . to be able to anesthetize one's flesh."[76] The metaphor of the locomotive, which Marvaux used to trick his mind into believing his body was a machine, explodes as the runner's heart bursts and Marvaux soars into the air buoyed by pure imagination: "I'm no longer a locomotive . . . What am I now? . . . Ah, I understand . . . I'm a helicopter. I rise into the air."[77] The play's potential tragedy is subsumed by this ending, and the race becomes a metaphor for a flight from reality into oneirism, a flight that was to parallel Gauvreau's own development in the years before his suicide.

Despite some similarities with the theater of Ionesco, Gauvreau's plays owe more to surrealism than to the absurd. His heroes are alone, armed only with their imaginations against a world in which languages and art are perverted so as to be tools for the acquisition of power. Gauvreau screams out, often in his own invented language, his unconditional refusal to accept the tradition and tyranny of the past and to conform to accepted aesthetic conventions.

In 1956 another Quebec playwright, Jacques Languirand, began a foray into *automatisme* which was to lead to something close to France's theater of the absurd, though far less successful. Languirand's first play, *Les Violons de l'automne* (The violins of autumn) was, he claims, an exercise in automatic writing. It is a play built on false identities and words that hide reality rather than reveal it.[78] Critics immediately compared its black humor, its flirtation with nightmarish fears, to the theaters of Adamov and Ionesco.[79] This and another absurdist play *(Les Insolites)* were presented abroad, in London and in Paris, but never convinced the critics. Languirand was to change techniques and to write, in 1965, a play called *Klondyke*[80] in which he abandoned the tradition of the theater of the absurd for an exploration of the relationship between man and nature; the play is more interesting for its postface on "Le Québec et l'américanité" than for what it does theatrically. Since that play Languirand has left the theater and prefers to write poetry which

he often presents, along with music and his own philosophy of
communication, on Radio Canada.

Languirand's plays are an interesting experiment but without
lasting impact on the evolution of Quebec theater. More important,
in the 1950s was a play written by Yves Thériault. While not as
experimental as the plays of Gauvreau or Languirand, Thériault's
drama breaks out of the restraints of realism and announces both
the themes and the discourse of the new Quebec theater. *Le Marcheur*
(The walker) is about silence and hostility; it is a play whose decor
and atmosphere represent a myth of the past that weighs oppressively
upon the characters. It was first presented on the stage of the Gésù
theater in Montreal in 1950 and played for two weeks there. The
Jesuit directors of the theater considered its ending so dark and
amoral that they had Thériault write a new one, complete with
priest and Church doctrine; luckily, even the Jesuits realized, after
one performance, that this moralistic ending could not be kept.

Authority, represented by the father, dominates the existence of
every member of the family in *Le Marcheur*. Victor is an evil father,
not because his intentions are evil but because he cultivates absolute
authority for its own sake. He tries to be faithful to the myth of
the habitant, the peasant backbone of Quebec: a close-knit family
where the wife submits to the husband's desires, where the children
stay on the farm and work to make it prosperous, where the daughter
remains a virgin to her wedding night, and so on. The extent to
which these desires run against human nature becomes the justification, in Victor's mind, for absolute control, complete tyranny.
When the children disobey, they are beaten and eventually banished;
a retarded, weakling son who cannot work is beaten almost to death.
The mother is simply a victim of Victor's power: after their marriage
and brutal wedding night, she recounts, "he wanted to nail me
down. Not only to nail my body. . . , as he had the right to do,
since I was his, but to nail my soul, my thoughts."[81]

What is remarkable about Thériault's play is that this despotic
father is never seen on stage. We, along with his family who have
come to wait for him to die, only hear his regular footsteps as he
paces, walks to meet his death in an explosion of prideful defiance
at the very laws of nature. The father's greatest sin is to want to
play God; his descent from the second floor, as he dies and falls
down the stairs in the final scene, signals the victory of human
nature over man-made order, the liberation of human beings from

the will of any person or institution that claims to control our minds and bodies.

As the *marcheur* dies, his family, reunited in the home after the children's banishment, cry out their resentment and hate of the father. This hate was too strong, too undiluted by Christian love for the Jesuits of the Gésù; in the scene they ordered tacked onto the play a priest enters and hears the dying man whisper a plea for pardon. There is no such plea in the definitive version, and it would be out of character for the mother or children to forgive. Only the father's death can free them of his omnipotent influence; as one son says to the mother, "He's going to die. For you it'll be a renewal. It'll be like a new springtime."[82] As a critic has noted, the children's homecoming is a rite of passage into adulthood, a "second birth . . . their true departure toward a conscious and free life."[83] In this respect, the return to the father's home is really a return to truth, for the father's presence forces each member of the family to confront one another. The aggressiveness of the victims of persecution is often as strong as that of their persecutors. Before the children can become adults they have to understand why one of them is afraid to get married, why another uses flowery words to hide his true feelings, and especially why the mother, having banished love from her existence, is, despite her resentment of her husband, his accomplice to the end. Was it simply human weakness that led her to remain silent while Victor banished his daughter for sexual sins she never committed? Or has the father's presence made a dent in the defenses of those who swore to resist him?

The strength of Thériault's play is that no easy answers can be found to explain the mother's silence and her gesture of companionship toward Victor as he dies. This is a play that exists on the level of emotions; it is a ritual that reflects what was happening to many Quebecers during the years preceding the Quiet Revolution, and Thériault, as Renald Bérubé points out in his preface to the play, managed to "make come alive on stage . . . the great problems that our poetry and novels would deal with in succeeding years."[84] Thériault has chosen the family home, in a highly stylized form, as the center of the drama of an entire society; the society is, perhaps, one large family (as Premier Duplessis or the Church would have had us believe), but the family itself is vulnerable to society, and its members, almost unconsciously, take on the attitudes that the state and Church encouraged in the 1940s and 1950s. The home is no longer a refuge but a torture chamber, and in the plays of the 1970s, especially in those of Tremblay, the themes advanced by Thériault will be taken up again and transformed into a bitter realism. In the development of Quebec theater Thériault's play is a step that will later be surpassed, but it is an important one because it shows that the fresh inventiveness of the 1970s would have been impossible without a break with the stultifying beliefs and myths of the past.

The Beginning

It is usual for critics to date the beginning of the new Quebec theater in 1968 when Michel Tremblay's *Les Belles-soeurs* was produced on the stage of the Théâtre du Rideau Vert in Montreal.[85] But as this chapter has shown, the new Quebec theater was born in the wake of a long and difficult theatrical development in French Canada. The conditions that made this theater possible are, to a great extent, linked to the political and social evolution of Quebec: to the Quiet Revolution and subsequent impatience with reform, to the fall from power of the Church, to education reforms, and most of all to a change in the makeup of the political and cultural elite as more and more young Quebecers moved into the middle class through access to management positions in industry and the Quebec civil service. But there was also a change in the situation of the theater in Quebec which made possible the development of new forms of drama.

In an article written in 1968 for publication in 1969, the theater director Jean-Louis Roux wrote: "We can affirm that the Quebec theater is on the right road, but that its evolution depends on the following conditions: the establishment of a national dramaturgy which can compete with other dramaturgies; the widening diversification of its audience; the increase of official subsidies which will allow important companies to make themselves into permanent troupes."[86]

In ten years, these conditions came to exist. The Canada Council increased its subsidies to theater from half a million dollars to 1.3 million dollars from 1964 to 1965[87] and similar increases occurred in the budgets of Quebec's ministry of culture and the Montreal regional arts council. Of course, subsidies alone were not enough, especially when these subsidies often encouraged a French or international repertory rather than the plays of Quebec's young dramatists. Nonetheless, by the late 1960s, the theater in Montreal had become diversified enough to allow the production of plays that were not in the traditional repertories.

The period from 1950 to 1965 saw the establishment of a number of permanent professional theaters.[88] Just as important was the appearance of a number of amateur or semiprofessional experimental theaters, for example, Les Apprentis Sorciers, L'Egrégore, or Les Saltimbanques, all of which presented readings of plays and produced plays that constituted too much of a risk for the professional theater. In 1960 Guy Beaulne founded the Association Québécoise de Théâtre Amateur which united all these groups and sponsored yearly festivals and meetings, and in 1962 the Conservatoire d'Art Dramatique came under the aegis of Quebec's ministry of culture. All these events had for effect the constitution of a new audience composed of young professionals and intellectuals, as well as of a new breed of actors who were open to experimental theater and improvisation.

Perhaps the most important single element in encouraging the new Quebec theater was the foundation, in 1965, of the Centre d'Essai des Auteurs Dramatiques. It was here that Tremblay's *Les Belles-soeurs* got its first dramatic reading; here plays of Gurik, Maillet, Garneau, and many others got their first chances. The Centre d'Essai saw itself as "a laboratory of dramaturgy, a place where a new form of dramatic discourse could evolve."[89] Public readings of texts were accompanied by workshops and a vigorous effort aimed at the promotion of Quebec texts (by 1981 the Centre d'Essai had in its repertory four hundred plays that could be borrowed without charge). The Centre d'Essai also published texts and edited a newsletter entitled *Dramaturgies nouvelles*. It was a principal force against the commercialization of theater and for increasing subsidies given to Quebec plays, and it helped create the sense of a collective effort, aimed at the creation of a new, national theater.

During the latter half of the 1960s a number of small theaters emerged in Montreal which, with the well-established ones, would be instrumental in presenting Quebec plays. The most important of these small theaters were the Théâtre de Quat'sous (founded in 1964), where the plays of Tremblay and Barbeau were often presented, and the Théâtre d'Aujourd'hui, founded in 1969 by Jean-Claude Germain, which presents an exclusively Quebec repertory. Two traveling troupes also appeared: the Théâtre Populaire du Québec, founded in 1966, and the Grand Cirque Ordinaire, born in 1969, which promoted the ideals of collective creation and improvisation.

By 1968, then, the conditions existed for the kind of revolution Tremblay, Barbeau, Germain, and others were to bring to theater. The means of production were in place, a new audience had formed, but, most important, a new group of authors consciously thought of themselves as the creators of a national dramatic art, one whose themes and techniques were rooted in Quebec's consciousness but were universal enough to have wide appeal. The experience of the past had shown how difficult it was for theater to exist in Quebec; the experience of the future was to show how important theater would become in the development and maturation of a young, vigorous, and fascinating culture.

Chapter Two
Toward a New Realism

Michel Tremblay

> "J'parle comme j'peux, pis je dis ce que j'ai à
> dire, c'est toute." (Marie-Ange Brouillette, in
> *Les Belles-soeurs*)

> ("I talk like I can, and I say what I have to say,
> that's all.")

The year 1968 was a turning point for Quebec: a year after De Gaulle's "Vive le Québec libre," René Lévesque founded the Parti Québécois which radically changed the political game in the province. The theatrical game was about to be changed too, for on 14 August 1968 Michel Tremblay's *Les Belles-soeurs* was first performed.[1] "A turning point in Quebec theater, in Quebec literature, even in Quebec thinking," said one critic.[2] The considerable dramatic innovations that appeared in this play and in the eleven others that were to follow would influence a whole generation of young dramatists, and open a new era in French-Canadian theater. But even more important than theatrical innovations was the way Tremblay saw and depicted Quebec society. His vision gradually came to be an important part of the collective consciousness of French Canada, and it is no coincidence that the period 1968–1977, which culminated in the victory of the Parti Québécois, also marked the beginning and end of Tremblay's "cycle des Belles-soeurs."

Tremblay's theater is intimately linked to the world he describes, and that world is a very specific one: the Plateau Mont-Royal, a working-class neighborhood in Montreal just north of the Parc Lafontaine. It is there that Tremblay was born in 1942, and it is from this neighborhood that he derives the inspiration of his plays. He was born of parents who were well into their fifties and who lived in a small apartment with another family—ten people in all, not counting Michel.[3] Before he could live off his earnings as a writer, in his late sixties, he worked, as his father had done, as a linotypist. Not that the doors to higher education had been slammed in his face; when in seventh grade he was offered a scholarship to enable him to take the traditional *cours classique,* passport to the universities and to a liberal profession. But after three months of *classique* Tremblay asked to be transferred back into the *cours ordinaire,* and this refusal to join the ranks of the middle class is important. "If I had done my *cours classique,*" he asserts, "I'd have been spoiled by the Jesuits. I'd absolutely never write what I'm writing."[4] For Tremblay, the act of writing implies identification with the milieu of his youth.

Tremblay's vision is at once personal, collective, and universal. The cycle of *Les Belles-soeurs* is an interwoven tapestry of characters and events that are taken or extrapolated from the author's experience but that, almost self-consciously, are representative of Quebec society on the one hand and the human condition on the other. The combination of these three elements is undoubtedly what makes Tremblay the most translated and widely performed of Quebec playwrights,[5] but it is also what has caused him to be a controversial figure in his own country.[6]

Les Belles-soeurs.   To understand the significance of Tremblay's quiet revolution in Quebec theater it is important to understand the play that started it all, *Les Belles-soeurs.* It is revolutionary, literally from the very first word, for never before on the Quebec stage had a play been presented entirely in joual, a French-Canadian slang common to Montreal's east end.

The use of joual was probably the biggest bomb in Tremblay's arsenal, for its effects are still being felt, some eleven years later; as Lise Gauvin observes, "Since 1968, the date of the first performance of *Les Belles-soeurs. . . ,* joual invades our literature."[7] The reactions were swift and severe. "It's the first time in my life that I hear, in the space of one evening, so many curses, swear words, filthy bathroom language," complained one critic;[8] another, with slightly less pristine ears, asserted that "the Quebec writer . . . has the strictest duty to describe reality in a universal language . . . classical French and nothing else."[9] These reactions must be put into their proper context; in the late sixties Quebec still suffered from an inferiority complex regarding its own accent and way of speaking, a complex kept alive by teachers of French and some elements of the educated middle class.[10] One doesn't show off one's lack of eduction and culture to the rest of the world, the critics of joual imply, even though, in France, the language of Tremblay's play was acclaimed rather than condemned.[11] What is important here is not to resolve the polemic (a decade after *Les Belles-soeurs* it would appear that joual is still widely used in theater but rather sparingly in poetry and prose),[12] but to see why Tremblay wanted to use slang rather than standard French in the first place. He was certainly not unconscious of the effect it would produce: "the theater I write is a 'slap in the face' which tries to raise people's consciousness," he asserted.[13] But he also had more personal reasons for using joual. "If I had these characters speak French, it would be as if I put myself on a higher plane than them."[14] By using joual Tremblay asserts his solidarity with the people he depicts; joual is the only language that can describe working-class Montreal *from within*. But can joual translate particularly Quebecois concerns into universal problems?[15] Tremblay's answer is simple: "one is never more universal than when one is local."[16] He is not being evasive here; he is expressing an accepted reality in English and American theater which the French theater (because of the value placed since the seventeenth century on standardized language) has never admitted.

The kind of language Tremblay's characters speak is inextricably tied to their social and psychological situation. When, as in *Les Belles-soeurs,* the characters are literally overwhelmed by the problems of daily existence, their language is crude, full of curses, harsh to the ear; when on the other hand characters break out of their daily lives and dream, as do La Duchesse de Langeais or Berthe in *Trois petits tours,* the language loses its harsher characteristics and becomes harmonious, lyrical.[17] In short, there is nothing gratuitous in Tremblay's use of language. As Laurent Mailhot points out, *"joual* isn't a carnival costume which the author has arbitrarily and artificially put on his heroines; it is their everyday wear, it sticks to their skin; it very literally is a part of them."[18]

Les Belles-soeurs establishes not only the language that Tremblay will employ in all of the cycle but also the major themes. It is a play about women—specifically, about Germaine Lauzon who has won a million trading stamps and has invited a group of feminine relatives and friends to help her stick them in booklets. In Germaine's small kitchen (made even smaller by the presence of extra chairs and large cases of stamps and booklets) fourteen women gather, ostensibly to help but in reality to give vent to their frustrations, hates, jealousies, and, in the end, to steal most of the stamps for themselves. The play unfolds somewhat like an opera without music: the narrative (arguments, chatter) of the women is punctuated by numerous "arias," or monologues in which one woman describes her particular private and painful existence, and by two "chorales" in which a group of women recite litanies ("une maudite vie platte," [Life is a damned bore] and "Ode au bingo").

On one level, immediately perceptible in 1968, the play is a harsh criticism of one of Quebec society's most sacred institutions: the family. Husbands are absent (either working or drunk), children are insolent, grandparents are a burden (the grandmother in the play bites like a dog and is calmed only when hit on the head), and relatives (sisters, aunts, in-laws) are jealous enemies. Gone are the peaceful family scenes, the silent and suffering mothers we see in the novels of Ringuet, Guèvremont, or Gabrielle Roy; Tit-Coq's dream of a warm, embracing family is ridiculed by Tremblay. The "blissful guardian of the home and of all virtues" has become the unhappy victim of a world that goes beyond her understanding;[19] as she desperately hangs on to the religious bigotry and sexual ignorance of the past, her husband and children leave her alone in the kitchen in order to get a breath of fresher air, even if it is the polluted atmosphere of the tavern or the club. "Bâtard, que chus tannée" [Damn, am I bushed] becomes the mother's refrain.[20]

Tremblay is not the first Quebec writer to show us an unhappy family. Albert Laberge had already done this in his novel *La Scouine* some fifty years before *Les Belles-soeurs,* and in the theater Marcel Dubé had chipped away at the family in 1965 with *Les Beaux dimanches.* But Tremblay's attacks in *Les Belles-soeurs* and in other plays of the cycle are more than just criticism: they go to the heart of Quebec culture, the Roman Catholic Church. It is the particularly Catholic idea of family that Tremblay attacks, "the family dominated by the priest, crushed by ignorance."[21] For Tremblay, the image of the Virgin Mary is part of the problem: how, he asks, can a religion whose central symbol is a virgin mother be a model for women who are called upon to have sexual relations with their husbands and to bear as many children as possible? How can women find solace or strength in the image of "an . . . inhuman creature, lacking will or autonomy, who, one day, had found herself pregnant without ever having wanted to be?"[22] Condemned to a life of obedience to the sexual will of their husbands on the one hand, and to the sexual prescriptions of the Church on the other, how can French-Canadian women possibly be the keystone of a happy, integrated family?

But Tremblay is less concerned with *denouncing* the family in *Les Belles-soeurs* than he is with describing it and attempting to understand its victims. As opposed to some of his other plays such as *A toi, pour toujours, ta Marie-Lou,* or *En pièces détachées,* the famaily of *Les Belles-soeurs* goes well beyond the limits of the nuclear or even of the extended family. Of the fifteen women present in Germaine's apartment, only six can be considered members of the same family (there is, significantly, only one *belle-soeur,* or sister-in-law); in addition, reference is made during the play to 117 other people who are relatives, friends, or acquaintances of the fifteen characters. In describing the problems of the women in *Les Belles-soeurs* Tremblay is describing the problems of an entire society.

Two themes predominate in his description of the world of *Les Belles-soeurs:* the degradation and alienation of its members and their search for some possible way out of their tragic situation. That the women are alienated one from the other is evident in the backbiting and arguments *(chicanes)* which run throughout the play. The stamps serve to reinforce this alienation both by their nature (Germaine has, in fact, done nothing to *deserve* them, as Marie-Ange Brouillette points out [22]) and by their number. They literally inundate the characters (at the end of the play even more stamps rain down from the ceiling [109]) and demonstrate, ironically, the emptiness of the women's lives. Other objects in the play have similar functions. The telephone hangs loose because no one has told Germaine's daughter that she had a phone call; the radio blares out the daily rosary but no one listens. Yvette Longpré keeps the first tier of her daughter's wedding cake under glass ("it's made like a church sanctuary, pure sugar" [45]), and this object also is a constant, mocking reminder of the failure of her own (and of the other women's) married life. The lack of a sufficient number of soft drinks in the refrigerator is symbolic of a profound frustration with life (the 93-year-old Olivine Dubuc's only words are "coke . . . encore . . . coke" [103]), of desires that will be forever unsatisfied. The game, the contest, becomes the symbol of alienation: each of the women spends hours each day solving puzzles in the newspaper, identifying voices on the radio, but only Germaine has ever won anything. In fact, of course, Germaine's prize is a curse rather than a blessing. The other women, by stealing her stamps, are figuratively picking her apart;[23]

like Rhéauna Bibeau, whom surgeons have progressively dismembered in seventeen operations ("I've got nothing left except one lung, one kidney, one breast" [63]), Germaine is being destroyed by forces that neither she nor the other women understand. The oft-repeated complaint of the women—"j'ai-tu l'air de quequ'un qui a déjà gagné quequ'chose?" ["do I look like someone who has ever won anything?"] (41)—is the desperate cry of those whom the consumer society has left behind and who lose even when they win.

The frustration and degradation that these women feel is the result of their being out of touch with their own lives. They seem to be trying to swim in unknown waters. The confusions and mistakes they make in their language show us how lost they are: *une étole de vison* (a mink stole) becomes "la grosse étoile de vision" (the big mink star), (48), and *une maison mal famée* (a house of ill repute), the detested symbol of their suppressed sexuality, is changed into "une maison mal farmée" (a poorly closed house") (54).[24]

Sex is the greatest concern and the principal problem in the lives of the women in *Les Belles-soeurs*. They detest sex both because it is condemned by the Church (except as a tool for the procreation of the species) and because it is usually a painful experience for them. "Maudit cul" (damned ass), cries Rose Ouimet whose husband asks his due twice a day (102). Yet neither Rose nor the other women can get sex off their minds. When the delivery boy brings Germaine the stamps, she looks him over and tries to fix her daughter up with him. The high point of Lisette de Courval's boat cruise was when a lieutenant ("a really nice hunk of man") gave her the eye (59), just as Marie-Ange Brouillette's excitement for the week was being accosted in a cinema (96).

Part of this preoccupation with sex is the result of ignorance. When the wedding night arrived, many French-Canadian women had no idea what to expect, and neither their mothers nor the Church was of any help. Rose Ouimet realizes all this: "You've really gotta be dumb to bring up your kids in such ignorance, boy! You've got to be dumb!" she exclaims, but then quickly adds, "I sure told my Carmen what men were worth a long time ago! As far as that goes, she won't be able to say I didn't warn her!" (102). Men, on the other side of the sexual fence, are of no help either. They are often brutal, sometimes drunk, never understanding. They are variously described by the women as *cochon* (horny pig) or *écoeurant* (disgusting), and they are associated either with violence, as in the case of

Thérèse Dubuc whose husband has taught her how to tranquilize his mother by hitting her, or with emotional cruelty, as in the case of Germaine's sister Pierrette who left her family to follow "Johnny" and was later abandoned. If men are physically absent from the play, it is because they have no part in the emotional lives of their wives.

On another level, however, sexual problems are symbolic of a more general lack of control these women have over their lives. Nowhere in the play are the implications of sexual frustration clearer than in the "Ode au bingo," a quintet punctuated by a chorus calling out the winning numbers. Frustrated with their marital and sexual lives, bingo (another form of contest, just as alienating as the green stamps) becomes the focal point for a kind of small pleasure, a sort of ersatz sexuality:

Boy, I love bingo! Boy, am I crazy about bingo! I get prepared two days in advance, I'm all jittery, I'm so excited, I can't think of anything but that . . . When we get there, we *take our things off,* then we go right into the apartment where we're going to play . . . Sometimes, *it's a bedroom* . . . Happens every time, *I go nuts.* My god, *is it ever exciting,* that business. I'm head over heels, I'm all hot, I don't know what I'm doing. (86–87, emphasis added)

More than a parody of a parlor game, this "ode" is, as one critic remarked, "the high point of the play" in that it expresses "a confession of impotence" on the part of the women. [25] In fact, impotence is a theme running throughout the play, and its implications go well beyond the sexual. "As for me, I eat shit, and I'm going to eat it for the rest of my life!" exclaims Marie-Ange (21). The daily existence of these women, as expressed in the quintet "une maudite vie platte" (22–24), is a repetition of the same activities, a closed circle from which there seems to be no escape. Caught within the prison of their own kitchens, the women turn their frustrations inward, against themselves and their neighbors. Because their sex lives are painful, they hate the Italian family that openly shows affection; because they are too ashamed of their condition to talk about it with their friends, they come to hate their friends in whom they see reflected their own miserable condition.

The women are the most hostile to anyone who has attempted to break out of the cell of the family and the Church. The nightclub is the principal object of their scorn; the priest has told them that it is a mortal sin to enter one and they are pitiless for Angéline Sauvé (the name, with its celestial overtones, is significant), an unmarried woman in her fifties, who has dared to brighten up her loneliness with a few drinks and a few laughs. "I was brought up in Church basements, and I want to get to know something else," exclaims Angéline (79). "I learned how to laugh at fifty-five years old!" (81). She is banished from the group, sent to Coventry ("Angéline, nightclubs are the devil's work!" [78]) until she goes to a priest and confesses her sin. A more inveterate club-goer is Pierrette, the black sheep of Germaine's family. She is the only woman to have escaped the prison of family life, and the nightclubs of the Boulevard Saint-Laurent (the Main) have provided her with a way out. But to be out on the Main, as we see in the later plays, is to accept another way of life and new values: it is the life of cheap shows, country singers, prostitutes, transvestites, and petty thieves. Life on the Main has its own frustrations, as Pierrette has learned, and the only way she can exist after the loss of her man is to get drunk: "All I can do now is to get tanked . . . I'm too old . . . I'm finished!" (94). Pierrette's liberation is, ironically, hampered by the same force (sex) that so torments the other women in *Les Belles-soeurs*.

But even if Pierrette thinks she is finished, she is not willing to do what Angéline did and to reenter the family. She maintains her difference and her will to resist until the end, despite efforts on the part of the other women to chase her out. She is, above all, a *positive* character, as is Lise Paquette, Linda's girlfriend who has just learned she is pregnant. Like Pierrette, Lise revolts against her condition; rather than become an unwed mother ("unmarried mothers are good-for-nothings and depraved" [100]) she will seek an abortion, an idea abhorrent even to her close friend Linda. Lise's decision is, in fact, the most hopeful element in the play both because it contradicts the accepted Catholic notion of a woman's role within the family and because it gives Linda the opportunity to be reborn, to start life anew: "I want so bad to get out of my crud!" she declares (90). Lise thus turns to Pierrette for an address, and the latter, in a gesture which Tremblay describes as "pure love," takes Lise into her arms and consoles her ("everything will work out, you'll see" [95]).

As the play ends, it becomes clear that the plot revolves around two poles: the kitchen, the women's prison from which escape is impossible because it is never contemplated, and the outside which offers at least the possibility of a new start. It is important to see that Tremblay does not glorify life on the outside; indeed, Pierrette's monologue is one of the saddest in the play and forecasts the disappointments other characters will meet in the later plays. But Lise's decision, and Pierrette's desire to help her, offer at least a ray of hope. Against the hate that the women have for each other, Pierrette and Lise represent the love and understanding that can exist between women; againt the despair of Rose Ouimet and the others, who constantly look backwards for the meaning of their lives, Pierrette and Lise represent a look into the future, cloudy though it may be.[26] "Women are caught by the neck and they're going to stay that way right to the end!" says Rose (102); in contrast, Lise's almost eloquent plea is as follows: "I came into the world by the back door, but I'm gonna get out through the front door" (90).

To what extent can *Les Belles-soeurs* be said to contain a realistic portrayal of Quebec society? When one looks at the techniques employed by Tremblay, it is obvious that he owes a debt to the theater of Ionesco and Beckett far more than to the Quebec theater immediately preceding him. The exponential proliferation of objects reminds us of *Amédée* and the long monologues of *Endgame*.[27] On the other hand, Tremblay's use of joual is obviously an attempt to introduce an authenticity that was absent in the plays of Dubé or Gélinas. This combination of social realism with psychological fantasies can be seen as revolutionary in a theater that, for the most part, defined realism as the illusion of reality on the stage. For Tremblay, realism goes well beyond the "slice of life" and brings to the surface the depths of consciousness; it is multidimensional in that it combines the subconscious with the conscious and refuses to accept appearances. In essence, this type of realism presumes that reality is not just what we see and hear, but includes the unspoken and unseen social and psychological forces that affect the lives of individuals.

The Cycle of *Les Belles-soeurs*. In *Les Belles-soeurs* Tremblay establishes the dramatic structure for the ten subsequent plays in the cycle of *Les Belles-soeurs*.[28] This structure is based on antithesis: the playing off, one against the other, of the home (the family) and the outside. But while these two poles of attraction are opposites, they also reflect each other; the world of the family only becomes understandable when we contemplate the Main, just as the Main exists primarily as an inversion of the world of the family.

The family, as it appears in the cycle, is much the same prison we saw in *Les Belles-soeurs*. For Thérèse in *En pièces détachées*[29] the home is so alienating that she can only cope with it when drunk; her husband is both physically and mentally lame and spends his time watching cartoons on television; her mother, representative of the Quebec of the past, plays the martyr role to the hilt until Thérèse falls to her knees and literally asks pardon for having been born. Thérèse's fifteen-year-old daughter is already becoming hardened to life and spends her time doing nothing. Thérèse and her husband have a bout of arm wrestling before going to bed; fighting has replaced love. Similarly, *Bonjour, là, bonjour* presents us with the picture of a family[30] in which people are mere tools for the satis-faction of other people's desires. Serge, the son who has just returned from Europe, finds that one of his sisters wants to use his apartment for her extramarital adventures, another wants to use him to procure the drugs without which she cannot keep her sanity; the third simply wants him to walk around the house in his underpants so that she can get a good look at his body. These three sisters and his two maiden aunts force him to eat quantities of roast beef and mashed potatoes, literally weighing him down, making escape impossible, figuratively forcing him to accept whatever kind of life the family "serves."

Given these impossible situations, how does one escape? One solution, which will be explored presently, is simply to leave. But what if, like Thérèse who works as a waitress on the Rue Papineau, one has to return to the family each night? Tremblay offers two possibilities. The first of these is escape into a world of total fantasy, represented by Thérèse's brother Marcel, a mentally retarded person whose mind is that of a child. Marcel in *En pièces détachées* fantasizes that he can make himself invisible with his dark glasses, and that he can understand everything around him, even English. He dreams of a revenge on society ("one day I'm gonna get'em all with my power!" [84]) and of becoming infinitely small so that, invisible, he can put an end to his suffering and to that of others: "I'm gonna get smaller and smaller and smaller, . . . and I'm gonna vanish . . . and then I'm gonna kill'em all!" (84). Marcel's fantasies are, of course, a dead end; he will spend his entire life in an asylum. But his illusion of power contrasts vividly with the defeatism of Thérèse and her family. While they repeat the refrain "chus pus capable de rien faire" (I just can't do anything) (90), Marcel, in his delirium, cries *"I* can do everything! I've got all the powers!" (92)[31]

Next to the escapism offered at the end of *En pièces détachées, Bonjour, là* presents the accommodation of the individual to some sort of family structure. In essence, this play deconstructs the family in order to rebuild an entirely new relationship. Rejecting his aunts and three of his sisters, Serge goes to live with his fourth and youngest sister, an unassuming young woman who loves him for himself rather than for any "services" he can provide. Serge's action is a double challenge: on the one hand he must fight society's condemnation of incest, and on the other he must combat the tendency for all love to degenerate and be replaced by selfishness and hate. It would appear that the only love possible in Tremblay's dramatic world is one that contravenes the structure upon which the family exists; only incestuous or homosexual love seems to endure. The intimacy that Serge and his sister shared in childhood finds its natural extension in physical love: "If what we feel for each other is sick, it's a goddam beautiful sickness!" (90). To the brother-sister couple, Serge adds his deaf widower father who had been wasting away in his aunt's apartment. The new "family" thus formed is composed of members who implicitly understand each other and who, unlike the other characters who speak directly to the audience, address each other and even exchange words of love. The title of the play thus represents both an end to an era of misunderstanding (*bonjour* is often used to mean *au revoir* in Quebec) and the possibility of a new type of existence.[32]

Like *Bonjour, là,* the plays of the cycle that deal with life on the Main show the replacement of the family by relationships that have been traditionally condemned by society. The Main is a bit like the underground world of Jean Genet: what the society condemns is glorified, and evil becomes good. "Give me air, even if it's poisoned," is the refrain of those who, like Louise Tetrault in *Demain matin, Montréal m'attend,* want to escape the family at all costs. Through the eyes of Louise, who comes to Montreal from the Beauce region, we discover the world of the Main: the "Meat Rack" bar where women are men and men women; the nightclub where Louise's sister (called Lola Lee) sings as long as she is willing to sleep with her boss; the brothel run by Betty Bird, where Lola Lee got her start. "The world is upside down / my head is upside down / my feelings are upside down / my life is upside down" sings the chorus line at the Coconut Inn (89).

Those who have left the family unit for the Main have traded one set of social structures for another which, if subversive of the established order, is just as constraining in its own way. Cheap prostitutes and singers dream of becoming Gloria Star ("that perfect body . . . beauty in all its splendor" (*Trois petits tours,* 57), but end up like Carlotta, the woman who must constantly play second fiddle to one of Johnny Mangano's "astonishing dogs" (*Trois petits tours,* 46).

In the upside-down world of the Main, the only way to exist is to wear a mask, to create a false identity that, little by little, becomes the real (the only) identity. "My name is the Name of the Game!" sings Betty Bird in English (*Demain matin,* 69); her real name is Béatrice, while La Duchesse de Langeais (a drag queen) is Edouard Tremblay and Hosanna (another queen) is really Claude Lemieux. In the hierarchy of values of the Main the falser a person is the more impressive he is. La Duchesse can reach a glory well beyond that of Betty Bird because the former is "more a woman than any woman" (*La Duchesse de Langeais,* 101); as she/he explains:

When you can get a man to believe that he is in bed with a great international star and that this great feminine star is really a man, because he actually wants to go to bed with a man, well, you're doing all right! (*La Duchesse,* 89)

Hosanna, for her part, aspires to be the queen of the Main and will take the disguise of Elizabeth Taylor's Cleopatra; it is in her mirror that Cleopatra takes shape and that, ultimately, Hosanna finds her identity.

In the world of the Main the transvestite has a special meaning, for his/her very existence is predicated upon illusion. The failure of men in Tremblay's theater ("men are jerks. There are no men in Quebec")[33] and the oppressed condition of women leads the author to create an androgynous being, a man who talks to himself in the feminine. Tremblay explains:

Since there are no men in Quebec, I wanted to make the prototype of the man-woman, that is, a homosexual who represents man and woman . . . So I managed to make a kind of man-woman who, through his very nature, is frighteningly human.[34]

These inverted men are, of all the characters in Tremblay's theater, the most sympathetic, the most *fraternels* precisely because their real self is evident to us beneath their disguises.[35] When Hosanna in her Cleopatra disguise is ridiculed and mocked by her friends, her mask falls. She becomes not a broken woman but a broken *man:* "I'm a man," she declares to her male lover, "You'll have to get used to that as well" (*Hosanna,* 74). La Duchesse de Langeais has a little more class than Hosanna; her disguises are more perfected and her masterpiece is Sarah Bernhardt playing in *L'Aiglon,* "with the wooden leg and everything!" (*La Duchesse,* 90). It is a curious and revealing disguise, for, just as Sarah Bernhardt would have used the pretext of her amputation to show off her remaining, very feminine leg, La Duchesse uses the disguise to show off his very *masculine* legs.[36] "Well, it's no wonder, I almost looked like a man," he asserts (90). Ironic though it may be, the only characters who, through their assumed identity on the Main, have moments of happiness are the transvestites; they are certainly the only characters who experience love. For most of the habitués of the Main, love is a game that is played in the same way as one accepts a false identity: "everybody pretends to love everyone else . . . and since everyone is playing the game . . . everyone ends up by believing each other. . . ," says Lola Lee (*Demain matin,* 51). But Hosanna and her lover share real moments of tenderness when Hosanna's disguise fails ("what's important is for you to be yourself," says his lover [75]), and La Duchesse is hopelessly in love with a Peruvian sailor:

I'm in love like an eighteen-year-old girl who's still got her cherry! And it's not even because he's good at making love! He's not even that! I don't know what it is, I don't know! I just can't do without him! It's . . . it's as if he were my child . . . what I feel for him is almost pure! (*La Duchesse,* 104)

The hostility, the sordidness of heterosexual relationships are completely absent from the homosexual love experienced by Hosanna or by La Duchesse; in fact, Hosanna and La Duchesse achieve a kind of purity in their love for men (the latter has always dreamed of becoming a Carmelite nun, and Hosanna compares herself to the Virgin Mary). The transvestite symbolizes the possibility (or even the necessity) of a definition of love that is not only outside the traditional family but also outside the accepted heterosexual context.

The eleven plays of the cycle of *Les Belles-soeurs* form an integral dramatic world, but three of them stand out as having a special role to play: *A toi, pour toujours, ta Marie-Lou* (Forever yours, Marie-Lou), *Sainte-Carmen de la Main,* and *Damnée Manon, Sacrée Sandra* (Damned Manon, holy Sandra). This trilogy chronicles the destruction of a family and explores two possible means of personal liberation: the Main and religion.

The keystone of the trilogy is *A toi* . . . This play consists of two scenes presented concurrently: on one side of the stage sit Marie-Louise (the mother), alone in front of the television, and Léopold (the father) alone in his tavern; on the other side, ten years later, sit the two daughters, Carmen, who has left the home and is now a "western" singer in a nightclub on the Main, and Manon, a religious fanatic, who sits alone day after day in her kitchen. As the play unfolds, it becomes clear that the marriage between Léopold and Marie-Louise is sheer hell. Marie-Lou ("Don't touch me" {51]) has let Léopold make love to her four times in more than ten years of marriage; each time he was drunk and virtually raped her; each time Marie-Lou found herself pregnant. Like Thérèse's family in *En pièces détachées,* this family is characterized by resentment and loneliness; as Marie-Lou admits, "when we get married, it's so that we can be all alone together" (90). The children are caught in the web of their parents' relationship. Manon, who physically resembles her father, strives to emulate her mother, a saintly figure; Carmen, on the other hand, resembles her mother physically but attempts to break out of the vicious circle as did her father (whose refuge was his tavern), but more effectively.

There are, in fact, four possible avenues of escape from the family. The first is suicide. Léopold, whose father and grandfather were insane, attempts to find a semblance of sanity in drink ("I'm all alone in the fog . . . peace!" [72]), but this solution fails since he, more than any of the other characters, sees *lucidly* the impossibility of his own situation as an individual and as a Quebecois: "we're just small cogs in a big wheel . . . and we're afraid of revolting because we think we're too small . . ." (91).[37] He decides to put his wife and their young son in the car and to drive them all to their death, an action which is an admission of his impotence to change either his social or personal condition.

Marie-Lou's solution is self-inflicted martyrdom. She yearns for the day when her husband will be in an asylum and "I'll be able to keep on knitting in peace, and at heart I'll know that people take pity on me" (73). In the meantime she makes sure that she is seen sadly reciting her rosary; her solution, because it internalizes the sources of her problem (Catholic attitudes towards sex and marriage), is totally ineffectual.

Manon's way out of the family problem is to develop her mother's religiosity to an extreme. She has closed herself into a sterilized universe: men, agents of the devil (like her father), are absent and are replaced by religious statues with which she entertains a particularly intimate relationship. She forces herself to pray for hours on end until she enters into a mystical trance: "it's as if everything gets bigger in your head! Everything gets big . . . I lose my balance . . . it's as if I were floating!" (78). Her trance isn't very different from that of Marcel behind his dark glasses, nor is it inconceivable that her father's insanity has been passed on to her. Her sister Carmen, on the other hand, rejects any means of escape that implies a denial of the problem or a retreat from reality. The day her father took most of the family to their death, she left the house for the Main where, for the first time, her life began to make sense to her:

I'm free . . . In the evening, when I step out onto the stage, in front of my microphone, and when the music starts up, I tell myself that if *they* hadn't died I probably wouldn't be there . . . I'm so happy they're dead. (93)

Carmen's revolt is a conscious one. It is the affirmation of life over death, and above all (as we shall see in *Sainte-Carmen*) of the power of art—even the cheap music of the Main—to transcend human suffering. "Rebel, Manon, it's all you've got left," she tells her sister, but Manon refuses to see the significance of the death of her family and plunges herself deeper and deeper into mysticism (92).

In *Sainte-Carmen* Tremblay explores Carmen's revolt: will she be able to build a new life on the Main? Can the Main fulfill the dreams of freedom that she (like Lola Lee or Betty Bird) hangs onto to justify her decision to leave the family?

The play is constructed along the lines of a Greek tragedy. Carmen has just returned to Montreal from a voyage (almost an odyssey) to the United States where, under the influence of country and western music, she has begun to write her own songs and lyrics. She is welcomed back to the Main by a chorus of prostitutes and transvestites who hail her arrival by chanting: "The sun has come into the world like a big red fist at the end of St. Catherine Street!" (6). Accompanied by her servant, Bec-de-lièvre, Carmen makes a triumphal entrance: she has become a saint and prophet in that she alone, on the Main, has been able to put into words and music the sufferings and joys of her people. She has come to give back language to the people of the Main and, because she has acquired a social conscience as well, she has come to convince them that they can take control of their own future: "with my voice I've decided to help the Main to get out of its hole" (63).[38] But most important, she has brought a message of love to the Main: "I realized that I had something to say to people because I, too, love them!" (25–26). Her motivation is not that of a Marxist revolutionary but of a Catholic worker-priest, even of Christ himself, and her message is not lost on her people. The chorus chants:

Carmen has said that within me I had strength . . . . Everyone has always been ashamed of me. But Carmen told me that I was beautiful and that I could leave the tavern. (53)

In her generosity, in her gestures of selfless love, Carmen resembles Pierrette in *Les Belles-soeurs*. But whereas Pierrette, discouraged and abandoned, needs to drink to hold onto whatever humanity she has left, Carmen finds enough strength within her own personality to spread her message of hope to the Main. And whereas transvestites like Hosanna and La Duchesse need disguises to reveal their true selves, Carmen no longer needs a costume. Her songs and her messages are no longer "western," they are her own:

I began with other people's words and other people's music but perhaps I can end up with my own words and my own music. Oh! To be able to step onto the stage without feeling the need . . . to be disguised! (66)

Carmen's solution to the problems of the Main is not to hide them under an illusion but rather to face them and, ultimately, to surpass them.

But Carmen's message of love and hope, her attempt to legitimize the characters of the Main, meets with the resistance of the nightclub owner Maurice who, like the other businessmen who profit from the Main, will do all he can to keep things as they are. Maurice's role in the play is not unlike that of Creon in Sophocles' *Antigone;*[39] his objections to Carmen's songs have a certain logic given his will to preserve *order:*

I know the Main by heart, it's my mother! She brought me up . . . there's not a square inch of the Main I couldn't recite by heart! And listen to this, little lady; there's no way that you're going to change her! You're not the first one she's met, you're not even the toughest; she can take a lot more than you can give! (60)

But Carmen is unmoved by Maurice's admonitions to stop singing her own songs and to go back to her "western" costumes "with as much bare leg as possible" (61). Her refusal to obey Maurice's orders will seal her fate, as did Antigone's refusal to obey Creon. Like Antigone, Carmen is acting in the name of a higher order than that of society: human dignity. But the wages of disobedience are death, and Maurice, who has already had a number of dissident people killed (including La Duchesse) arranges for his bodyguard Toothpick to dispose of Carmen. True to the tragic style, Carmen's death occurs offstage; she is immediately replaced by Gloria Star who, with her Latin-American costumes and music, puts the Main back in order.

There are obviously many levels on which *Sainte-Carmen* can be interpreted: a call for more authentic Quebec culture rather than cheap imitations of foreign models, a criticism of the defeatist element in Quebec society, even a call for political self-determination. Within the context of Tremblay's theater, however, the play constitutes the destruction of the myth of the Main as a place of hope. Not only does Carmen die, but her assassin attempts to destroy her image and her dream. Toothpick arrives on stage to report (falsely) that Carmen was killed by Bec-de-lièvre after the singer confessed to her servant that the new Carmen, the "saint," was but another disguise to hide a cold, calculating performer interested only in duping the public. Bec-de-lièvre then appears on stage and tells the truth ("Carmen is dead, assassinated by Toothpick" [80]), but her words fall on deaf ears. Toothpick enjoys the protection of the authorities who must, to preserve their power, reinforce the notion that the people are helpless, and that life's rules cannot change.

The ending of *Sainte-Carmen* has given rise to a number of theories. Some critics see a kind of catharsis in the outcome of the tragedy; Carmen may be dead, but her message, her songs, will remain after her; art will, in effect, triumph over death.[40] On a different note, other critics interpret Carmen's death as the final revenge of the Main and its people who refuse to listen to her message of hope.[41] It is indeed curious that Tremblay never presents any of Carmen's songs; what we see on stage is the effect of her message rather than its content. It is also curious that the chorus, whose traditional role is to represent the people and the author, is silent after Carmen's death; their eloquent chants have degenerated into inarticulate grunts (81). It seems that the play confirms the power of the system, its ability to crush any form of *individuality* (this, after all, is also the message of Antigone), any form of deviation that puts the individual on a higher plane than the state. There is, in *Sainte-Carmen,* a sense of helplessness which may, in part, account for the play's lack of success with the public.[42] In any case, the play signifies the end of the myth of the Main as "the promised land, somewhere you can be like everyone else or just yourself."[43]

Having put Carmen to death, Tremblay, in the last part of the cycle, turns his attention to Carmen's fanatical sister, Manon. In *Damnée Manon, Sacrée Sandra* Manon shares the stage with Sandra, a transvestite who had minor roles in other plays. As Manon sits alone in her white kitchen, dressed in black, remembering aloud her past ("God is the answer . . . to everything" [27]), Sandra occupies the other half of the stage dressed in white, in a black room, repeating her credo: "There are no ifs, no ands, no buts, no whys, no wherefores, there's only one answer: ass" (27).

The play has no plot, and is essentially Beckettian in its structure. Manon and Sandra are alone, each speaking directly to the audience; they exist not through any action but rather through memory; they are each *waiting* for some sort of release from their lives. Manon's world of spiritualism is beginning to dissatisfy her; she feels the need for contact with physical objects and has bought an enormous set of rosary beads that she fingers as if they were the sexual organs of a live body: "when I touched them I felt as if there was something alive inside them . . . they're heavy and warm and alive" (33). Her prayers, rather than freeing her from her senses (and her sexuality), have the opposite effect: they increase her desire for a physical communion with the object of her devotion. The crucifix becomes a living body: "I passed my hands over the body of Our Savior . . . and all of a sudden . . . I felt an awful need to kiss him" (43). Sandra, for her part, finds her life of sensuality increasingly unsatisfying ("a kind of empty feeling in my stomach" [37]) and realizes that "Beauty doesn't keep" (48). She would like to be rid of her body, to become a free spirit; she decides to paint herself in green and finds that "my own face doesn't exist any more . . . I don't exist any more" (53–54). But just as Manon is literally weighted down by her enormous rosary beads, Sandra is attached to the physical world by her (his) penis: "It's my cock that runs the show, I just do the work. A slave? Sure am!" (54).

Manon is obviously the opposite of Sandra; born the same day in the same neighborhood, she is, as Sandra admits, "my antithesis, my contrary" (62). At the same time, the two characters complete each other ("it's probably true, she's my twin sister, I feel her, I know her, she's me," says Sandra [63]), the exaggerated sexuality of Sandra being, in essence, the answer to Manon's prayers just as Manon's spiritualism offers an escape to Sandra. We have, in this play, the final incarnation of the antithetical or dialectic structure that began to take form in *Les Belles-soeurs:* the conflict between the family and the Main, between masculine and feminine, between religion and sex, are summed up in the existence of Manon and Sandra, "two halves of the androgynous egg."[44]

In the final scene of the play a sort of reconciliation takes place between the poles of attraction represented by Manon and Sandra. This coming together is possibly only because Tremblay, for the first time in his theater, puts himself in the middle of his own work. In fact, we learn that Sandra's real name is Michel (the author) and that Manon had, in her childhood, been in love with him. But Hélène, the young rebel whom Manon calls "the fallen one" (50),[45] exerted her influence over Michel and convinced him to cover himself in green, an act symbolic of disguise and transformation. Hélène's influence is above all sexual; if, as Manon says, she has pulled Michel "into her hell" (52), it is she who, disguised as the Virgin Mary, comes to Manon in the middle of the night to caress her body: "She ran her hands over me just as I had run my hands over the body of Our Savior, then she whispered softly: 'Do you like that Manon?' " (51). As the caresses become more intense, Hélène becomes Michel, or rather an androgynous Hélène-Michel figure that suddenly appears in Manon's dream: "She stopped caressing me and said: 'I'm not Hélène . . . don't you remember me?' " (51).

The circle is thus complete. The two sexual poles merge into one, and then *absorb* the religion/sex conflict creating one primary force.[46]

It is not by accident that Manon is "damned" and Sandra "holy."
Manon's actions take her further and further away from the state of
religious perfection she desires, whereas Sandra, with her Martini-
quais lover named *Chrétien* (her "black God" [46]) whom she will
receive disguised as the Virgin Mary, actually achieves a kind of
sanctity; her "communion" with her lover will have, in her eyes at
least, a very spiritual dimension. But neither the damned Manon
nor the holy Sandra can exist on their own; Sandra, observing Manon
through the window, realizes that "if Manon hadn't existed, I'd
have invented her" (63).

Manon and Sandra are thus both part of Michel Tremblay, and
part of contemporary society, in Quebec as elsewhere. They reveal,
in Tremblay's words, "a need of the absolute"[47] which can take the
form of a religious or sexual search. But Tremblay sees both religion
and sex as dead ends, human inventions which are incapable of
satisfying man's needs for a transcendent meaning to life. In the
final scene of *Damnée Manon* Tremblay transforms himself, as author,
into the absolute his characters seek. As Manon goes deeper and
deeper into a trance, as she becomes lighter and leaves her body
behind, she is drawn toward an enormously bright light: "Only
your very own Light . . . which makes Truth burst out, the only
Truth, your Truth, only your very own Light is the right Light!"
(64). But this light is not that of God; it is that of the author who,
like a god, has come to call back his character into a state of pre-
creation. For Manon's great revelation, and that of Sandra, too, who
asks Manon to take her along on the voyage, is that they are invented
characters, that *they no longer exist:* "Take me with you because I too
no longer exist," says Sandra, "I too have been invented" (66).

Damnée Manon, with its deus ex machina, stands in contrast to
the other plays in the cycle. In the latter Tremblay had stuck to a
social and psychological depiction of life; salvation, even for Sainte-
Carmen, means escape from a physically and psychologically oppressive environment. But in *Damnée Manon* both the problems and
their solutions are essentially *metaphysical:* the conflict between the
physical and the spiritual becomes the *only* important human problem. Tremblay's resolution of the conflict is both artificial and
unconvincing. The voice of the author may well, as Tremblay implies, be the ultimate truth, but we are called upon to accept this
truth without knowing what it is. In the end it is the *person* of the
author who descends on stage and absorbs the contradictions of his

characters into his own ambiguous personality. But characters have their own independent existence, as Pirandello shows in his *Six Characters in Search of an Author*. Tremblay may have destroyed Carmen, Manon, and Sandra, but the characters he created in the cycle continue to exist, independent of the author's desire to put them to death or to take them back. As one critic notes, the cycle remains unfinished[48] and the contradictions it uncovered remain unresolved.

Conclusion. As we look back on the entire cycle of *Les Belles-soeurs*, Tremblay's contribution to Quebec theater comes clearly into focus. His use of language stands out above all; in *Les Belles-soeurs* it was pure joual but, as the cycle progresses, he develops a language that combines joual with more poetic elements to form a specifically theatrical language. In this sense, Tremblay's theater resembles that of Bertolt Brecht, Luigi Pirandello, or Sean O'Casey in that it uses the spoken idiom rather than the written word as its basis.[49] But at the end of the cycle, Tremblay moves away from realism toward another concept of theater that combines reality with classical and sacred elements.

Tremblay's use of the stage is also innovative. The dramatic space he creates has a double function: it is limiting and reinforces the sense of loneliness and isolation his characters feel, and it is expansive, transforming the family or the Main into theatrical spaces that have meanings that go beyond the specific worlds they depict. For Tremblay, the stage is a privileged space that need not be subject to any distinctions between the real and the unreal. His use of space, like his use of language, tends to assert the independence of theater as a form of art.

The context of Tremblay's plays is inextricably linked to the development of Quebec society, and purposely so: even if he makes few political inferences in his plays, he is far from being politically indifferent. His cries for the political independence of Quebec are muted, but they are there, in the contrast between Carmen and Manon, for example, and especially in his depiction of the transvestite. "We are a people who disguised itself for years in order to look like another people," he asserts, "we have been transvestites for three hundred years."[50] For Tremblay, a nation that, not knowing its own identity, creates a false image of itself in order to survive is doomed to suffer the same contradictions as Hosanna or La Duchesse.

Less specifically political, but tied to the social development of Quebec nonetheless, is Tremblay's depiction of the breakup of the family. It is not just the traditional family that cracks under the pressure of modern society but also the "family" that Quebec society formed prior to the 1960s. This more or less homogeneous group of Catholic French Canadians also breaks apart as Quebec becomes a pluralistic society and exchanges its ethnic status for that of a nation. Even if Tremblay's vision of this transformation is bleak, his plays have—perhaps despite his intentions—shown us a ray of hope. Individuals like Carmen, Pierrette, or Hosanna, freed of the shackles of the past but also terribly alone, bring a new message of love to society. They are not out to change the social order—indeed, none of Tremblay's characters has an acute enough political sense even to contemplate such a change—but they do intend to make changes within their own lives. That they are defeated in their purpose only underscores the validity of their choice and the necessity for society to pay attention to their message. For, when the mask falls, we must see that Tremblay's characters are really ourselves.

Jean Barbeau

> "J'suis pas bien dans ma peau
> J'aimerais mieux être Zorro"
> (Ben-Ur)

> ("I wish I didn't feel so low
> I wish that I was Zorro")

Jean Barbeau, who became known to the theater-going public in 1970,[51] is a playwright who has much in common with Michel Tremblay. Like Tremblay, Barbeau tries to present the reality of contemporary Quebec but rejects traditional realistic theater. Like Tremblay, Barbeau is interested principally in social reality rather than in specifically political problems; "I'm not very well versed in politics," he declares, "but there are things that oppress me and I try to communicate them, to say that those things might be changed."[52] And like Tremblay, Barbeau uses joual in his plays to create a specifically oral (as opposed to literary) medium and to permit his characters to speak "their everyday language."[53]

But there is a great deal of difference between these two Quebecois playwrights. The reality Barbeau presents is not circumscribed to a specific social milieu or geographical location; his plays take place equally in the city, in the suburbs, and in the countryside, and his characters are sometimes middle class, sometimes working class. Nor does the location of the play have the same importance for Barbeau as, for example, "the Main" does for Tremblay. Barbeau's inspiration is sometimes personal, but his subjects are almost always dictated by specific circumstances; his theater has a very utilitarian side and is specifically designed to reflect "the current preoccupations of Quebec."[54]

Jean Barbeau was born on 10 February 1945 in Saint-Romuald, near Quebec City, in a working-class family (his father was a bus driver). "I come from a Catholic milieu, where we had a very simple faith in religion, where we never asked questions."[55] Typically, his mother was the strong figure of the family; his father was "resigned, . . . absolutely neutralized. . . , a reject."[56] The image of a powerful mother and ineffectual father haunts Barbeau's plays; as for the Church, it partially replaces the absent father but its influence is oppressive, permitting neither free thought nor free expression of emotions.

Barbeau attended the Collège de Lévis (the "cours classique" that Tremblay rejected). It was there that he witnessed a student production of Ionesco's *La Cantatrice chauve (The Bald Soprano):* "All around me five hundred spectators were doubled over with laughter. It was fascinating. An amusing detail: the feminine roles in the play were taken by guys, which made the performance seem even crazier. For me, it was a revelation."[57] Shortly thereafter, taking up the challenge of one of his professors, Barbeau and two classmates wrote a text entitled *Caïn et Babel* which was presented at the Collège in March 1966. "What *Caïn et Babel* did was to initiate me to teamwork and to the stage, as well as to the mechanisms that govern a theatrical presentation."[58]

From 1966 on, Barbeau's career takes two distinct directions. The first is the continuation of the collective theatrical experiment begun at the Collège de Lévis. First at the Collège and then at Laval University, with a group of young actors called La Compagnie des Treize, Barbeau created plays in which the distinction between author, director, and actor disappears, replaced by a common effort. Barbeau wrote a kind of skeleton text that was then modified by the actors as the play took shape. But as time passed the distinction between author and actors became greater, and, by 1970, Barbeau was looking at collective creation more critically. The hierarchy of author/director/actor that he had once rejected began to appear to respond to "natural criteria."[59] When Barbeau presented his first play *(Le Chemin de Lacroix)* with the new Théâtre Quotidien de Québec, he did so as an author, and, from that time on, his plays were published.

In 1973 Barbeau left Quebec City to live in Amos (Abitibi) with his wife, and this move confirmed the direction his theater had already begun to take with *Le Chemin de Lacroix* and *Goglu.* Barbeau has become a dramatic author, and, though he still comes south to participate in the mise-en-scène of his plays, ("I am there, with the director, to answer all questions, to get a handle on things."),[60] it is in the writing of the text that he puts his principal effort.

These two distinct directions—collective creation and personal authorship—imply a certain evolution in the subject matter of the plays themselves. The earlier, collective efforts were often circumstantial works, presented with a specific event in mind. *Le Frame all-dress,*[61] presented in 1969, concerns an allegorical float that an Optimists Club and a chamber of commerce decide to send to France, to represent Quebec in the July 14 parade. *Le Chemin de Lacroix,* less collectively authored than *Le Frame . . .* but presented only four months later, was in response to police repression of demonstrators opposing Bill 63 (which gave Quebec Anglophones free choice of English or French schools); its title and dramatic form (the "stations of the cross" experienced by a young Quebecois who is wrongly arrested by the police) were inspired by its being composed during Lent.

The plays Barbeau wrote as a playwright, after 1970, show the development of a certain number of subjects that are both personal and social. More recently, Barbeau has turned his attention to the collective subconscious of Quebec society: "now that I am more and more alone as an author, I am trying to explore the individual, the 'I' in relation to the experience that is called Quebec."[62]

In the following pages I will analyze two plays, representing the two theatrical tendencies of Barbeau: *Ben-Ur,* where the problem is that of the existence of the individual in Quebec society, and *Le Théâtre de la maintenance,* where the problem is the existence of theater, collectively or individually created.

   Ben-Ur.   *Ben-Ur* is a key play in Barbeau's dramaturgy because it provides us with the best, most complete presentation of a French-

Canadian antihero. Victims abound in Barbeau's plays (in *Citrouille, Le Chemin de Lacroix, Goglu*), but *Ben-Ur* seems to touch on the motivations, actions, and reactions of all Barbeau's victims. Moreover, the play can be seen as a long reflection on antiheroes, heroes, and their relationship to Quebec society. "Even in the choice of our heroes," says Barbeau, "we suffer the effects of colonization."[63] In *Ben-Ur* the playwright takes a critical look at the models of Quebec popular culture.

In its dramatic form *Ben-Ur* creates a distance between performance and audience which is similar to the alienation effect defined and used by Brecht.[64] Barbeau rejects the use of the stage to create a slice-of-life effect; in *Ben-Ur* "the stage is a multifunctional place, representing the poles of attraction in Ben's life, that is: the paternal house, the presbytery, the office of the manager of the Brook's Security Company."[65] The play's characters are in a cupboard and are rolled out on vehicles that represent their values and ways of thinking; hence the mother comes out on a chair to which she is attached by a rosary and the priest enters on his prie-dieu. Moreover, each character holds between his or her teeth a *fiche signalétique,* or identity card, which, when read, gives us a cold, ironic view of the character's personality. The mother, for example, is presented like this:

Name, forename? Madame Hubert Théberge. . . . Color of hair? Grey. Color of eyes? Closed. Height? Resignation . . . Weight? Religion . . . Profession? Slave of the dishes and of the rosary. (15–16)

Songs punctuate the performance; sung by a chorus of five actors, they comment on the play's action and criticize the characters' attitudes. The scenery (in the 1971 performance directed by Albert Millaire) adds to the distance between actors and audience by providing a satirical backdrop for the plot. What Barbeau is aiming at here is the Brechtian goal of a critical audience, one which, rather than accepting the play as it is, sees how the situation could be different. "When I write a play," says Barbeau, "I step back from the problem I'm dealing with. . . . I would want the people who come to the theater to do the same thing, to step back [from the play]."[66]

The play tells the story of a rather dull, working-class Quebecois named Benoît-Urbain Théberge, nicknamed Ben-Ur. There is a certain irony in the nickname with its overtones of William Wyler's epic film, but Ben sees no humor in the teasing and tormenting that he gets because of his name. The first part of the play is a series of flashbacks into Ben-Ur's childhood and adolescence. He comes from a family in which the father is, literally, asleep whenever he is home; his mother, "old prototype of a devoted mother, . . . of limited usefulness" (16), teaches him to accept his fate without asking questions just as she has accepted a husband that "God has put in my path to let me earn my place in heaven" (18). As he gets older, Ben learns that he is locked into a life that he hasn't asked for and that seems both meaningless and demeaning. He does poorly at school and has to repeat grades; his schoolmates make fun of him, his teachers call him stupid, and his family (his mother) forces him to serve at mass. "Ben-Ur equals cheap, . . . stupid, little mama's boy," he complains (19), but sees no way out of his situation until he quits school and looks for a job. "I feel that I'm different . . . I have something to give the world," he says (25), little realizing that the generosity he expresses will be either refused or exploited. Predictably he goes from menial job to menial job until, at the age of twenty-one, his parish priest, now a successful businessman, lands him a position as a guard for the Brook's Security Company (a thinly disguised name for Brinks, but with Canadian overtones for "Brook's" was founded in 1867). He is given a pistol and a uniform and, dressed in this new costume, finds that "this uniform transforms a man. . . . I no longer see things in the same way" (42). But Ben-Ur's way of seeing the world is completely out of focus with the world's view of him. Despite his wish to be a useful member of society, all society finds in him is a disposable tool to carry out its less interesting tasks. With his sixty-dollar-per-week job, he thinks of marrying Diane, his former neighbor, but before she consents she wants her man to be cultured. She brings in an encyclopedia salesman who is an anglophone Canadian from Toronto (his mother was Italian, his father German, and his name is Mike). Because Diane has a blind faith in the kind of "culture" that is seen on television quiz shows ("What is the parthenon? Name me the oldest university in Europe. . . . *That's* culture." [52]) and because Ben is too weak to resist the fast-talking Mike, Ben-Ur buys a set of the *American Encyclopedia,* written in English (of course). The purchase, like his job, is a dead end; he has committed almost his entire salary for two years in order to receive an encyclopedia that he can't even read.

Most of the characters Barbeau presents in the first part of the play (the mother, the priest, Diane) are stock characters, and purposefully so; Barbeau wants the audience's point of view to be like Ben's but lucid enough to see that optimism and generosity are not justified. Ben's naïveté is exasperating, but it is also endearing, for he alone in the play has human characteristics. It is precisely these human failings that are explored in the second act where the point of view shifts from the outside (Ben in society) to the inside (the recesses of Ben's mind).

Ben's principal weakness was evident from the time he first put on his uniform. He is a hero-worshipper. "I'm going to become like a hockey player . . . I'm going to spend my time signing autographs," he dreams when he puts his uniform on for the first time (42). But hockey players are only one part of Ben's panoply of heroes. Comic books are his first and primary source of inspiration, and as the second act begins, we see him alone in his room, ignoring his wife and child, resolutely trying to get past the letter *B* in the encyclopedia and delving, in his frustration, into his formidable collection of comic books. He is immobile, childlike, and childish as he dreams of his favorite heroes. In his first dream he is the Lone Ranger who defeats the Indian chief Sagouin Racaille (the name signifies "filthy rascal") and forces the tribe to a reservation; the West is thus made safe for the railroad of the empire-builder Mr. Swinggate. In his second fantasy Ben is Tarzan; he saves the life of an anglophone missionary nun (who, for the African natives, calls God Pady-wack and man Nick-nack) and declares: "A little civilization in these savage regions will only do good" (86). In the third dream Ben is Zorro who has arrived in California to make sure that the territory is annexed to the United States; he has to combat Renato de la Vaca (René Lévesque, of course) who wants the territory to be independent. In the fourth dream Ben-Ur invents his own contemporary comic-book hero, a kind of superman who carries cans of spray disinfectant and is called Anti-Pol ("He who . . . kills all germs that cause pollution, pollution of the air, the water, the earth, of silence, of ideas, of morality, of tranquility." [103]). Anti-Pol attacks a group of hippies, sprays them with disinfectant and, like Christ, sends them away with the words "go to the barber and sin no more" (105).

But Ben has one last dream, and it is not a fantasy. In the course of his work he has shot and killed a man who was trying to steal some of the money he was guarding. This action has made Ben himself a hero: his company gives him a free trip to Mexico, his wife and his mother are proud of him. But Ben, faithful to his gentle and generous character, is troubled; "I only wanted to scare him," he says (106), and he asks the others "why are you applauding? I killed a guy . . ." (107). He is seized with a sudden movement of revolt against his heroes, against those men in the service of the established order who persecute the weak, the Indians, the Africans. He begins to tear up the comic books but, hearing his baby cry, stops: "I can't do it . . . What will the other Ben-Urs do, after me? . . . How will they get rid of their frustrations? What will they use to dream with?" (108) He goes to lie down on his father's divan. "I'm tired . . . I'm going to bed . . ." (108).

Ben's last line, reminiscent of his father's refrain, confirms that the play's principal dramatic effect is irony. There is irony in Ben's job, where he guards quantities of money while he himself is poor, and in the sudden transformation of the priest into a businessman. But it is the character of Ben himself that is a model of ironic contradiction.

When a child, Ben, like most North American children, played cowboys. This game was a kind of refuge from the constant harassment Ben was subject to, since "when [the kids] needed me, they stopped yelling 'Ben-Ur' and came to find me" (58). But here, as in his adult life, Ben is being used rather than useful: "With the neighborhood gang, I always played the good guy. . . . The other good guys always betrayed me for gold, and I found myself all alone in front of a dozen bandits. . . . And I got shot down" (59). Not that Ben *wants* to be a good guy; on the contrary, he would rather have been a bad guy and won. But his destiny is like that of his mother (he's even called a "mama's boy") who has the same sort of martyr complex we saw in some of Tremblay's characters (Marie-Louise, Manon): "I got shot down, but I didn't hate that at all . . . because I was the best of them," says Ben (61). When his neighborhood gang leaves the poor area of town and goes to play with the rich kids, Ben's personal fate becomes the fate of his entire social class. Armed with sticks and hockey pucks for guns, and under a stolen papal banner, the French-Canadian kids confront the English Canadians. The French lose of course, but this time it is they who

are the bad guys: "Everything was weird in the rich neighborhood
. . . There it's the good guys who win. I was never on the right
side," Ben laments (59). But the rich "good guys" are more violent
and cruel to Ben than the poor "bad guys" in his own neighborhood.
What is "good" and what is "bad" is not a function of virtue but
rather of power, and this a lesson Ben will never learn.

It is thus ironic that Ben, in his play, in his work, and even in
his dreams does everything to protect and defend the system that
oppresses him, and that he is incapable of identifying the source of
oppression. The Lone Ranger, guardian of an oppressive social order
(at least from the Indians' point of view), glorifies Tonto and other
Indians who have betrayed their own people; the Indians, the Africans, the Californians, are all metaphors for the Quebecois, but
Ben-Ur doesn't see this. Nor does he understand that his comic-
book heroes represent "the worst values of American society: racism,
imperialism in all its forms, violence."[67] But why should Ben see
through the comic-book heroes to the truth? Like religion for his
mother, comic books are the only refuge he has from a painful and
demeaning existence: "Life wasn't rosy when I was young, but at
least I had my comics. . . . OK, I took it on the jaw more than
the others, but my heroes, they didn't take any crap" (62). Like all
of Barbeau's protagonists, Ben gets so caught up in compensating
for his weaknesses that he can never go beyond his state of victimization and become a "creative nonvictim"[68] like Tremblay's Sainte-
Carmen. He ends up emulating his oppressors, like the feminists
in *Citrouille* who ape the worst characteristics of the chauvinist
male.

Why is Ben-Ur so miserably incapable of breaking out of the
straightjacket that keeps him a victim? Ironically, because the original Ben Hur led a revolt of Jewish slaves, it is Ben's *name* that
imprisons him. He was baptized Benoît for his mother's father and
Urbain for his mother's cousin who is a priest (and for numerous
popes); from his birth on he is caught between a matriarchal family
structure and the Church. In a very real sense, Ben is a bastard, for
his father (who, when not asleep, beats him) has literally deserted
the family and has been replaced by the priest, the only male authority his mother obeys. "Go hide, Ben-Ur," sings the chorus,

> pick up your crap;
> shut your trap, Ben-Ur,

> And go away, to your mother's arms
> To the priest's skirts
>
> (14)

Ben's name is his birthright, and nothing is more understandable than that he should want, one day, to "debaptize" himself and to become an adopted child or an orphan that his mother has found "on the church steps . . . or at the dump, or in a garbage can wrapped up in the sport pages of *La Presse*" (19). To have a new name (or no name), or to be an orphan is to be free of the identity that imprisons Ben and over which he has no control.

Like most Quebecois, Ben is not attacked by society for what he *is*, but for what his ethnic identity represents. "For a long time I didn't know my name, and who I was, except from the outside. My name is "pea soup." My name is "pepsi." . . . My name is "damn Canuck," writes the poet Gaston Miron.[69] Ben's name sticks to his skin and brands him as "just a cheap little French Canadian" (17). But his name is also his language (French) and there is more than irony in the fact that the encyclopedia is in English. In the "A.B.C. of Unemployment" the chorus sings:

> To get ahead
> Put your tongue in your pocket
> Speak white, men,[70] or else
> They'll just pass you by
>
> (29)

For Ben to put his tongue in his pocket (*mettre sa langue dans sa poche*) he must (as the expression implies in French) not only hold back his words and ideas but also put away his own language and use another. Surrounded on all sides by pressures to speak English, he sees his own language as the equivalent of unemployment and "bad luck" (29).

In a country that, like Quebec, has been conquered, in which the language of the majority was, until recently, the language of the poor, in which the dominant institution (the Church) taught resignation or collaboration with the oppressors, can there be any heroes? "It's too bad all our heroes are Americans," reflects Ben, "not that I have anything against Americans, but . . . I think it'd be fun if . . . if we had our *own* heroes" (98). The Church and the middle class proposed, as the classic French-Canadian hero, Dollard des Ormeaux (another ill-fated defender of New France against the Iroquois), but, as Ben notes, there are no Dollard cartoons and his effectiveness in saving the colony is disputed by historians. What is left besides hockey players and popular singers (Diane Dufresne, Robert Charlebois)? But they aren't *really* heroes, "a hero is immortal. . . . Take Tarzan, the Lone Ranger, Zorro . . ." (98). What about Ben-Ur himself then? "Let's see . . . Ben-Ur, national hero . . . No, I really must be nuts to think like that . . ." (99).

Other playwrights (Germain, Ferron) will take this question of national heroes one step further and propose a new mythology. What interests Barbeau is less the myths themselves than the *need* for myths. Ben's childishness in the second half of the play is deceiving; this man who appears inoffensive has killed an unarmed person. Even if society approves of Ben's action there is something left in Ben's generous nature that questions whether money is worth more than a man's life. Comic-book heroes provide more than a refuge for Ben; they provide a justification for his own unjustifiable action and, at the same time, obliterate the humanity in him that led him to question, however feebly, his own values.

Arthur Miller would have made *Ben-Ur* into a tragedy, like his *Death of a Salesman,* the individual crushed by the system. But Barbeau sees nothing tragic in Ben; "I laugh at these ghosts of the past that one always sees in the street," he remarks.[71] If *Ben-Ur* is a funny play, it is because comedy is the only way to extricate oneself from an impossible situation. But the play is above all a lesson. Even if its message is directed primarily at the Quebecois public, the questions it poses are, unfortunately, universal. Is there any society where the myths that provide a refuge for the oppressed do not justify the oppressors?

Le Théâtre de la maintenance. Le Théâtre de la maintenance (The theater of maintenance), first performed in 1974 but not published until 1979, was, unlike *Ben-Ur,* solicited from Barbeau in order to teach students in tenth and eleventh grades what theater is all about. In its first versions (unpublished) it contained numerous extracts from other French-Canadian dramatic works; these were eliminated in the second version that became a play in its own right.

As its title implies, *Le Théâtre de la maintenance* concerns a crew of maintenance workers (four women, three men, and a boss) who begin their day's work in a theater. Part of their job is to clean the stage, and, as they begin their work, it becomes clear that three of the workers are on loan, as it were, from another play—Edmond Rostand's *Cyrano de Bergerac*. An unattractive young man named Bergeron attempts, with the text of the nineteenth-century French play, to show a handsome but unsuccessful Christian how to seduce the beautiful young Roxane. To the displeasure of the boss Guérin, Christian and Bergeron spend more time rehearsing their lines than cleaning the stage. The other workers bring out their mops, buckets, and brooms but are easily distracted by Bergeron who, taking advantage of their interest, begins to explain to them the function of the various parts of the stage as well as the nomenclature used in the theater. Little by little, the maintenance workers warm up to the idea of presenting a play on the stage. Taking advantage of Guérin's temporary absence (he has gotten his head stuck in a bucket), they rehearse a scene from *Cyrano* under the direction of Bergeron; they later present a second skit, an improvisation directed by Lyse Maheux, the most militant and feminist of the workers. Lyse's skit is a kind of sociodrama with a very specific purpose: she wants to force Guérin to rehire one of the workers (Hélène) whom he has fired for being drunk on the job. The skit succeeds and Hélène is rehired, but we learn at the same time that she is really not drunk, that her behavior is merely an *act* used to gain attention. Meanwhile, Bergeron, Christian, and Roxane live out the plot of *Cyrano de Bergerac;* Rostand's lines and their own lives become so intertwined that it is impossible to tell where theater ends and reality begins. In short, it becomes clear that the entire play is a game, and that the maintenance crew is a team of actors with fictitious personalities. Admitting to this reality, the actors begin to put on a play for the benefit of the audience; it will be, of course, *Le Théâtre de la maintenance . . .*

The didactic purpose of the play is so obvious in the many scenes in which Bergeron presents his ideas of theater that it needs little comment. Bergeron is not only a teacher, he is a director and the author's mouthpiece. For him theater is art, poetry; it is the perfect expression of "exquisite sentiments . . . using metaphors, comparisons" just as Cyrano does when speaking to Roxane.[72] Theater presupposes a boss, a director: "the director's work is to supervise the actors . . . to help them find the right tone, the right movement, the correct intonation" (57). The text is important, but it is not the final authority; "we don't 'put on' the play as it is, we use it. . . . We extract the words from it and adapt it to our situation," says Bergeron (72). In sum, Bergeron's theories are almost a carbon copy of the ideas of Jacques Copeau in France,[73] a director who brought together painters, actors, and authors in an attempt to create, on the basis of a text, a composite art form which was specifically theatrical.[74]

Opposing Bergeron's idea of theater is Lyse Maheux. If theater is an art, says Lyse, "it's not for workers. It doesn't have anything to do with our interests" (57). What she proposes is a kind of collective theater, similar to the Bread and Puppet Theater or the Teatro Campesino in the United States. "We won't borrow a text from anyone," she tells the other workers, "we'll make it up ourselves. It'll be our ideas, put into our sentences, and said in our own words" (81). Theater is not an art but a tool to be used to gain specific results in specific social or political situations. The actors have no boss; the person who suggests the ideas for the play becomes a natural, but temporary director. Finally, the play appeals to the audience's intelligence rather than to its emotions. Brechtian techniques of alienation are achieved by actors who "present themselves on stage as actors playing a character and not as the character himself" (89).

It would be hard to reject one of the above definitions of theater for the other. Together, these two theories trace Barbeau's own evolution and, if Bergeron, like the author, no longer participates in collective creation, he at least understands it and sympathizes with its purposes. "The theater has come down from the clouds," he says upon seeing Lyse's improvisation. "It passed through this house, Hélène's house, and it is returning to the street where it began" (97).

But beyond the controversy between personal and collective theatrical creation, Bergeron understands something about drama which the play itself shows to be an elementary truth: theater is an essential part of life, as necessary to human beings as eating, breathing, or sex. Clara, a middle-aged worker who is unmarried, naturally improvises a skit about an unwed mother, thereby compensating for her own loneliness. "You're all actors but you don't realize it," says Bergeron to the others (71). Roxane, even when trying to be herself rather than a character in *Cyrano,* cannot help but recite the lines written by Rostand; after all, in the circumstance, these lines are better than anything she herself could have thought of. "For once

I wish . . . that it wouldn't be theater," she complains to Bergeron who answers: "Sorry, but it *is*" (86).

Besides being a director and a teacher, Bergeron is a giver of *words*. The French expression *donner la parole* (to give the word), often used in the theater, has a special sense here, for *la parole* in French implies the spoken word much more than its synonym *le mot*. Bergeron teaches the maintenance crew the names of various objects in the theater (flies, proscenium, backdrops, e.g.). *Cyrano de Bergerac* becomes a metaphor for the entire play. As Bergeron provides Christian with words, with a text, so that Roxane will love him, he also provides the crew with the tools that would enable them to use theater for their own purpose and, beyond this, gives the audience an introduction to a form of expression that will one day become their own. Without Bergeron's initial instructions *Le Théâtre de la maintenance* would have been an impossibility.

In Quebec, and in Barbeau's theater, language provides a focal point for national concern. To be able to shake off the anglicized French that is the result of two hundred years of English domination and to use a language that is autonomous, in which every object or thought has a French (or a Quebecois) name is a way-station on the road to cultural independence. It is no accident that so many of Barbeau's plays concern language. In *Le Chemin de Lacroix* a Frenchman "corrects" the joual of the main character, a Quebecois; in *Joualez-moi d'amour* a Quebecois finds it impossible to have sex with a Parisian prostitute until she trades her argot for his joual. Barbeau's characters are caught up between the impoverished language they speak and the authoritarianism of French culture that would replace *a French-Canadian way of speaking French* with Parisian slang and Continental expressions. But Bergeron, in *Le Théâtre de la maintenance,* seems to escape the dilemma. Sure of his own Quebecois way of speaking while possessing a more than adequate French vocabulary, Bergeron has none of the characteristics of powerlessness and impotence we see in Barbeau's other characters. Ben-Ur kept his tongue (and language) in his pocket, but not only does Bergeron possess his own tongue, he offers it to others and makes it so accessible and familiar to them that they can *play* with words and say, for example, "je cours dans le jardin, je jardine dans la cour. Le nez dans les frises" (50).[75] Power, here, does not come from the barrel of a gun but from a well-supplied arsenal of words. Bergeron has enabled his crew mates to conquer their language so as to conquer their own lives.

In *Le Théâtre de la maintenance* as in *Ben-Ur,* Barbeau uses theater as a means of instructing as well as entertaining. "When people are seated in the theater," he says, "I prefer that they have a good time. But I don't want them to forget anything."[76] His theater is a constant attack on accepted cultural and social values, as well as a firm encouragement to break out of the victimization of the past. The audience learns a lesson from Ben-Ur's problems; both actors and audience profit in a very practical sense from *Le Théâtre de la maintenance.*

The lessons contained in Barbeau's theater, however, go beyond the dramatic world he has created. Unlike Tremblay, whose plays created their own universe on the stage, Barbeau's theater refers principally to a reality that exists outside the theater. Ben-Ur's problems are due to an economic and political situation that we never really see on stage (except indirectly in some of the satirical backdrops), whereas Tremblay takes care to make us feel the oppressive atmosphere of the family, or the harsh and unforgiving character of the Main in the play itself. Ben-Ur's situation is tied to the political and social evolution of Quebec, a force over which the theater has but limited influence. Even in *Le Théâtre de la maintenance* the everyday existence of the actors, reflected in the firing of Hélène as well as in the love affair between Christian and Roxane, is separate from the play we see. If, for Barbeau, theater is as important as life itself, it is because life is too complex to be contained on the stage; theater has to descend into the street and become part of life before it can become a form of art.

Barbeau's theater is thus never a place of refuge for the spectator, tired of his daily existence, looking for an amusing diversion. It is a place of denouncing, of demystifying, of preparing for a battle that will be fought outside the theater. "In the theater, things always finish badly. That's what I hate," says Hélène in *Le Théâtre de la maintenance* (58). To which Barbeau would probably answer: When the political and cultural climate is better, when the Quebecois are at home in their own country, you'll like the theater a lot more.

Michel Garneau

The theater of Michel Garneau bears, at first glance, little resemblance to that of Tremblay or Barbeau. His plays are written in free verse, punctuated with very lyrical songs, and played in decors where place and time—even social context—are uncertain. Garneau does not react against traditional realism; he is oblivious to it.

Yet Michel Garneau's theater is characterized in Quebec as one of "poetic realism."[77] When we look carefully, it becomes clear that this dramatist's purpose, far from being an escape into the imaginary, is the transformation of day-to-day reality into a new kind of expressionism where the conscious serves as a symbol for the subconscious. Garneau is to theater what Ingmar Bergman is to the cinema in that the emotional or affective reality of life dominates political or social reality. And Garneau affirms a common purpose with the Swedish filmmaker whom he sees as apolitical in any partisan sense but as provoking *"des hosties de prises de conscience"* (a damn lot of consciousness raising).[78]

Garneau came to the theater after a number of other activities. Born in a middle-class Outremont (Montreal) family in 1939, he began his literary career by writing poetry at the age of thirteen; when seventeen, he left home to become a radio announcer in Rimouski. His talents were soon recognized by the Canadian Broadcasting Corporation which offered him a contract in Montreal. He wrote songs and lyrics, he continued to write poetry, and in the late 1960s he left broadcasting to devote himself entirely to writing; it is from this time on that he began producing the most prolific theatrical repertory in Quebec—twenty-one plays in ten years.

Two events stand out in Garneau's life as influencing the course of his career. The first was the untimely death of his brother Sylvain in 1953, when Michel was fourteen. The notion of death, of his own as well as his brother's, began to haunt him and he tried to express it:

It all began when my teacher asked me to write an essay on death. My brother Sylvain had just died and I was reading Hemingway; I was hung up on this sentence: Death is full of shit, and all I could write was: "I'm fourteen years old, I don't know much about death but Hemingway wrote . . ." My studies ended there.[79]

Where his studies ended, his writing began; two years later he began to write (stories, poems, outlines for plays), and in 1962 his first collection of poetry, entitled *Languages,* appeared. Of this early poetry, the critic François Ricard has noted the "central inspiration and major themes" of all the work to follow: "an entanglement of suffering and the desire to live."[80]

The second influential event in Garneau's early career was his imprisonment during the October 1970 crisis and the imposition of martial law. It became clear to him that his own future was inseparable from that of Quebec and that the struggle for political independence was linked to the personal anguish he had expressed in his writing.

In fact, it was during the decade of the seventies that Garneau was the most prolific, and that he became a socially committed playwright. This *engagement* does not imply the rejection of his earlier personalist and poetic work but rather its integration into a political context. Garneau sees no contradiction between poetry and social commitment, and if, after 1970, his verse most often takes the form of drama, it is because theater is a public art. "In the theater," he says, "the author can never fall into pure aestheticism. . . . It is very healthy for poetry to live in that context. It makes it socially responsible."[81]

Garneau is, along with Barbeau, the Quebec dramatist who has thought the most about the implications of theater as a phenomenon. If he accords so much attention to poetry and music in theater ("theater is a poem, a great song, a square dance"),[82] it is because words, for the poet, are an end in themselves. "Language," he says, "is marvelous, crazy, an absurd and incomprehensible human trait. . . . To be conscious of language is to be conscious of the means that permits consciousness of everything."[83] Garneau, like Tremblay and Barbeau, uses a written form of joual, but he achieves a lyricism never attained by these two playwrights. This is because both Tremblay and Barbeau use joual as a means to describe a certain reality; Barbeau tries to capture the social reality of his characters, and Tremblay is at his best when his language is transparent, when it seemingly fuses with the inner existence of his characters. Garneau's language is more opaque; it is a semitransparent screen between the characters and the public, "a language of the whole being."[84] Many of the passages in his plays could stand on their own as poems or as songs (for example, the quartets in *Quatre à quatre,* or the duets of a besieged young couple in *Sur le matelas*); moreover, Garneau is less interested in painting characters who stand out (like Ben-Ur or Sainte-Carmen) than he is in describing the "visible and invisible relationships" between people,[85] a complex web of feelings that poetry alone can express.

Garneau's interest in poetry does not preclude a very intimate involvement with the practical aspects of theater. Like Barbeau, he began his career as a playwright by participating in collective productions: tours within the province with actors in 1968 and 1969, during which "we didn't come to present a show but to compose a play using elements found on the spot."[86] These sorts of experiences led Garneau to formulate a theory of the theater production that he has outlined in a booklet entitled *Pour travailler ensemble* (For working together) written for his participation in a *cellule de création* at the 1978 Avignon Theater Festival in France. Unlike Barbeau, Garneau has not changed his attitude but has maintained consistently that the written text is but a preliminary step in a collective effort. "I discovered," he says, "that my role was to pretend not to write the play."[87] He is, to be sure, in command of the productions that he directs, but he leaves a great deal of room for improvisation: "we improvise / from the results / of the writing workshop / we rewrite / from the results of the improvisations / we re-improvise," he writes in *Pour travailler ensemble.*[88]

There is a seeming contradiction here between authorship and improvisation which is made more complex by the publication of twelve of Garneau's plays: in their written form these plays become the literary creation of a single author. Garneau attempts to resolve this contradiction by calling himself the repository for the collective consciousness: "I consider myself a collective working alone."[89] In fact, as we shall see, Garneau transposes his personal concerns into collective concerns and uses theater to express society's subconscious.

Garneau's theater is remarkably consistent in its themes and subjects. His characters are almost invariably young adults who attempt to find love and happiness in an oppressive world. His dramatic universe is one of contrast between, as one critic has put it, "desire and repression"[90] or, as another critic has said, "the angel and the beast."[91] The personages in his plays try to reconcile these contradictions and build some sort of authentic life within the phonyness of the worlds they live in, but they are not always successful. In the early (1971) play *La Chanson d'amour du cul* (The love song of ass) an employee of an advertising agency, Maurice Baribeau, finds his life hopelessly mixed up by the ideas he is supposed to sell: the commercialization of sex and its exploitation in sales campaigns.

When an adolescent, love seemed to be quietly resting one's head on a girl's lap, without moving, because "I was afraid that if I moved I'd break the world in two."[92] But, with the help of sex magazines and life-size inflatable plastic girls, the notion of love has irremediably broken up and Maurice has become, as his coworker puts it, an *"obsédé sexuel"* (27). Baribeau is a latter-day Don Juan, condemned to perpetual frustration not by divine will but because "everything was organized, I soon realized, to keep sex on one side and love on the other, far apart" (29). He tries to compensate for this unnatural division by believing that, by having sex, he is making love, but he ends up in love not with women but "in love with love" (40). His explicitly sexual song of love falls flat; he attempts to kill himself by jumping out the window but stops short, realizing that he's on the first floor.

The conflict between love (emotional and physical) and sex is a perpetual one in Garneau's theater. The young couple in *Les Célébrations* (1976) is sexually incompatible, and the husband, to compensate, takes vicarious pleasure in long, succulent (but lonely) meals. The refrain *je t'aime* punctuates each of the play's scenes, but this is, as the woman realizes, another aspect of the "verbal Ping-Pong" that they play and that prevents them from living their love.[93] A ray of hope is offered in *Adidou adidouce* (1977) where an unattractive young man and an equally homely young woman, both of them sexually naive, decide to marry. Even if the young man's bachelor party, complete with pornographic movies and *plottes* (whores) almost ends in tragedy, the play closes with the happy noise of the newly married couple making love to the accompaniment of a sweet love song sung by the rest of the family.

In the end, love is really a metaphor for life, for the desire to live without being subject to the encroachments of society. In *Sur le matelas* (On the mattress) these encroachments are clearly labeled. As Alfred Rimbaud and Charlotte Verlaine (the names evoke, besides poetry, another kind of love, condemned by society) attempt to live their love in their small room which contains only a mattress and which Garneau labels a "butterfly cocoon," they are subject to the intrusion of a number of people whom the author calls "hairy caterpillars." They first have to endure the questions of an investigator for the archbishop who is doing a survey of sexual habits. The investigator, a modern, attractive lady representing a contemporary, computerized version of the once-reactionary Church in Quebec, poses a long series of questions (such as "how many times a week do you make love?," "can there be sex without love and love without sex?," "should priests marry and if so should they do it only with nuns or with any lay woman?")[94] which enrages the young couple who see this survey as an inexcusable invasion of their privacy. Furious, they put the investigator physically out of the apartment. But she has gone to the police and, in a manner like that used in October 1970—quoting a "special law on riots at home" (36), a policeman enters. He is but the first in a series of intruders whom the couple manage to expel but whose presence will have serious consequences for their relationship.

Besides the representative of law and order, Alfred and Charlotte are visited by a (bad) poetess who attempts to live the life of some vaguely nineteenth-century tragic heroine; a revolutionary appropriately named Che who fears an imminent invasion by the American hordes; Charlotte's mother who is scandalized that her daughter is living in sin; a very modern priest named Father Watts, who has married couples in snowmobiles, acrobats in the air, divers under water, even homosexuals; and a woman named Brigitte (Bardot?) who is an expert on sexual technique. Some of these characters are very obviously aggressive: the policeman, though he protests "we're not fascists" (36), nonetheless intends to pay a visit to a nursery school where "even little kids are making seditious drawings" (43), and Che, who does not hesitate to use his karate on the young couple, declares "everything must be sacrificed to the revolution" (59). The aggressiveness of others is more insidious. Brigitte, for example, preaches the liberation of men and women from the sexual taboos of the past, but her solution is purely mechanical (erotic technique, pelvic exercises, and a sure hand in the kitchen) and reflects the same exploitation of sex for its own sake that we saw in *La Chanson d'amour du cul*. Charlotte's mother and Father Watts want the couple to be married, to be officially man and wife (Father Watts will even marry them in bed), but once their love is labeled, officially certified, it will become something abstract, detached from those who are in love.

Alone finally, at the end of the play, Charlotte and Alfred try to make love but realize that they're being watched by two hundred spectators in the theater. "They'll hold it against us if we make it . . . they'll be sad if we don't make it," says Charlotte (89). It now becomes obvious to them that love cannot exist on stage, that it cannot be public. Charlotte suggests that everyone, audience included, go home and make love; only in the privacy of the home, in secret, can one escape the images of love that society imposes. But this ending brings us full circle to the beginning of the play, where Alfred and Charlotte naively believed that a home is "a place that no one can enter" (20). Neither the couple nor the author have been able to isolate themselves from the essentially destructive influence of the outside world.

Sur le matelas is a kind of blueprint for Garneau's other plays, since it outlines the basic dramatic structure that pits an individual (or a couple) against exterior forces. Sometimes these forces are social or cultural in origin; sometimes they are psychological and contained within the characters themselves. In the following pages I shall look at two plays representative of these tendencies: *Quatre à quatre,* in which the conflict arises within an individual, and *Strauss et Pesant (et Rosa),* in which the problems are those of an entire society.

Quatre à quatre. First performed by secondary students in Ste-Thérèse in 1973, *Quatre à quatre (Four to Four)* is Garneau's most successful play and, after its run in Paris in 1976,[95] his best-known. Its popularity is undoubtedly due to its universality, for it is one of the most personalist and intimate of Garneau's plays. It is an attempt to explore, through poetry and music, the personality of a single woman.

The play takes place within the mental space of Anouk, a twenty-year-old Quebecoise living, presumably, in Montreal. "I exist just inside myself," she says as the play begins.[96] But, unfortunately for her, she can't separate her own life from that of the three generations of women who preceded her. As she sits alone watching television, those generations—her mother (Céline), grandmother (Pauline), and great-grandmother (Anne)—appear to her to talk about their lives, their husbands, their searches for love and happiness, their failures and loneliness. At first, Anouk listens; then suddenly taken with a violent revolt, she attempts to be rid of these ghosts of the past, to deny their relevance to her life. This moment of revolt is followed by a calm, a moment of acceptance. Anouk realizes that the past generations are part of herself, that she cannot get rid of their influence. "You want to go under us / but you must pass above us," says the great-grandmother Anne (49), and Anouk understands that the way to her own destiny is through a reinterpretation of the past in the light of her own experience.

The play exists on two levels. The first of these is Anouk's attempt to free herself from the influences of the past. In the generations preceding hers a certain mental structure has been formed. Anne, who lived on a farm in the style of Maria Chapdelaine, is the most naive of the women; not only has she never traveled further than her parish church, her mind has never dared break out of the strait-jacket that agricultural society has put it in. She is a "slave of man / slave of the priest" (46) and was afraid to play her husband's violin once he was dead; she is "the naive one / the sunlit hymn of sugar / the beautiful slave who lays myths" (45). Her calm acceptance of her place in society contrasts with the strident cries of the grand-mother, Pauline. Pauline is a drunkard. She learned early in life what men wanted of her (every man in the parish has slept with her except the priest, who is a homosexual) and takes refuge in an alcoholic revolt, a torrent of imprecations against her fate (and especially against men) which leads nowhere. If Anne is a sheep, Pauline is a wolf who bays at the moon, perhaps even a werewolf, "an ordinary monster, the hypocritical pride of the parish" (59) which uses her as a lesson in bad morals and as a convenient whore. Experience has embittered her ("I've drunk up all the legends" [59]) and has made her "black like the eclipse of a family" (31), but for all her lucidity and cynicism, she is still very much the slave of her sexual desire and lets herself be "planted like hay / in all submis-siveness" (46) by men.

Céline, Anouk's mother and Pauline's daughter, is the most con-tradictory of the women. She is the first to have been brought up in the city; she is also the first to understand, however unclearly, her condition as a woman. She is alone, abandoned by a husband who is a traveling salesman and spends his time in innumerable Hôtels Saint-Louis. At times Céline is like Tremblay's Marie-Lou, alone in her self-pity, refusing to leave the house, rejecting human contact. But at others she is warm, understanding, and hers is the most lyrical and beautiful song of the play:

> j'ai eu trois enfants mais chu encore vierge
> ah que j'voudrais don pouvoir er'commencer
> ah que j'voudrais don
>
> l'amour existe c'est sûr
> pour qu'on souffre autant

ah que j'voudrais don pouvoir er'commencer
ah si j'pouvais don

(42)

(I had three children but I'm still a virgin
Oh would I love to be able to begin again
Oh would I love to

Love exists, that's for certain
Why else do we suffer so much?
Oh would I love to be able to begin again
Oh if only I could)

Where Tremblay's Marie-Lou had lost all hope, Garneau's Céline still keeps alive a naive faith in love as an ideal, as an image. Some day, she hopes, her husband will come back to her. But Anouk realizes that "my mother has no future, just a past" (37) and, looking at her own situation, knows that her mother's past could become her future. Like her mother, Anouk spends lonely hours in front of the television, deserted by her boyfriend who "was a liar like a T.V. commercial" (15).

"Stop dreaming inside me," Anouk screams at her three ghosts, "stop asking me to live for you / stop singing me your songs / I want to hear my own" (47). But the autonomy she craves is illusory. Like it or not, she has within her aspects of all three of her predecessors. Like Anne and Céline, she is in love with love, with the romantic ideal; like Pauline, she is an *amoureuse pornographique* (a pornographic lover), an easy prey for less-than-scrupulous men. "The world dreamed of me / well before I was born," she realizes (57). Her present (and her future) are inseparable from the past. To be sure, there is an evolution from Anne to Anouk that parallels that of Quebec society. Pauline sold the family land (to an English-Canadian speculator); Céline, who worked in a factory and "almost went crazy" (34) still harbors a longing for the past ("I'd have made a good farmer," she laments [38]); but Anouk, having been born in Montreal, is free from the myths of the previous generations. She alone is in a position to understand the past rather than be a slave to it. But even such understanding does not guarantee happiness in the present; the solution to life's problems is not contained in an analysis of the past.

So the second level of the play is a search for happiness, for love, for a meaning to life that is similar in all four generations and that transcends any historical context. Each in her own way, the women had looked for a solution. For Anne, happiness was a result of a love that, beginning with one man and one woman, gradually spreads out to encompass an entire family unit. "I'm happy," she says to her daughter, "your father will be with me this evening / . . . / he sings songs of love / . . . / he says he'll build me a house all of cedar / he says we're going to be a family" (30). But Anne's dependence on her husband leaves her alone and unable to help herself after his death. Pauline, in a reaction against her mother's way of life, decides that love and happiness don't exist, and that alcohol and sexual pleasures are the best guards against disappointment and loneliness. "I never understood that there was anything / to understand," she says (43), but her solution falls apart when she realizes that the desire for sexual pleasure is, in its own way, a search for an absolute that will never be fulfilled. She can find no one who will have "honest" sex with her, who will give her the pleasure she seeks, and, just before dying, she sees that her pursuit of pleasure for its own sake was a search for oblivion, and for death: "I always saw my life / falling into bed / going down like the sun" (60).

Céline is perhaps the saddest case of all. Like Anne, she believes in family life even though her husband is never home; she keeps her house spotlessly ready for her daughter's visits, even though they can't talk to each other. But Céline is also, in some ways, like her mother Pauline. Even if she never puts into practice her mother's debauched way of life, she still, in her loneliness, dreams of a purely sexual pleasure that just might be the answer to her problems. "I'd like to get laid by someone I don't know," she sings, "it's been years since I have made love" (41). In the end, this contradiction between love within the family context and pure sex becomes in itself a roadblock to happiness. "Everything is pornographic / nothing is loving," she sings at the end of the play (54).

After listening to the stories of the three other women, Anouk is ready to formulate her idea of love and happiness. Will it be any different from her mother's or from Pauline's or Anne's? Can Anouk succeed where the others failed? Garneau is careful not to answer this question. "I don't know what to do / with the fruit of your wombs / I can hardly move / inside my own," Anouk says to her predecessors (61). If she has learned anything from her experience, it is the importance of knowing herself, of exploring the "clearing within me / where I want to enter softly" (61). But despite everything, she has not renounced a belief in an "unconditional happiness / for which I search at arm's length" (57), and the play ends with Anouk confessing, over and over again, that love exasperates her.

If Anouk's problems are first and foremost those of an individual, they are also very specifically those of a woman. Men are remarkably absent in the play: Anne's husband is dead; Pauline's, after believing he was a bird, has been incarcerated in a mental hospital; Céline's and Anouk's men live in hotels or taverns. This lack of a male presence, far from setting the women free, only reinforces their predicament. Their obvious physical desire for a man reveals a deep psychological dependence on males, an inability to exist without them; "I never knew how to do anything," admits Céline (38). Marriage has become for the women a trap, a trick men play on them to keep them emotionally dominated: "he put me in love with him / and he didn't love me," says Céline of her husband (41). But Garneau is no feminist. He sees the dilemma of the characters in *Quatre à quatre* as transcending the division of the sexes. If women are the victims in this play, in others (*Adidou adidouce, Sur le matelas*) both men and women suffer the problems caused by those who seek dominance in a relationship, be they male or female. Even more important, neither men nor women are exempt from the tendency to pursue ideals of love, sex, or happiness, a pursuit that inevitably ends in disappointment.

Strauss et Pesant (et Rosa). *Strauss et Pesant (et Rosa)* is one of Garneau's most complex plays, since it combines the personal with the social and offers a penetrating and devastating analysis of the mentality of Quebec society before (and, to some extent, after) the Quiet Revolution.

The play presents the last moments in the lives of Joseph-Albert Strauss, a sixty-six-year-old retired police captain, his sixty-eight-year-old wife Rosa, and a seventy-year-old retired bishop, Emilien Pesant, a childhood friend of Strauss. Unlike most of Garneau's other plays, *Strauss et Pesant (et Rosa)* is about old people, dying people—the end of an era, perhaps, but also the ritualistic putting to death of the past. And whereas the names of characters in Garneau's other plays held little significance (in *Quatre à quatre* the author simply chose the names of the actors), every Quebecois will see in Joseph-Albert Strauss a reference to the former hard-line Liberal, turned Conservative, Claude Wagner, and in Emilien Pesant (the name means weighty) the archbishop of Montreal, Paul-Emile Léger, whose name means light.

As the play opens, Rosa and J.-A. Strauss are returning home after a party to a room with an enormous bed that constitutes the decor and picks up a theme seen in *Sur le matelas:* the bed as the center of life, the place where one is born, one makes love, and one sleeps, and one dies. J.-A. is a little drunk, and he keeps singing the refrain from the song "Les Chevaliers de la table ronde" which goes "c'est qu'les hommes sont tous des cochons" (men are all pigs), to which he adds, for his wife's ears, "c'est qu'les femmes aiment les cochons" (women love pigs).[97] In effect, Strauss is a pig; as his wife complains of severe stomach pains, he starts undressing with the idea of having sex with her ("I can still do it, you too" [20]), thus beginning, with his retirement, "a new youth" (20). But this happy prospect is not to be, for Rosa, in more and more pain, disappears into the bathroom where she falls dead. At first, J.-A. believes Rosa is faking death because she doesn't want to make love, but he soon realizes the truth. Like a child he bewails his loneliness: "What am I going to do . . . my laundry is dirty. The house is dirty . . . I've got to find a woman" (28). For J.-A. Rosa was a *moman,* a mamma, a housekeeper, anything but a wife.

"I'm going to die if I stay alone," sobs Strauss (29), and, with Rosa gone, his life does indeed begin to fade away. But he will not die entirely alone. He is visited by his old chum Emilien Pesant, whose philosophy is both traditionally Catholic (Jesuit) and specifically Canadian, for he sees life as a "grandiose hockey game" in which "the Lord is the referee, the only referee" (38). Through suffering one earns one's place in heaven, "a hundred thousand times better than Florida" (43). Even if Strauss would have preferred a real retirement home in the sun to a celestial Miami Beach, he is forced to recognize the gravity of the situation, that all mortals are "little birds in the great apron of Providence" (37). All that is needed now is for Strauss to confess, and what could be more convenient than to have one's best friend, a bishop, on hand for the last moments?

But there are problems, serious ones. What on the surface seems to be a respectable middle-class situation is actually a sordid mess.

Strauss and Pesant are the hideous mirror image of a society where religion and proper conduct hide degrading, animal behavior.

Rosa's ghost periodically crosses the stage singing the refrain about men being pigs, and for good reason. As we see in flashbacks, both Emilien and J.-A., during their teenage years, used Rosa for their sexual pleasure in return for small amounts of money. As they grew older, Emilien chose the religious life and J.-A. joined the police force. Rosa became pregnant, and J.-A. married her, but their marriage, if not sterile, was singularly unproductive (twenty-seven miscarriages, for each of which Rosa lit a candle and prayed every night). Emilien, for his part, moved from his early heterosexual experiments with Rosa to homosexual ones with the Cub Scouts in the troup he once headed and this behavior did not go unnoticed by Strauss who at one point wrote letters denouncing his old friend. Emilien's conduct earned him an early retirement in a house of retreat. As for Rosa, she followed in the path of Tremblay's Marie-Louise; the Virgin Mary appeared to her:

> I was washing the toilet bowl.
> She appeared
> With her blue eyes and blond hair.
> She said, J.-A. must not make any more angels,
> he's made enough.
> Tell him to leave you alone.
>
> (68)

As the play draws to a close, as J.-A. and Emilien delve deeper and deeper into their past, each tries to get a confession from the other, some sort of confirmation of their own worth as human beings. But their lives have been utter failures. Strauss is not a real police chief but "the chief's right arm" (52), and his only "success" was to shoot a seventeen-year-old boy guilty of stealing an apple. As for Emilien, he still keeps alive a desire for Rosa, for the sexuality she represents and whose fulfillment with male substitutes brought about his downfall. Totally broken, Strauss and Pesant confess each other ("Ego to absolvo" [75]) and die, while Rosa's ghost continues to wash the floor.

The play is structured around the *"duplessiste* triangle" (as one critic has put it),[98] the internal order of Quebec society during the Duplessis government (roughly from 1936 to 1960), whose three

points are the Church, the state, and the family. The Church and
the state are here (as they were in reality) intertwined. As Emilien
says in a flashback to Strauss, "I'm going to be the police of the
soul / and you're going to be the police of the body" (53). It is not
just a common past that links these two characters together, it is
also a common purpose. Their concerted action, above political
parties ("the interests / of the Church and the interests of order go
beyond / ordinary politics," says Emilien [61]) leads them into graft
and corruption, with the blessing of Maurice (Duplessis?), a name
that brings fear to their hearts. Moreover, the sexual bestiality of
Emilien reflects the social bestiality of Strauss. The apples that the
almost-bishop presents to Strauss at the beginning of the play have
a double meaning; they are the forbidden fruit of which Emilien is
so fond and they are also the symbol of Strauss's act of police
brutality. "You no longer have any right over me," screams J.-A.
to Emilien at the end of the play (71), and, in effect, the Church
has relinquished any spiritual authority it might have had by its
incursions into the affairs of the state.

Both the Church and the state have an interest in maintaining
the traditional family unit, where behavior is learned and where
social values are perpetrated. The mother is the keystone of the
family, and Rosa, as Emilien assures J.-A., was "a true saint" (35).
But the Strauss family is, in the Catholic sense, incomplete, in
comparison with the large families of the past when political power
was thought to depend on the "revenge of the cradle."

The reason Rosa had so many miscarriages is, of course, medical,
but it is not perceived as such by Rosa herself or her husband. For
the former, the dead foetuses are divine payment for past sexual
activity: "Mary, I wanted to be a virgin and to have a son," she
prays (35). For Strauss, the problem is that Rosa "screwed / like a
dead cow" (57). Even Emilien, despite his assurances that Rosa's
suffering will earn her a place in heaven, cannot erase from his mind
the image of "the ignoble Joseph-Albert / giving himself to bestiality right before me / murmuring Rosa Rosa Rosa . . ." (59).
The problem here is not the family unit but of sex. The Church's
condemnation of sexual pleasure only adds to the difficulty that
J.-A. and Rosa (like Alfred and Charlotte in *Sur le matelas*) have in
living their love. The miscarriages are symbolic of social and personal
failure. In *Strauss et Pesant (et Rosa)* sex is the forbidden look in the

barn, or the sneaked feel at the Cub Scout meeting; it is never fulfilling.

Beyond the hyprocrisy of the Duplessis triangle, Garneau sees another force at work in Quebec society. The play, which began as a simple "fable on the church and the state," rapidly took on, in the author's eyes, a more metaphysical sense: "the idea of evil . . . came into it, this idea of evil introduced by the religious mentality and protected by the police mentality."[99] J.-A.'s and Emilien's confessions are not in response to the judgment of a higher order but reveal the absence of all judgment, the bankruptcy of a religion that closes its eyes to the evil it is helping to perpetrate. In fact, only one sin is ever mentioned by these men who have dealt in corruption, repression, and cruelty: that of sex, and they can't decide if it is a mortal sin or a venial one. Strauss and Pesant are unconsciously evil because their functions are evil. As for Rosa, she is a victim not only of society but also of her husband's and Emilien's images of her. Until his dying moment, Emilien lasciviously remembers her eyes while J.-A. evokes her culinary prowess ("I can't digest anymore / I miss Rosa's cooking" [74]). It is not by chance that Rosa's leitmotif is "women love pigs," for she is incapable of breaking out of her prison, just like her counterparts in *Quatre à quatre.* She is locked into a certain complicity with the evil world of her husband, and in taking a vow of chastity as in washing the floor after her death, she tries to introduce cleanliness and purity into a life that is irremediably soiled.

Strauss et Pesant (et Rosa) was received principally as a play about Quebec society, an exorcism of "all the Strauss and Pesant that swarm within us and around us."[100] It is certainly representative of the playwright's desire to create "Quebec archetypes,"[101] figures who incarnate social tendencies in the same way as the women in *Quatre à quatre* incarnate psychological tendencies. But even if the specific archetypes presented in *Strauss et Pesant (et Rosa)* are understandable only within a French-Canadian context, the institutionalized violence, sex, and corruption that they represent can have a more universal meaning.

Michel Garneau's theater is one of frustration. Between the desire to live or to love and the realization of that desire a shadow falls across man's path. The shadow may be society, it may be the past, it may even be some unnamed and unnameable flaw within human beings, but it is always present. It is no coincidence that Garneau's favorite Shakespearean play, the one he has adapted into joual, is *Macbeth*. The inexplicable reason for failure can and does appear as the presence of evil, and of a desire to repent evil actions and thereby reestablish some sort of metaphysical order. But the reality Garneau presents is that of a world without order and with an empty heaven above. Man is definitively abandoned to his own devices, and carries within himself the entire responsibility for his acts. It is a world such as that described by Jean-Paul Sartre in *Les Mouches* or Albert Camus in *Le Malentendu*. But Garneau is not a philosopher, and the starkness of existentialist theater is foreign to him. For within an indifferent universe Garneau sees one small ray of hope: that of human love, the fragile but possible link between solitudes.

Chapter Three
The Deadly Games
of Réjean Ducharme

> "Je suis fatiguée de jouer.
> La comédie est finie."
> *(L'Océantume)*
>
> (I'm tired of playing.
> The comedy is over)

One of the most enigmatic figures in contemporary Quebec literature, Réjean Ducharme is a playwright and novelist who keeps a good distance between himself and the community of critics and academics. He was born in Saint-Félix-de-Valois in 1942; he has worked at a variety of jobs, from that of a salesman to a pilot in the Canadian Air Force. But he does not make his private life public, and, like his American counterpart J. D. Salinger (with whom he shares much in common), he gives very few interviews, preferring to let his works speak for themselves. Ducharme's indifference to critics earned him in 1967 the ire of the literary world, especially in Paris where, it was asserted, Réjean Ducharme was merely a pseudonym for some well-known French author who didn't want to reveal himself. But a letter to *Les Lettres francaises* by the poet Gérald Godin who had just met and interviewed Ducharme brought an end to *l'affaire Réjean Ducharme,* and, since that time, no one has doubted the authenticity of his works.[1]

Ducharme is best known as a novelist, and for good reason; he has published five novels in prose and one in verse,[2] but so far only two of the five plays he has written since 1968 (*Inès Perée et Inat Tendu* and *Ah! Ah!*) have been edited. This situation arises not from any lack of quality in the plays themselves but rather from the manifest desire on the part of the author that dramatic texts, which are merely the "pretext" for the performance, not become fixed works of literature.[3] Even if Réjean Ducharme takes little interest in the production of his plays (he once asked to be considered "as a dead author")[4] his texts are really working documents for an eventual performance.

In a sense, it is ironic that Ducharme is known principally as a novelist, since, in all his prose works, he essentially writes *against* the novel. Ducharme's attitude toward literature is to refuse to accept that writing involves the description of reality. Ducharme believes that "the novel is related to passionate love, to possessive love, to urban life and its network of interests, to dubious historical occurrences."[5] This attitude is rooted in a rejection of everything the modern, adult world has to offer; like Salinger's Holden Caulfield, Ducharme's youthful characters perpetually see the hypocritical, seamy side of adult life and are digusted by possessiveness, sex, pollution, and selfishness. They search for a new way of seeing things that brings into focus not so much what things are but what they can become in the human mind. This perspective is what Ducharme calls "falseness"; it is essentially a poet's way of looking at the simplest object and transforming it: "look at a cabbage and imagine that when it's ripe each of its leaves will fall off by themselves and begin to fly, to sing, to be a goldfinch."[6] Without the connivance of the reader, of course, this transformation is impossible. Ducharme wants his readers to listen to the *voice* of his characters rather than to believe in their descriptions of reality[7] in order to "follow the path of 'falseness,' of the imaginary, of the perpetually new miracle of existence."[8]

Ducharme rejects not only the passive reader but the passive narrator. His characters are desperately looking for some kind of *action* that will remove them from literature. Bérénice Einberg, heroine of *L'Avalée des avalés (The Swallower Swallowed),* finds herself suffocated by everything around her:

Everything swallows me. When my eyes are closed I'm being swallowed by my stomach . . . When my eyes are open, I'm swallowed because I can see . . . I'm swallowed by the river which is too large, the sky which is too high, the flowers which are too fragile, the butterflies which are too fearful, my mother's face which is too beautiful.[9]

Bérénice, like all Ducharme's narrators, is trying to find a way out of the restricted world which she observes around her. But more important, she is trying to escape the limitations that the novel form puts on her as a character/narrator. To avoid being "swallowed" by the reality she sees, she must constantly keep that reality in motion either by subjectively transforming it or through some act of violent destruction. As Bérénice puts it, "that's what I need to do to be free: swallow everything, spread myself into everything, encompass everything, impose my law on everything, master everything . . . But I'd rather destroy everything."[10]

Ducharme's hostility to the traditional novel form and to the passive reader implies the necessity of a genre that is not constrained by the written word and in which action takes the place of contemplation. It seems likely that one of Ducharme's principal motivations in writing plays is precisely to replace the printed page with the movement of the drama. Moreover, theater is the antithesis of the *real*. Everything on the stage is *false,* from the actors who ask us to believe they are characters to the pieces of wood and cardboard that magically become a castle. In the theater every performance gives evidence of "the perpetually new miracle of existence."

Ducharme's first play, *Inès Pérée et Inat Tendu,* was first produced in 1968. The title is a pun (*inespéré* means "unhoped-for" and *inattendu* means "unexpected") and indicates that here, as in all Ducharme's works, words and their meanings are extremely important. The names of the characters in the play (Isalaide Lussier-Voucru suggests *l'eussiez-vous-cru?,* which means "would you have believed it?"; Mario Escalope is a pun on *Marie-salope,* a dirty woman, and *escalope,* a veal cutlet), the dialogue, and even the stage directions ("Première Rake," "Deuxième Make") have a multiplicity of senses that, far from being gratuitous, are at the very center of Ducharme's intentions. We have seen how joual plays an essential role in the plays of Tremblay, who through its use asserts his solidarity with Quebec's working class. In a similar vein, but with a different purpose, Ducharme's use of puns and word games is a refusal of traditional middle-class theater. But Ducharme isn't particularly interested in the working class (or in any other class), and it is out of disaffection with the world in general that he chooses to turn words over and over, to play with them rather than to use them merely as tools.[11] By playing with words, by exploring them, Ducharme explores the possibilities of change and ambiguity. Tremblay uses joual as a way of finding roots, a personal and social reality; Ducharme uses puns to remove words from their usual meanings and to escape being pinned down by any reality.

Inès Pérée is a young woman dressed as a bathing beauty (but wearing boots and a rubber glove). Inat Tendu, her companion, is a young man dressed as a bank clerk. Together they roam the earth searching for someone to take them in, to welcome them into their home. Like all of Ducharme's protagonists, they are permanent adolescents; they live together but have never made love and have a relationship based on friendship. They are not entirely human ("I wasn't born. I found myself on earth all of a sudden, with Inat, my hand is his," says Inès);[12] they have no notion of work ("Life is free. I have never paid for it and I never will," says Inat);[13] and they carry with them a violin and a butterfly, symbolic of their "good ideas," their ideals of music and beauty which will be perfectly useless to them and of which they will soon be deprived.

In fact, when Inès and Inat need to survive on earth is neither a butterfly nor a violin but brute force, and of this they are virtually incapable. Their search for a welcome is not like begging for alms but rather is like claiming one's due: "We didn't care to look for charity, but to take our share from you, to take our place next to you," says Inat (71). Their adventure consists of three stages, in each of which they meet people who threaten to destroy their innocence and idealism. In the first step, in the "disused funeral chapel" of a veterinary clinic, they encounter Isalaide Lussier-Voucru who, as her name implies, is ugly *(laide)* beyond belief (she is a veterinarian infested with as many fleas as the dirtiest of animals). Not only does Isalaide treat Inès and Inat with a cruelty bordering on sadism, but she does so as representative of the established order, of the fraternity of professionals who judge some people normal and some abnormal: "you are abnormal enough to be committed and I'm as normal as a normal school," she tells Inès (1st, 25). The veterinary hospital is a disguised mental clinic, and Isalaide's boss and erstwhile lover is Dr. Mario Escalope, a traumatized Italian psychiatrist who gets sexual pleasure from stealing and runs an insane asylum from which no one escapes. "The only way an inmate [he says *passionaire* instead of *pensionnaire*] will get out of my establishment is over my dead body. I'm too good at making them feel good," he says (29), and his involuntary(?) Freudian slip reveals the basic opposition between his way of seeing human existence and that of the two searching adolescents. Inès and Inat believe in passion—if not in passionate love, at least in passionate *life*—and they are thwarted at every juncture by people who, like Isalaide and

Mario, reduce life to a system of controlled reactions and predictable behavior. Or, to put it another way, Inès and Inat represent poetry, and poetry implies dissatisfaction with the state of the world, a kind of anguish that the psychiatrist, preoccupied with making people feel good, cannot accept. Mario Escalope says of Victor Hugo's poems: "they short-circuit the neurons, they screw up my science of exercising influence" (56).

To escape from the evil Dr. Escalope, from Isalaide and from the cruel miniskirted nurse Pauline-Emilienne[14] who throws cans of pet food at them, Inès and Inat would need only to assert themselves, to let each of their persecutors stew in their psychological juices, and to run for the door. But Inat is too tired and he soon falls asleep, and Inès has an irresistible urge to find a mother, a point of origin, a past to which she can attach her very fragile present. Having never been born (I've always been as I am" [35]), Inès is fascinated by the fetal life of Isalaide's daughter: "What did the baby do when he was in your body? Did he explore you like a geography lesson? Did he pull himself up to your mouth and then slide down to your feet?" (35). She declares her love for Isalaide and asks to be adopted: "When a boy and a girl knock at your door, and tell you they are your children, you have a duty to be their mother" (1st, 37). At the same time Inès is terrified of being alone with Inat, and of their having to build their own life, as orphans, from nothing: "Sometimes I tell Inat: 'Let's build our own house.' That's when I'm discouraged. What a horrible thing to have to live in one's own house" (36).

In the behavior of Inès and Inat toward the menace of Dr. Escalope and Isalaide we can see two of the themes that lie behind all of Ducharme's theater, and indeed a great part of Quebec literature: defeatism and the search for an identity. Inat solves his problems by refusing to face them. On the surface, he is polite, nonviolent; when the situation gets too difficult for him, he can always sleep. Inès, on the other hand, is not only a more aggressive character but is actively searching for a *space* in which she can settle. It is not by accident that, in the quote above, Ducharme has used spatial images. Isalaide's fetus is seen by Inès as exploring his mother's body in the same way as Champlain came down the St. Lawrence to explore Quebec. Ducharme's imagery here joins the tradition of Quebec literature that, from the novelist Savard to the poet Miron, is searching for a *pays,* a land whose space can be explored, mapped, made familiar. Inès cannot conceive of building her house in a void, without roots in the past or in the land. Unfortunately, her choice of an adoptive mother is ill advised, since Isalaide, even if momentarily sympathetic, will, by the end of the play, turn against Inès and Inat and join their oppressors.

"Children have come and they have rung the hour of terror," says Isalaide at the end of the "Premier Rake" (58), and, as the play progresses, the sage of Inès and Inat begins to take on apocalyptic overtones, like a black version of Saint-Exupéry's *Le Petit prince*. It is not by accident that, once having encountered the world of psychology, Inès and Inat find their second challenge in the world of religion, in the cell of Sister Saint-New-York-des-Ronds-d'Eau[15] to which they have escaped after a period of internment in Dr. Escalope's mental hospital. Inès is without her violin, Inat without his butterfly; these objects were stolen from them by the psychiatrists along with their "good ideas." The couple is rapidly becoming a shadow of its former self. Drugged at the hospital, their minds emptied both of anguish and ideas, Inès fills the void within her with junk food; when she has eaten enough chips and drunk enough coke, she feels "well stimulated, full of wicked energy" (1st, 82). As she becomes cruder, more violent (but without purpose or direction), Inat becomes even less aggressive, even more detached, preferring to elevate his soul rather than to fight for his right to exist: "I'd rather have a crown than a mouthful of bread. And your crown falls when you bend down to pick up a morsel of bread" (64).

At first Inès and Inat seem to have found a kindred soul in Sister New-York. Her ideas, a kind of naive and romantic ecology, are not without resemblance to their rebelliousness: "The word belongs to the forests and the forests aren't made for those who cut down trees, oh no! They're made to grow, to give more and more shade to lovers, who are so hot, and so that fearful birds can build their nests higher up" (68). But Sister New-York immediately adds, "I am the servant of the R.M.B.: the Reverend Mother Banker" (68), thus calling attention to her real nature, indicated visually by the revolver she carries, the safe in the middle of her cell, and by her tendency to show off her thighs (her defense is that "Christ certainly showed his thighs on the cross" [76]). Sister New-York's links with wealth and capitalism on the one hand (the "New-York" of her character), and her ostentatious display of her body to Inat on the other, make her a double threat: the adolescent ideal Inès and Inat represent accepts neither sex nor money. Inès's newfound violence is sparked and she finally goes into action, tying up the ever-present Pauline-Emilienne. But a new character enters, a gentleman thief named Pierre-Pierre Pierre who, accompanied by Isalaide's daughter, the "firewoman" Aidez-Moi (help me!), quickly grabs Sister New-York's revolver and turns the tables on Inès.

Pierre-Pierre Pierre is part of the third and final threat to the existence of Inès and Inat. He is, despite his good manner, violent and materialistic: "We have come to take everything," he asserts (84), and his philosophy is based on force, disharmony, and the work ethic. In the third act he finally lives up to his name. He has already subjugated, by his mere presence, Isalaide who had begun to emulate the adolescents by roaming the world carrying the violin and butterfly Mario had stolen; slowly but surely Pierre-Pierre begins to close in on Inès and Inat. He takes up his place in a bathtub in the middle of Sister New-York's cell in which he has replaced the crucifixes with pictures of sex and violence. Inès, dressed as a cowboy, fires her pistol in the air and orders him to raise his hands, but he merely ignores her and she puts away the gun. Inat threatens to hit Pierre-Pierre Pierre, but he gets confused and says "je t'é-ponge" (I sponge you off) rather than "je te ponche" (I punch you) (104). Smiling, Pierre-Pierre presents Inès and Inat with something to eat—eggs. But as Ines and Inat look closely, the eggs reveal themselves to be stones *(pierres)*: "Pebbles! We've come all this way for pebbles!" (117). It is the final disappointment, and even if Inat makes a last desperate effort to break open the stones and find a meaning in them ("maybe they contain something, a sign, a message?" [117]), the game is irrevocably lost. Inès and Inat, dying of hunger, fall to the ground and expire.

The two themes which I have already mentioned—the search for a space and a tendency toward defeatism—can be seen as typical of a nationalist current in Quebec literature. But Ducharme is very subtle, and his protagonists are motivated not so much by nationalism (either in the sense of Abbé Groux or of René Lévesque) as by a naive desire for freedom. They are searching for a welcome, an *acceuil,* but they refuse the charity of Sister New-York or the work ethic of Pierre-Pierre Pierre because they want to be accepted for what they *are* rather than for any usefulness they might have for someone else. They insist on this aspect of their search which sets

them apart from more common mortals: "We aren't made of the
same water as other people . . . The land is ours as much as theirs.
They didn't make it; they didn't earn it" (72). For Inès and Inat
the idea of a country, a land with specific borders, is inconceivable;
their journey is in a land without limits, from house to house "in
a straight line" leading toward the ocean (104).[16] The space they
claim for themselves is that of limitless imagination,[17] and this
space is as necessary to them as air, food, or water.

The dramatic structure of *Inès Pérée et Inat Tendu* is closely related
to the play's meaning. It is above all a play of *words* (some critics
have gone so far as to suggest that Ducharme's plays are better as
literature than as performances—a conclusion with which the playwright would probably disagree),[18] but of words in free play, free
to have a variety of meanings (one could find, for example, numerous
senses to the words *inespéré* and *inattendu* within the thematic context
of the play). Affinities with Ionesco and Beckett, and especially with
Boris Vian's *Les Bâtisseurs d'empire*, will be immediately evident:
Ducharme's theater contains elements both of the absurd and of
surrealism. The world of Inès Perée and Inat Tendu has no specific
point of reference in our world. The elements that compose our
everyday reality are completely detached from their contexts, set
loose on stage to be whatever the playwright wants them to be.
Even the protagonists are not like us; they are not the recognizable
Quebecois adolescents of Jean Barbeau's *Ben-Ur*. Ducharme's plays
refer principally to themselves, and as such, they are "a window on
another world"[19] whose contours are those of a desperate search for
a way out of an oppressive universe.

Le Cid maghané and *Le Marquis qui perdit,* Ducharme's next plays
(produced respectively in 1968 and 1970), are a departure from the
kind of theater the playwright had created with *Inès Pérée et Inat
Tendu* in that they are parodies of other works rather than original
creations. Ducharme himself claimed, having written *Le Cid maghané,* that this play wasn't really his: "I only wrote one play *(Inès
Pérée et Inat Tendu)* since the *Cid,* as messed up as it is, isn't written
by me but rather by some Castro whose first name I can't recall and
by Pierre Corneille."[20] Despite this quip, Ducharme's purpose in
writing these plays was very serious indeed; behind the parodies,
the gags, and the laughter lie some very sombre reflections.

Ducharme wrote *Le Cid maghané* (*maghané*, messed up) to make the classic French play "more understandable here, less serious and uglier."[21] In fact, it is the coexistence of two very different centuries and civilizations that impress us first. The play is to be done "en costumes d'époque dans des meubles 1967"; some lines are to be declaimed *à la française* whereas others are to be spoken *à la québécoise.*[22] Parodies of Corneille's verses abound. For example, Don Diègue's exhortation to Rodrigue: "Va, cours, vole et nous venge" (Go, run, fly and avenge us),[23] becomes "Quick, my son! Take the bus, take a taxi, take the train, take the plane, hurry up, go ahead, break him into a thousand pieces" (12). The heroic and noble sentiments of Corneille's characters become the common sentiments of common people. The confrontation between Rodrigue and Chimène in act 3, scene 4, in which Chimène finally avows her love for Rodrigue ("va, je ne te hais point" (Go, I hate you not) [625]) becomes, in Ducharme's version, a burlesque and juvenile love scene in which Rodrigue tickles Chimène's feet, Elvire throws herself onto the couple, the three of them roll together on the floor, and Chimène ends up by making a date with Rodrigue for a night at the local motel ("OK, bum, OK creep. Eight o'clock. Motel Sunset" [34]). And the scene corresponding to act 4, scene 3, where Don Fernand pardons Rodrigue and says to him "henceforth be the Cid" (634), becomes a barter in which Rodrigue demands of the king something more tangible—a new car (43).

As in most parodies, complexities of character are reduced to caricature. Rodrigue, in Corneille's play, is very reticent to carry out his father's wishes to fight with Don Gormas and, in act 1, scene 6, makes the painful vow to "venge a father and lose a mistress" (601). No such thoughts torment Ducharme's Rodrigue. His deliberations are reduced to: "this business isn't all that complicated. I lose my honey anyway, whether I kill my honey's father or not. I'd be really nuts not to kill my honey's father" (13). L'Infante, in the seventeenth century version, is caught between the knowledge that Rodrigue loves Chimène and that the rules of her society make any marriage between herself and Rodrigue impossible; at the end of the play (5:7) she generously exhorts Chimène: "accept without sadness/this generous victory from the hands of your princess" (652). No such generosity inspires the heart of Ducharme's Infante. Her rivalry with Chimène has made her a quarrelsome character who does not hesitate to express her jealousy to Chimène: "What have you got that I haven't got? What did you do to him so that he doesn't look at me anymore?" (40). There is certainly an element of exaggeration in Ducharme's charactures, but it is the childish naïveté of the characters that dominates and provides a link with *Inès Pérée et Inat Tendu*. Characters end each scene by giving each other a "petit bec," the kiss of friendship, as if they were children rehearsing a play just for the fun of it. Rodrigue has a slogan—a king of macho warning—that he, like the Lone Ranger, repeats before going into action: "Qu'ils viennent les maudits si c'est pas des peureux!" ("Let the bums come on if they're not chicken" [12]). One often has the impression that the play is an interpretation of Corneille by children who understand concepts of love, honor, and death only in their own very simplified way.

Despite first appearances, however, Ducharme's *Cid* is not a simple parody of Corneille. In fact, the play, which until about midway seemed a straightforward line-for-line parody, suddenly takes off on its own and changes considerably for the Corneillean plot. The most important of these plot changes concerns the development of the characters of Rodrigue and Cimène. Rodrigue does not come to bid his "last adieu" to Chimène "in full daylight" (642) but rather does so in the middle of the night, in her room. She is in pajamas and he is drunk. To prove his courage, and in preparation for his fight with Don Sanche, Rodrigue decides to descend the fifty steps from the apartment to the street on skis.[24] This feat costs him a broken leg, and the injury, on top of his inebriated state, makes Rodrigue no match for Don Sanche. Chimène, sure that Rodrigue has been killed, feels none of the pain and despair of Corneille's character (5:6) but rather a great relief, as she says to Elvire: "How I wish you could put your hand on my soul and touch the marvelous peace that is settling upon it second by second." (55). In fact, contrary to Corneille's play, Don Sanche *has* killed Rodrigue ("The pocket-size Cid is dead! Long live the king-size Cid!" [56]), and Rodrigue's body, "in skis and boxing gloves, with catsup spread over it" (59) is brought to the middle of the stage at the play's end.

Rodrigue's death is not the only point on which the end of Ducharme's play differs from Corneille's. Whereas Corneille's king establishes order and satisfies both the need for honor and love by sending Rodrigue to battle for a year, Ducharme's king is not nearly so powerful. Not only does he have problems with his telephone service and with a police force on a perpetual coffee break, but he is incapable of imposing any kind of order on his society. Ducharme's play ends in perfect anarchy. Characters insult each other and a free-for-all ensues during which the women gain the upper hand. The king vainly tries to establish order by drawing his sword, but he is quickly disarmed by the valet Blackie who says to him: "Quit waving your sword around or I'll stick it in your nose" (61). The play ends with all the actors dancing a *ronde* around Don Rodrigue's body while singing *O Canada*.

These plot changes indicate that Ducharme's intentions go far beyond dressing *Le Cid* in modern clothing. By presenting a king who is powerless, by ending the play in disorder, by giving us a Rodrigue who is full of hot air and drink, Ducharme (as most of the critics remarked)[25] holds the mirror to Quebec society. He sees a society that resembles the world of the western movies more than the well-ordered France of Louis XIV.[26] The real courage of Corneille's Rodrigue is replaced by the comic-book bombast of Ducharme's character: "Nothing can harm the Cid. I can catch Indians' arrows with my bare hands just like tennis balls," boasts Rodrigue (49).

To be sure, Ducharme is not the only Quebec dramatist to comment on the tendency to use American comic-book heroes as role models; Jean Barbeau's *Ben-Ur* is perhaps the bitterest satire of a young man who uses comic books to hide from reality. But what charcterizes Ducharme and sets him apart from Barbeau is the emptiness of his characters. Underneath Rodrigue's boasts, behind Chimène's great right arm which, like that of Muhammed Ali, knocks out most of the noblemen in the play's last scene, there is only a gaping void. Ducharme's characters *are* the masks they wear and nothing else; they are, as one critic put it, "disjointed puppets."[27] The most striking example of this aspect of the play comes in the scene corresponding to the Infante's introspective monologue in Corneille's play (5:2). Ducharme's Infante tries but is incapable of uttering her monologue; instead, she lets her mask drop and appears to the audience as an actress: "it's not the Infante who is speaking to you, ladies and gentlemen, it's Antoinette Buffon, actress" (51). Not only does this technique remind us that we are in the theater (as opposed to Corneille who demands complete suspension of disbelief) but it also reveals an actress whose personal life is as painfully empty as that of the women in Tremblay's *Les Belles-soeurs*. Her boyfriend has left her and she last saw him on television being interviewed on his reaction to the high cost of bureau drawers: "I cry into my tube of toothpaste when I brush my teeth and I cry into my ashtray when I smoke," she sobs (51). Incapable of remembering her lines in the play, Antoinette Buffon pours out her soul and shows us an alienation that the seventeenth century ignored: that of people living alone in apartments, waiting for the telephone to ring, seeing their former lovers through the intermediary of television.

As in *Inès Pérée et Inat Tendu,* however, Ducharme also expresses a personal philosophy in *Le Cid maghané.* Ducharme uses *Le Cid* as a pretext to create his own Corneillean situation, that is, one in which there is no way out.[28] *Le Cid* is a tragedy despite its happy ending; for Corneille, the fact that Rodrigue was "a man more virtuous than wicked, who, through human weakness, . . . meets a misfortune that he doesn't deserve"[29] was sufficient to give the play an Aristotelian sense of tragedy. But Ducharme rejects the tragic element in *Le Cid.* His Rodrigue lacks the physical and moral superiority of Corneille's and the fundamental honor/love conflict is reduced to a childish but deadly game. Ducharme's Chimène is not concerned with avenging her father's death but with finding the macho heroic man of her dreams: "the really virile and masculine man I'm looking for is not to be found here," she declares (46). The duel she sets up between Rodrigue and Don Sanche will, she believes, give her boyfriend the chance to prove his masculinity, but when he leaves her apartment too drunk to fight, she has no feeling of regret: "Ouf! Another good deed done!" (50). This lack of tragic element creates a darker and more pessimistic play than that of Corneille. Rodrigue knows the rules of the game and has ignored them: his death is deserved and inevitable.

If *Le Cid maghané* turns its back on history by the confusion of costumes and decor, and by its plot changes, *Le Marquis qui perdit* (the Marquis who lost—a reference to Marquis de Vaudreuil, who, in 1759, lost New France to the English) is an attempt to re-create the history of the British conquest of North America). It can also be seen as an attempt to *conquer* history in order partially to avenge the conquest not only by England but equally by France (before and after 1760), by the old generation of Quebecois (defeatist—with some exceptions), and by women (the matriarchy of a Marguerite Bourgeoys). It is the most political of Ducharme's plays since it puts into question popularly accepted myths regarding Montcalm's heroism, Levis's sanity, and the reasons for which France was defeated in the first place.

Ah! Ah!, arguably Ducharme's best play,[30] represents both a continuation of, and a departure from his previous dramatic works. Unlike *Le Cid maghané*, or *Le Marquis qui perdit*, it is not a parody. Yet there are hints of these two plays in some of the lines as well as in some of the themes.[31] There are also affinities with *Inès Pérée et Inat Tendu*, especially in the emphasis Ducharme puts on the cruelty that human beings inflict on each other. Overall, however, the play presents us with a much more ambiguous situation than Ducharme had used before; it is both real and unreal and seems to transcend any single categorization as a philosophical, psychological, or social drama.

This is how the publicity department of the Théâtre du Nouveau Monde summed up the play:

Roger and Sophie are living together; Bernard, a childhood friend of Sophie, and Mimi, his supernumerary, pay them a visit. In a setting at once filled with real elements and detached from exterior reality, transcending time and space, they will love each other, hate each other, destroy each other.[32]

The plot is deceptively simple, the characters and decor deceptively realistic. Sophie and Roger are the classic couple in their late thirties; she is "passionate, complex," he is "rather ugly, rather blubbery." Bernard and Mimi are younger, wealthier, better looking (he is a "handsome, well-dressed man"). The apartment seems normal enough (thick purple carpet, Tiffany lamp, expensive but tasteless furniture). But there are items that are unusual, strange: next to the modern stereo set and lazy-boy chair there is a tall ashtray with small flashing lights on top; Roger wears too many rings and his language is hopelessly confused; Roger and Sophie sometimes speak while holding their noses. Roger's moods vary from serenity to violence and he is completely unpredictable. Sophie has to pay Roger each time she wants to make love; she earns this money pushing mescaline. Bernard becomes morose, drunk, helpless. In the midst of all this Mimi, the youngest of the four, is a scapegoat for the others who take pleasure in making her suffer.

"A great Quebec tragedy," said one of the critics.[33] To some extent *Ah! Ah!* is a sort of French-Canadian *Who's Afraid of Virginia*

Woolf? in that it defines the relationship between people as a battle
for domination. But Ducharme has another interest besides psychology: games, play, theater—all used by people to escape from
the present and from reality.[34]

During the second act, Mimi tells of a nightmare:

There were lots of people, like at Dorval Airport during the holidays. But
no one was waiting for anyone or for any planes. We were all paying
attention to ourselves . . . We were watching out not to hurt each other
but there were too many of us to avoid bumping into others or hitting
them . . . At the beginning everyone was polite. When we accidentally
touched each other we said hello, we smiled, we said excuse-excuse-me-
I-didn't-do-it-on-purpose . . . But suddenly it all changed. Nothing
really happened but we noticed that all those who had been touched had
marks on them which ate through their clothes like burning wounds . . .
Then we heard them announce on the loudspeaker that it was an epidemic
. . . We all wanted to leave, we fought and pushed to get out. It was
hideous. Because the more we bumped into each other, the more marks
we got . . . Then someone yelled out: Stop-stop-it's-not-the-end-of-the-
world-it's-only-a-game-of-tag. But it was too late. I looked at myself, I
was completely rotten. (2:5)

This dream is a précis of the play as it appears to Mimi and, because
she is the underdog, the audience interprets the play from her point
of view. As she so clearly sees, contacts between people, despite
attempts to be polite, exist only at the level of aggressiveness. People
are looking to exercise their power and they need a willing victim;
Bernard and Sophie take turns playing this role with Roger. Roger
dominates all the characters. He possesses, psychologically and physically, both women; he obliges Sophie to recite newspaper clippings
with her nose plugged; he tears Mimi's skirt while she tells her
dream; he obliges Bernard to drink from the toilet; he keeps all the
money in the stuffing of his sofa. Sophie takes her revenge on Mimi
whom she treats as a child; Bernard (like Rigaud) takes his revenge
out on the bottle. What sets Mimi apart from the others and what
explains her emphasis on physical wounds is her exaggerated sensitivity. "I'm a strange person . . . When someone touches me it
hurts," she explains to Sophie (1:5), but rather than finding sympathy she gets nothing but derision: "Oh, when you're as sensitive
as that, it's no longer sensitivity, it's . . . it's . . . I won't say
innocence . . . you're terribly suspect," says Sophie (2:6). What

enables Roger, Bernard, and Sophie to disdain Mimi's sensitivity is their ability to play the game. "It's a game! It's not for real! We're pretending! That doesn't hurt!" says Sophie to Mimi (1:7) but the latter is unable to distinguish game from reality until the end of the play ("I'm a good enough actist . . . artress, artist . . . to be on the stage" [2:6]). By then it's too late—she has lost her innocence and has become, as in her dream, "rotten"—and she will leap to her death at the end of the play while the others yell to her "it doesn't count . . . Ah! Ah! . . . TAG!" (2:6)

The game that Roger, Bernard, and Sophie play is called, throughout the play, *le phone,* and this deformation of the word "fun" is significant. The game is *phoney,* of course, but it is also alienating. It keeps people at a distance from each other, just as the telephone, at numerous times during the play, allows characters to converse without seeing their partner. *Le phone* is also a deadly game. Sophie goes so far as to compare the sound of her voice to that of a machine gun, but this gun is filled with words, not bullets, and Roger has taught her how to protect herself from words. He knows how to make words into objects. The lights on his ashtray flash, he plugs up his nose to deform the sound of his voice, and he recites: "Sh h h h sh't'ava pourtant ben nana ben n'avarti!" (1:5). The message ("But I had warned you") is lost in voluntary alienation. Roger and Sophie empty themselves of all feeling and fill themselves with words which, like the newspaper clippings rolled into balls that they throw in the air (1:7), gradually come to dominate the entire play.

It is not some perverse desire to play deadly games that motivates the characters in *Ah! Ah!* but rather a very clear vision of themselves as irretrievable losers. Like Ducharme's Rodrigue or like Inès and Inat, the personages here are looking for some way out of the inevitable failure of their lives. Inès and Inat had, in the beginning at least, their "good ideas"; no such ideals are present in *Ah! Ah!.* Sophie compares life to a hockey game being lost: "Our greatness can be measured in the empty hockey rink, in the multitude of inhabitable solitudes which have reverted back to the bleachers. It's a matter of losing the match and *may our cry alone fill up the entire amphitheater*" (2:1) (my emphasis). The loss is accepted—even more, it is proclaimed as the human condition. All that is left is the game that, in turn, becomes its own pleasure. Roger's quote from the

Polish playwright Witkiewicz is apt: "something within me revels in this endless sacrifice, in this bottomless mediocrity." (1:1)

There is a second level of meaning to *Ah! Ah!*. The entire drama can be seen as a play within a play with Roger as the director. Sophie implicitly recognizes that the play has been planned out in advance and that she is but an actress reciting a part: "and to think that . . . the drama was all written, corrected, censored, performed" (1:7). She goes on to pay homage to her director: "Master, you have shown me that I was full of my role, full and round like a ball, that I had only to let myself roll" (1:7). Roger is apparently certain that he is in complete control of the play: "I write my life in advance: I choose it before anyone else does it for me . . . I am a creator, my creator: I PREDICT MYSELF!" (2:3). But although he is a director he is also an actor and is as imprisoned by his words, his lines, as other characters. He and the others accept to play their roles to the end ("isn't acting fun [*"le phone"*]?" asks Sophie [1:7]).

It is impossible here to distinguish between games and reality; between actors and the roles they play. The game is all the more deadly serious because there is nothing else. We see here a transposition, on the level of theater, of the image/substance dialectic that was at the basis of *Le Cid maghané* and *Le Marquis qui perdit*. In these two plays the search for an identity became the search for an image; if Rodrigue or Montcalm were powerless in fact, at least they could try to transcend that reality and to become fiction. In *Ah! Ah!* it is the play itself that provides the images and enables the characters to believe in some (fragile) existence. Lacking any existence outside of their games, the play (in its strictest sense) becomes the only reality.

More than any of Ducharme's other dramatic works, *Ah! Ah!* is self-conscious theater. The playwright uses the phenomenon of theater to explore not only the lives of his fellow Quebecois but to explore his own purpose as a dramatist. If life is a series of empty and false contacts with others, then theater becomes a privileged form of expression because it allows an audience to perceive both the false and the real, and to distinguish the false—the game—from what is real (the illusion-making machine called theater). In the end the *real* disappears. As soon as an actor appears on stage, he loses his identity as a human being and becomes a character. This process is all the more evident when, as in *Le Cid maghané,* a character reveals herself to be an actress. We the audience know that the actress (appropriately named Antoinette Buffon) is just as fictitious as the character she is supposed to play; even if the real actress were to use her real name and tell us the real story of her life, we would accept her story as essentially theatrical, that is, as something invented. The stage has a magic power that turns everything upon it into an illusion, into game, and it is this magic that Ducharme uses to create a dramatic universe in which the false envelops the real and becomes the only mode of human existence.

Ducharme's contribution to Quebec theater, like his contribution to the world of fiction, is considerable and exists as much, if not more, on the level of structure and technique as on that of theme. His theater is far from literary; it is "a theater of victory over words, a theater of cruelty and innocence, a completely *theatrical* theater."[35] The comparison with Artaud's theater of cruelty is not without foundation. Like Artaud, Ducharme is interested in a theater of metaphysics, where the very existence of human beings is put into question. That this theater contains political overtones is inevitable; a Quebecois's existence as an individual presupposes, in the eyes of most artists and intellectuals, his existence as a member of a French-Canadian nation which has not yet gained control of its own destiny. Or, to put it another way, Montcalm's and Rodrigue's defeats are part of the reason that Roger, Sophie, Bernard, and Mimi play their games to the death. But Ducharme is one of the least *engagé* of Quebec writers, and the significance of his plays can be appreciated in any society. This is not the least of his merits.

Chapter Four

Toward a New Mythology

Antonine Maillet

> 'Le printemps, c'est fait pour ceuses-là qu'avont
> eu de la misère à travorser l'hiver"
> (*La Sagouine,* 122)

> ("Spring is made for them that's had a bad time
> gettin' through the winter.")

The French-speaking region known as Acadia (northern and eastern
New Brunswick, as well as parts of Nova Scotia) might have been
forgotten in Quebec and in the rest of the world if it had not been
for the efforts of Antonine Maillet. Born in the heart of Acadia, in
the coastal village of Bouctouche, New Brunswick, in 1929, Antonine Maillet is the author of numerous novels (*Pélagie-la-charrette*
won France's prestigious Prix Goncourt in 1979), seven plays, and
a volume of short stories, all of which concern her native province,
its people, its legends.

Antonine Maillet's best-known play, *La Sagouine* (first presented
in Montreal in 1972), created a sensation similar to Tremblay's *Les
Belles-soeurs.* For the first time the Acadian people were presented
speaking their own language (a form of French that preserves structures and expressions of the seventeenth century) and telling their
own story. Maillet's Acadia is as far removed as possible from the
romanticized descriptions of Longfellow, and it is undoubtedly the
author's authenticity that has given her such international acclaim.
"My initiation to the theater," she claims, "didn't take place on
the stage but on the steps of the church, on Sundays in July, when
I heard the village blacksmith yell to the barber that he had seen
his wife's garter belt, and when this mild comment touched off a
volley of replies which ended up with acrobatic gestures right out
of the commedia dell'arte."[1] Like Jean-Claude Germain, the Quebec
playwright whose work will concern us in the second part of this

chapter, Maillet believes that "culture, in the most primitive and most profound sense, is the common and original experience of a group or a people."[2]

But although Maillet is best known for her plays and novels, she is also the author of a comparative study of Rabelais and the Acadian folk tradition *(Rabelais et les traditions populaires en Acadie).* This essay, written as a Ph.D. thesis for Laval University, is not without significance for the author's drama and fiction. What interests her in comparing Rabelais with the farmers and fishermen of New Brunswick is how the latter managed to survive and to keep their language intact for almost four hundred years, despite the deportation *(le grand dérangement* of 1755), and despite past (and present) efforts to assimilate the French-speaking communities of New Brunswick into the English-speaking majority. This survival was possible, she implies, because the legends and traditions of fifteenth- and sixteenth-century France, which Rabelais transcribed in his *Cinq livres,* crossed the Atlantic, were transplanted and took root in North America, and provided the Acadian people with a distinct and unique identity.

The Acadians are, for Maillet, the very symbol of transplantation. They came from France during the seventeenth century and settled in remote regions of the provinces known today as Nova Scotia and New Brunswick. In 1755 the English, now masters of Acadia, deported them aboard ships; their isolation became even more complete, more personal, as families and friends were separated and sent off on different boats. In the following years more than three thousand Acadians returned to France (although not all stayed), while smaller groups settled in New England and along the Atlantic coast of the United States, in Louisiana (where they became Cajuns), and in Quebec. But a very persistent if small group of Acadians transplanted themselves back into Acadia. They slowly, and with much trepidation, made their way to New Brunswick, there to hide and to flee all contacts with the English for two or three generations.[3]

Antonine Maillet describes this period of transplantation as the most fertile episode in Acadian history. The Acadians slowly rebuilt their settlements; they cleared the land, built docks and dams, stayed for a while, then moved on to a new, better area along the coast; they met new families, old friends, and relatives, and storytelling became the favorite way to pass the time.[4] A popular culture was born which was oral in its expression and which translated the desire

of the Acadians to persevere even if this meant beginning anew over
and over again.

Stories and legends are the stuff from which Maillet's works are
made. She is part of a popular tradition of storytelling and monologues that goes back to the earliest beginnings of New France and
that went public, on the stage, in the Quebec of the early twentieth
century.[5] "Proportionately," she says, "we have more storytellers
than any other people in the world . . . because we have never had
the means to express ourselves in any other way."[6] The monologue
is the natural expression of a people whose definition of itself is
hesitant, unsure; as Laurent Mailhot points out, it is "a search for
identity and unity, a pause before acting, preparation for a social
language."[7] Maillet's narrators in her stories and the monologuists
in her plays are speaking for themselves first, and, in so doing,
reaching out for a contact with readers or audiences who will affirm
both their solitude and their solidarity with the rest of humanity.

Maillet's monologues tell and retell the same story of the deportation and its lasting effects, and they always do so from the point
of view of the little man or woman, what the author calls "little
history," or "the life of this people which gets tossed about by great
events and great men."[8] The little people and the little history of
Acadia are presented to us in the novels through a narrator whose
expression is the popular idiom (with some modification) and who
has already digested reality and changed it into legend. In the plays
there is no narrator to interpret the events, of course, but the
audience's complicity is urged, even required, when actors and actresses address themselves directly to the spectators and invite them
not only to be witnesses of events but to guarantee the veracity of
the interpretation presented.[9] Maillet's plays always demand the
sympathy of the audience, never its criticism. She draws the public
into her own world, her own family (in the extended, Acadian sense),
and repeatedly presents the same characters who, like La Saguione,
are not so much consciously invented as they are the almost invol-
untary expression of the Acadian soul, a kind of "automatic
writing."[10]

But for an Acadian writer to lay bare the soul of her country in
front of a non-Acadian public is dangerous business. The plays could
easily become museum pieces, complacent portrayals of a disappeared ethnic group. Maillet is keenly aware of this problem and
has attempted to make her work part of a political and cultural

movement that favors the rebirth of Acadian expression and (in the form of the Parti Acadien) an autonomous Acadian province within Canada. But rather than write political plays or novels, Maillet prefers to wage her battle for Acadian survival along cultural lines.

Acadia is threatened, according to Maillet, both from without and from within. Economic and social conditions have created a situation in which more and more Acadians leave their villages to work in the cities, and slowly but surely lose their culture and language. Maillet evokes this problem in her first novel, *Pointe-aux-Coques* (1958), where a young educated woman chooses to return to her native fishing village rather than to live in the city (significantly, her name is Cormier, Antonine Maillet's mother's maiden name). A subtler presentation of the problem is made in *Les Crasseux,* a play written in 1966. Here, the bourgeoisie of an Acadian village ("les gens d'En Haut," the people from the hill) want to expel the poor fishermen of the same town ("les gens d'En Bas," the people from below) when it is revealed that a young boy from "En Bas" is courting the daughter of a merchant and that the barber's son is dating a working-class girl. The "Gens d'En Bas" end up being evicted from their homes when the mayoress obtains a ministerial order providing for a public garden on their land, but the poor have the upper hand in their battle with the rich. They pick up and transplant themselves right behind the barber's shop, on a vacant lot which they have obtained for a dollar through the same governmental department that issued the expulsion order. As Don l'Orignal (Don the Moose) comments at the end: "à force de se frotter aux renards, je finissons par avoir du poil," an expression meaning roughly that when you deal with foxes, you end up being as clever as they are.[11]

The triumph of the "Gens d'En Bas" over the "Gens d'En Haut" is the victory of the Acadian people as a whole. La Sagouine divides Acadian society into three levels: "them that's got their pew up front, them that's got their pews in the back, and them others who stand."[12] The people with pews up front are the Acadian bourgeoisie, those who control not so much the Acadian economy (this is in the hands of a much wealthier, Anglo-Canadian middle class) as they do the educational establishment, and who set the tone for Acadian culture. It is they who favor the power of the Church, who invented an Acadian flag (the French tricolor with the *stella maris* in papal yellow), who proclaim the Acadian national holiday to be the Feast of the Assumption, who, Maillet says, try to "save the heritage and the identity of an Acadia that has become almost mythical and that for a century has no longer had any meaning on a national scale."[13] The people who sit in back of the church are the working class, living on concessions outside the towns, who have a little bit of money and have been, or shortly will be, part of the migration to the cities. What is left is the poorest class, those who can't afford to sit down in church, the fishermen and their families, who, without knowing it, are the repository for the Acadian language and an authentic, popular culture.

The battle lines are thus drawn, for Maillet, between the anglophone Maritimes middle class with its francophone Acadian counterpart, and the "gens d'En Bas." If *Les Crasseux* was the first of Maillet's weapons against the Acadian establishment, *La Sagouine* is her most famous. The play is deceiving at first glance: a charwoman (*sagouine* in the Acadian dialect means unclean, not in the moral but in the physical sense) alone on the stage describes her life and that of her fellow Acadians with a resignation that is not surprising, given her age (seventy years) and her social condition. "We're nothing but poor people," she says, "but that's no reason to complain" (70). Following an auction of church pews which almost upsets the social order (the poor bid higher than the rich only to find that they cannot buy their pews on the installment plan), she agrees with her husband Gapi that "you have to know how to keep your place" (94). But beyond this outward acceptance of her lot in life, La Sagouine expresses a profound, if subtle protest against her world and its social order.

As she kneels over her bucket in the middle-class house she is cleaning, La Sagouine says: "Mebbe my face is black and my skin all cracked, but my hands is white, yessir! . . . Y' could say I was filthy: I spends me whole life cleanin' up everybody else's filth" (47). Her physical position gives her a rare lucidity; she clearly sees the dirt (both literal and figurative) that escapes the eyes of the middle class, and even if she knows she can't change society, she sees through the hypocrisy of the social order. As she pays lip service to the Church, to the political system, she reveals an ingrained skepticism regarding everything that the "gens d'En Haut" would want her to believe. She knows, for instance, that the missionary priests sent down to the parish to preach morality are there to please the "gens d'En Haut" and that it is the rare worker priest, who visits the poor and helps with the work without preaching morality, that really represents the spirit of sacrifice. She knows that election campaigns bring a momentary prosperity to her village (welfare checks, gifts of record players, irons, beer) but that "once the elections is over with, the government ain't got the time to bother with us" (68). She realizes that, from the perspective of the "gens d'En Bas," social and religious myths give way to stark reality, and so-called disasters (wars, floods, depressions) benefit the poor (who receive regular pensions or relief checks) as well as the rich.

But La Sagouine's skepticism goes beyond the social and political to the realm of the metaphysical. Life and death are realities that the teachings of Catholicism cannot hide from her: "God and religion ain't none of my business," she says (125). She recognizes no distinction between a mortal body and an immortal soul; this is the meaning of the story of Jos, whose father was once buried alive (but came back to die a natural death) and is so afraid of the decomposition of his own corpse that the villagers build him a double coffin, cover it with insecticide, and plant it deep enough to keep it out of reach of the rats. "That way," she reflects, "he's all protected: he won't freeze, nothin'll eat 'im, and he won't be comin' back from his coffin neither 'cause we stayed up five nights so's to be sure he was good 'n dead" (106).

If we look closely at La Sagouine's attitudes, we see that they reflect a kind of humanism reminiscent of the Renaissance (Rabelais, of course, but also Erasmus, Montaigne). In contrast to Gapi, who asserts that "what comes after death is death" (129), La Sagouine poses questions that, she knows, will forever remain unanswered: "If only I could know. Know before I gets to the other side . . . If there ain't nothin' on the other side, then there ain't no need to worry 'bout it. . . . My Lord, is it possible that we'd begin to suffer there, too? Ain't we had enough already?" (143). Her agnosticism won't admit of a heaven or a hell, even less of a resurrection. Yet she likes to dream that someday she will rise from her grave, not in conformity with some divine scheme, but to reestablish human justice on earth. "An eternity to remake the world like you wants to! To take it into yer hands an' sand it an' polish it an' make it look beautiful" (129).

If La Sangouine is unsure of where she's going, she is also uncertain where she comes from. The federal government census takers don't help matters, since they refuse to recognize "Acadian" as a nationality, and La Sagouine knows that she is neither American ("they're rich, them Americans, an' we ain't") nor Canadian ("they're English, an' we're French") nor French ("the French is what comes from France") nor French-Canadian ("French-Canadian is what comes from Quebec" [135]). "It's tough to make a life fer yerself," she reflects, "when ya don't even got yer own country, an' ya cain't even name yer nationality. Ya end up not knowing what the heck you are" (135). But having no afterlife and no nationality are not problems that weigh heavily on La Sagouine. Her reality is on earth, in the present, and depends not on any national or ethnic labels but on what she does with her life. "As fer me, I'll tell that government: I don't know nothin', I don't belong to nothin', mebbe I ain't nothin' at all. But I'm still alive, sure as shootin'. And right now I believes I'm still called La Sagouine" (138).

La Sagouine's humanism, her faith in herself, do not sit well with a society that invokes divine providence as the reason for its survival. The challenge that la Sagouine presents to traditional Acadian society goes to the heart of its mythology. She has heard the story of the deportation in which the Acadian people play the role of a "peuple héroïque et martyr" (a heroic and martyred people) told in Church basements by members of the *Monument de la Recounnaissance* (sic) (roughly equivalent to the D.A.R.) but, she says, "I liked my late dad's stories a lot better" (136–37). In contrast to the passivity of a "peuple martyr," the Acadians in her father's stories are agressive, clever people. Pierre à Pierre à Pierre, for example, dressed himself up as a woman and took to the trees to escape the deportation; no martyrdom for him, or for Capitan Belliveau who, finding himself prisoner on a British ship, "threw them English overboard . . . and took the helm hisself" (137).

This countermythology, to which la Sagouine alludes briefly, is Maillet's way of attacking what she calls "l'évangélinisme," the imposition on the Acadian people of a story that was first recounted by the Nova Scotian Haliburton (in his *History of Nova Scotia,* 1829) and then poeticized and popularized by the American poet Long-fellow (1847). As a way of debunking the Evangeline story even further, and of providing a positive response to it, Maillet wrote in 1975 a play called *Evangéline deusse* (*Evangeline II, deusse* being the feminine form of *deux* in the Acadian dialect). The play is a conscious attempt to juxtapose reality and legend: "Evangeline has been a symbol of hope for Acadia. . . . But I know Evangelines who are much more real and who have been not symbols but survival itself."[14] But it is also a transitional play, the action taking place in Montreal rather than in Acadia and including non-Acadian characters. *Evangé-line deusse* represents the culmination of anti-*évangélinisme* and the beginning of a new direction in Maillet's theater; as such it merits a detailed analysis.

The play was presented in Montreal in the winter of 1977, with Viola Léger, the actress who had incarnated La Sagouine, in the title role. But, unlike *La Sagouine,* in which the spoken word had an immediate and privileged role to play, *Evangéline deusse* is, at first, a play of silence. Four characters appear on stage, each of whom, seemingly, has nothing to say to the others.

The setting is a small Montreal park, and the first character to enter is a virtually mute Quebecois whose job it is to cross people from one side of the busy thoroughfare to the other, holding up a small stop sign. He is called, appropriately, "le stop," and, though he lives in the city, he came originally from the Lac Saint-Jean region (made famous in Hémon's *Maria Chapdelaine*). "Je travarse le monde," he says,[15] using a pun that defines him immediately as a wanderer, an exile (the meaning in French is either "I help people cross" or "I cross the world"). We first see the Stop help across an old rabbi, he too an exile, having been chased from eastern Europe by the Nazis, thence to France, to South America, and now to Canada. As the rabbi sits on a bench and opens his Yiddish news-paper, Evangéline comes on stage, crossing the busy road on her own. She is eighty years old but acts as if she were sixty, and she has just moved from New Brunswick to Montreal to live with her son and daughter-in-law. She carries with her a small fir tree, sent from Acadia, which she proceeds to transplant at the foot of a rather large sycamore. The symbolism of this tree is obvious and corre-sponds to the author's own rerooting of herself in Quebec, now the central locus for francophone expression in North America. The Stop suddenly leaves to help the last member of the group of exiles across: a Breton fisherman, born in France, who has spent the last fifty of his eighty-two years in Canada. He carries with him a wooden model boat which he is carving and which identifies him in the same way as the tree identifies Evangéline or the Yiddish newspaper charac-terizes the rabbi.

It is Evangéline who, literally, gives words to the three silent characters. At first there is little communication from anyone but

her. The rabbi is too shy, too deferential to speak; the Stop, though
full of good intentions, finds it almost impossible to express himself,
and the Breton seems preoccupied with his own thoughts. But as
Evangéline talks, as though to herself, the others warm to her.
Significantly, it is language that helps her break the ice with the
Breton. Whereas neither the rabbi nor the Stop seem to understand
her when she asks the latter " 'a houque-t-i' des tapis, votre mère?"
(32) ("does your mother hook rugs?"), the Breton suddenly remembers: "*houquer* . . . I do remember that word. It's used in Normandy
and perhaps in northern Brittany." As for the rabbi, the Breton's
story of exile from his native land awakens the former's interest and
he makes common cause with the others. The French language has
become here an instrument enabling people from diverse back-
grounds to communicate, but more than that it has provided a
common linguistic and cultural ground for uniting the characters
of the play. As Evangéline remarks: "if a person understands your
language, he's sure as shootin' gonna understand you, too" (100).

As Evangéline talks about herself, the comparisons with La Sagouine become evident. Evangéline, too, is one of the "gens D'En
Bas," she too is uncertain of anything except her will to endure, to
survive. "At eighty years," notes the author, "she begins again, like
her ancestors before her, in exile, to eat at other people's tables, to
enter other people's houses. But Evangéline won't slack off, and
won't let the city pigeons dirty the tiny needles of the young fir
tree she has transplanted from her country to Montreal."[16]

But Evangéline is more than just a survivor; she is, of course, an
anti-Evangéline. And if the author's attempts to show this side of
her character are heavy-handed, they are nonetheless effective. During the second tableau the Breton reads to Evangéline from the
French translation of Longfellow's poem. Presumably, Evangéline
has never heard the story in detail before, at least not in the official
version, and her reactions point out the contrast between her mentality and the tradition of martyrdom. When the Breton recounts
how the English shut the Acadian men up in a church in Grand-
Pré just as Evangeline was about to marry Gabriel Lajeunesse,
Evangéline Deusse is astonished: why weren't the women shut up
with the men? Why did the men let themselves be shut up? "Our
men needed a woman or two in the church with 'em, to organize
'em, to whip 'em into shape, an' to make 'em 'shamed of 'emselves"
(45). When the Breton reads that Evangeline hid her face in her

apron and cried when her fiancé was made prisoner, Evangéline Deusse responds that when a similar disaster struck her small town— a storm causing a shipwreck that claimed fifty-three men—she and the other women didn't hide their faces; they fought the storm, hauled in the cables, sorted through the shipwreck, and waited until all the work was done before breaking down in sorrow. And when Evangéline Deusse hears that the British set fire to the church at Grand-Pré, she is indignant: "They set fire to the church? [*She picks up her bucket.*] They let the church burn? Was all the wells dried up? You jest let someone come and set fire to the church under my nose. In them cases, we get a bucket brigade going" (46).

Evangéline Deusse, in her refusal to submit to force, is unlike Longfellow's heroine but her fate parallels that of her predecessor, or at least it partially does. At eighty, she will fall in love with the Breton, and, like her legendary counterpart, will be separated from the object of her affection. But the love that grows between Evangé- line Deusse and the Breton is purely symbolic. It is not an emotional attachment but a coincidence of heritage, language, and destiny. Their love is born of a common memory: the life Evangéline led on one side of the Atlantic is like that in a small Breton fishing village on the other. Not only are their memories of ships, storms, and rum-running comparable but, as they begin to talk, the differences in their respective types of French begin to disappear. The Breton finds, hidden in his mind, more and more old words that are pre- cisely those found in the Acadian dialect that Evangéline speaks: "Brittany was full of old Acadian words," he says, "if I try I'll be able to dislodge them all." (89). He gives Evangéline the wooden ship that he has finished carving and that he has now baptized *Evangéline.*

For Evangéline, the Breton is less a person to be loved (signifi- cantly, he has no name in the play) than the manifestation of her own inexhaustible energy and desire for adventure. She has had lovers in the past, most noticeably a rum-runner named Cyprien who perished in a shipwreck but who left her an illegitimate child. Like Cyprien, the Breton is symbolized by the sea. He, too, is a dreamer, and he too searched for fortune and adventure running contraband liquor between Saint-Pierre-et-Miquelon and the United States. He did this because, as he says, he is one of those who dream of finding "lost paradises" (68). The Breton's romanticism is not to be taken literally; Evangéline Deusse would be content to find a beautiful, calm sunrise over the water. But the sense of timelessness offered by the ocean is an essential part of Evangéline's will to survive and see herself as part of an endless process of death and rebirth.

Like Gabriel Lajeunesse in Longfellow's poem, the Breton will die in Evangéline's arms. Victim of a heart attack, he evokes, as he expires, the sea, the coast, the ghost ships that are his and Evangé-line's common mythical heritage. The scene and his last words ("Evangéline . . . go to Louisiana . . . look for . . . Gabriel" [94]) parallel Longfellow's poem almost exactly:

> Vainly he strove to whisper her name, for the accents unuttered
> Died on his lips, and their motion revealed what his tongue would have spoken.
> Vainly he strove to rise; and Evangeline, kneeling beside him
> Kissed his dying lips, and laid his head on her bosom.
> . . .
> And as she pressed once more the lifeless head to her bosom,
> Meekly she bowed her own, and murmured,
> "Father, I thank thee."[17]

The parallel is poignant because Evangéline Deusse is the last person in the world to accept her fate with a meek "Father, I thank thee." Her reaction is rather one of resentment: "They've taken everythin' away from me, piece by piece" (97). But it is not merely the contrast between the two Evangélines, the legend and the reality, that the author wants to point out in this scene. The curious remark of the Breton, telling Evangéline to look for her lost Gabriel in Louisiana, is followed by an equally curious exclamation from Evangéline; as the Breton expires, she cries out: "Cyprien!" (94). The Breton is, symbolically, Cyprien or any other passion, just as Evangéline herself is the symbol of the woman who will forever search out this passion, and their love represents Evangéline's love for all men, for life.

If, in the end, Evangéline Deusse does not distinguish between the Breton and Cyprien, it is because she sees herself not simply as an Acadian exile but as part of all the exiled of the earth, all the wanderers. In this sense she is different from La Sagouine and Mail-let's previous characters who remained resolutely within their Aca-dian ethnic context. It is not simply her coming to Montreal that makes Evangéline Deusse cosmopolitan; it is really her contact with other exiles whose existence she had never suspected that leads her to accept the rabbi, the Breton, and the Quebecois as if they, too, were Acadians. For their part, the other three realize that they are, in a sense, all "Acadian." The Breton, of course, has emotional ties with Evangéline, but the rabbi too finds the story of the deportation strangely similar to his own. The Stop is the most enigmatic of the characters; he never sees his similarity as a Quebecois to Evangéline's fate until the very end of the play when, finally, the sense of the story of the deportation sinks in. At that point, he tells Evangéline the story of Maria Chapdelaine, emphasizing that the Quebec heroine stayed on her land and refused the temptation to leave for the United States. Evangéline immediately sees that this story is radically different from her own and that, by extension, the fate of the people of Quebec, unlike that of the Breton or the rabbi, does not parallel hers. She tells the Stop: "That means that folks like you ain't left their land, not like folks like us what gets themselves deported. That's fate." (104–5). But for all that, this Quebecois is still an *exilé,* though in a more subtle sense than the others, for he cannot recall his own name and seems to have no idea of his own identity. He and his ancestors may in fact have remained on the same land for more than two hundred years, but this land does not yet have a name, and the country to which these people belong does not yet have a destiny.

It is not only the universality of the Acadian experience that defines *Evangéline Deusse* as a transitional play in Maillet's repertory. Maillet's earlier works were an attempt to find a definition of the self that took into account the individual's reaction to a specific society. Acadia was essential here because it provided both a cultural tradition and a social context for her characters. But with *Evangéline Deusse* the notion of place has changed, and with it the existential dilemma. Unlike La Sagouine, Evangéline does not spend two hours on stage defining herself and her society. Evangéline's role is rather that of a witness to the lives of others and also, as her name implies, that of an evangelist, the bearer of a message. Her granddaughter, she says, had accused her of having no future: "she said to me that ya gotta have yer future behind ya to talk like I does, an' that *she'd* got *her* future in front of her" (33). Far from finding this remark insulting, Evangéline recognizes an essential truth in it. She does, in fact, have her destiny behind her. Life, for her, is a series of actions that take on meaning only when compared with the past. We have seen that Evangéline's love for the Breton was a continuation of her previous love for Cyprien. Similarly, her future in

Montreal is but another step in the process of deportation and resettlement that began in the eighteenth century. As she herself says at the end of the play, "old folks and deported folks is the only people I know what knows everythin' 'bout life, 'cause they're the only people who've begun their lives over an' over again, and who've already been to the end of their road" (107).

Beginning with *Evangéline Deusse,* then, Maillet's characters begin to see themselves as part of a cycle. In her only significant play since *Evangéline Deusse,*[18] *La Veuve enragée* (The enraged widow), the visit of an Irish sailor, Tom Thumb, to a coastal Acadian village is the occasion for a battle of will between a religious fanatic (La Veuve) and a group of gypsylike women (Les Mercenaires) who regularly entertain visiting seamen. The Mercenaires win their battle and chase away La Veuve (who wanted to put them off their land); moreover, they convince Tom Thumb to settle down and marry into their community. Like the Breton, this Irish sailor sees reflections of his native fishing village in Acadia; "it's in America that Ireland is beautiful," he says.[19] But his role is more positive than that of Le Breton, for he is to ensure that there will be a future generation of Mercenaires. Without knowing it, he is being faithful to the past, to the first Mercenaire, a Frenchman who, like Tom Thumb, deserted his ship to settle in Acadia. The cycle continues, and the survival of a small, marginal group of people is assured.

The sense and evolution of Maillet's theater is clear. From a theater of refutation, where the Evangéline myth was debunked, where reality replaced legend (or re-created it), she has moved toward the fabrication of a new mythology in which the notion of deportation is replaced by that of regeneration. *La Sagouine* ended with a monologue entitled "La Mort," during which La Sagouine, conscious of her own imminent death, said "tomorrow I'll go see the doctor" (144). *La Veuve enragée,* in contrast, ends with a prenuptial feast and the assertion that "icitte la vie recoumence" (here, life begins anew).[20] "It isn't the deportation that is the most important part of [Acadia's] history," says the author, "it's that people came back."[21] The universality of her theater lies precisely in this refusal to lament one's fate or to see in the course of history anything more than the proof of man's capacity to transcend his destiny. Antonine Maillet's theater is above all a theater of hope.

Jean-Claude Germain

> "L'illusion . . . ya rien quça dvrai . . .
> l'ILLUSION."
> (*L'Ecole des rêves*, 109)

> ("Illusion . . . only that is true . . . ILLUSION.)

If any Quebecer deserves to be called a "man of the theater" it is Jean-Claude Germain. He exercises almost every activity associated with dramatic production: playwriting, directing, teaching, criticism. Moreover, he is keenly aware of the role of theater in society and of society's (and the state's) role in supporting dramatic art. Through his plays, articles, and public appearances he makes his voice heard, loudly.

Born in 1939 in the same Montreal neighborhood as Michel Tremblay, Germain's career took a different turn from that of the author of *Les Belles-soeurs*. From the beginning Germain was less interested in the portrayal of the milieu of his youth than in the cultural evolution of Quebec and Canadian society. After a less-than-successful try at founding an avant-garde theater appropriately named the Théâtre Antonin Artaud in 1958, Germain became a journalist, first for *Le Petit Journal* where he reviewed plays, then for a journal he helped found called *L'Illettré* (The uneducated), and finally for the popular monthly *Le Maclean*.

Germain saw his task as more than the criticism of plays from an aesthetic or technical point of view. The works he described and analyzed in his columns became the pretext for a personal interpretation of the cultural history of Quebec.[22] It was inevitable that these reflections on Quebec culture should lead Germain to put his ideas into practice and to found, in 1969, the Théâtre du Même Nom (whose acronym, TMN, is a deliberate confusion with Montreal's solidly middle-class Théâtre du Nouveau Monde, or TNM), later to become the Centre du Théâtre d'Aujourd'hui, on the Rue Papineau in Montreal's east end. Just as Germain's newspaper articles are not merely criticism of plays, so the Théâtre d'Aujourd'hui is not merely a place where plays are produced. "The theater," says Germain, "does not only exist in relation to the text or to the performance, no, the performance, like the text, reflects the image of an entire functioning organism."[23] In the image of Jacques Copeau's Théâtre du Vieux Colombier in the Paris of the 1920s, Germain has created a center where actors, playwrights, and directors collaborate closely, and where the public can feel involved in a small intimate house whose stage extends into the audience. But the Théâtre d'Aujourd'hui is more than that; it is also the crucible for the development of Germain's concept of culture.

Germain's theory of Quebec culture is rooted in his interpretation of history. When, in 1759, the French abandoned North America to the British, French Canadians had already developed, over the course of more than a century, a folk tradition that included songs, stories, and even theater. This tradition was essentially oral and included such "theatrical" manifestations as the "Easter sermons" of priests ("the people preferred the speeches about the sixth and ninth commandment," says Germain; "they liked anything having to do with sex."),[24] passion plays that toured the province, and, later, reviews and sketches in music halls. In sum, a popular culture existed in Quebec that was indigenous to the French-Canadian population and that "for a long time alone portrayed Quebec realities."[25]

For Britain's Lord Durham, however, who issued his *Report on the Affairs of British North America* in 1839, French Canada had no culture. In terms that have become infamous for Quebecers, he characterized the French Canadians as an "uninstructed, inactive, unprogressive people" having "no history and no literature," and went on to remark that "their nationality operates to deprive them of the enjoyment and civilizing influence of the arts."[26] French-Canadian reaction to Durham's comments was, according to Germain, to accept his presuppositions. "Creating a rather amusing paradox," Germain says, "the only way to prove to a European that we had a culture and a literature was to make a culture, a literature, and a history in the European style."[27] An almost direct result of the Durham report was, of course, François-Xavier Garneau's epic *Histoire du Canada* whose first volume appeared in 1845; as for literature, a tradition of writing modeled on authors from France began and later did show some evidence of originality and native inspiration. But in the schools and universities, in the museums and fashionable clubs, and especially in the theater, culture came to mean French culture, the classic dramatists of the seventeenth century, especially Molière (expurgated, of course, of such plays as *Tartuffe*).

The problem, as Germain sees it, is not the coexistence of two cultures, one elite and the other popular, but a kind of cultural schizophrenia because the elite culture is not Quebecois but French, that is, foreign. Since culture is a way in which a people perceives itself, slavishness to the French model implies that Quebec culture, if it exists at all, is a second-rate version of French culture. A parallel situation exists in all of Canada with respect to what Germain calls the "Mid-Atlantic Seven Arts Club Band"—the East Coast American establishment that confers cultural legitimacy and "questions the reality of certain indigenous cultures," like that of Canada.[28] In the desire by some Canadian and Quebec writers to be of universal significance, to appeal strictly to international audiences, Germain sees not only the rejection of three hundred years of cultural history but also of the dream of a truly independent country. For the artist, he asserts, "independence and its natural expression which is the feeling of belonging to a distinct, particular, autonomous, and sovereign cultural entity is never seen as a goal to attain: it is an a priori, a prerequisite to creation, and an ontological evidence."[29]

No other Quebec playwright is as preoccupied with his country's development as Germain. For most of these dramatists, the expression of a certain reality—personal (Tremblay), social (Barbeau), political (Gurik, Ferron)—is the principal reason for writing plays; the ways in which these plays influence the cultural evolution of Quebec is a side product of the original inspiration. But Germain sees culture itself as the major inspiration and subject of his plays. His main function as a playwright is to "translate the culture that surrounds us, to make it pass from what I would call its folklore stage to a cultural stage."[30] For Germain, folklore is culture with a small *c,* the forgotten plays of Félix-Gabriel Marchand, whom he rehabilitated, or Ernest Guimond, whom he has yet to resurrect, the music halls of Montreal, and the town halls of provincial villages. But folklore is not a time machine and Germain never ressurects the past for its own sake. His efforts aim toward the integration of the folk culture of the past with that of the present, which includes country and western music, radio talk shows, sleazy nightclubs, Ben's smoked meat, and a language full of anglicisms. Through reevaluating, updating, and even rewriting the cultural inheritance of the past (his version of Marchand's *Les Faux brillants,* for example, is a "paraphrase" of the late nineteenth-century vaudeville play)

Germain is self-consciously reevaluating the past as a function of the present.

Because, unlike most of his fellow Quebec playwrights, Germain is the artistic director of his own theater, he has a great deal of control over the way in which his plays are presented as well as over the policies that govern the operations of his theater. This control has led him, in the tradition of such French directors as Jean-Louis Barrault and the late Jean Vilar, to formulate theories that serve as guidelines for the concepts his theater stands for. He tries to steer a middle course between the idea of a "popular" theater (that is, for the common people) put forward in France by Jean Vilar and Roger Planchon, and a more intimate theater created for the happy few who are attuned to the cultural avant-garde. Germain takes from Vilar the idea of "a theater accessible to the 'people,' " theater as a "public service."[31] But where Vilar had used a very large house (the Palais de Chaillot in Paris) and had wanted to present the classical and contemporary repertory to a segment of the population to whom it had too long been inaccessible or incomprehensible, Germain prefers a small house, an "intimate theater of complicity."[32] A culture with its roots in popular tradition does not imply a theater of the masses, and Germain wants his audience in small doses: "Theater must not be considered a 'popular' art which can come in contact with great numbers of people," Germain says. "It is an exclusive art which appeals to small minorities."[33] But exclusive does not mean elitist, and Germain makes a conscious attempt to discard the European-French trappings of intimist theater (inspired in Quebec by Father Emile Legault's Compagnons de Saint-Laurent) in favor of what he calls a "popular language"—that is to say, joual. Where Tremblay uses joual because it is an intrinsic part of his characters, Germain uses it largely to attract the average Quebecer who usually does not attend the theater. Popular language is therefore more than popular speech; it is also "cultural allusions, clichés, body language, the way the stage is organized," all of which translates the preoccupations of the vast majority of Quebecers.[34] It should be noted that Germain eschews the class analysis advanced by such theorists of "popular" theater as Roger Planchon; the Théâtre d'Aujourd'hui sees its audience strictly as a national and cultural entity, a characteristic which supersedes class differences.

Jean-Claude Germain's theater is above all entertaining; he takes seriously Molière's dictum that theater is the art of pleasing the audience. His plays are intended to produce laughter, not only at the subject being presented but also at the manner of presentation itself (which is often a parody of other kinds of drama). Germain's purpose is to provoke a reaction both to the social or political situation in the play and to its dramatic language; a distance is created between the spectator and the play so that the audience, rather than believing in the reality of what is on the stage, feels free to criticize. Despite similarities with Brecht's alienation effect, Germain's idea is not so much to present a new reality beyond appearances (for Brecht this reality was the economic and social structure of society) but to show that all reality, personal, social, and political, is essentially a theatrical game.[35] The affinities with the drama of Jean Genet are obvious, and Germain acknowledges them: "What Genet does is very important. I think that audiences now identify with theater itself, and that's why my characters are always people who are playing."[36] But Germain's purpose is much less personal than Genet's, and the falseness he denounces is not only existential. It is the result of Quebec's profound and complex problems of identity within the Canadian confederation.

The dramatic structure of Germain's plays follows from his theories. As he consciously rejects the style of theater brought to Quebec from France by Father Legault, he looks at the popular theater of the past for inspiration and attempts to "renew contact with a theatrical tradition that existed before the Compagnons de Saint-Laurent and to find in it the premises of modern [theatrical] practice on the level of form as well as of themes."[37] The most important of the elements that Germain takes from the past is the oral tradition. Like many Quebec authors (Jacques Ferron, Roch Carrier, Louis Caron), Germain is a born storyteller and his plays are geared to the rhythm and pace of the raconteur.[38] Episodes replace linear plots, and audience reaction is encouraged. "In Quebec," he says, "most people live, survive, and relive by using words; it is their way of speaking, of telling stories that gives meaning to their existence."[39] Music, too, is an element of the oral tradition that Germain incorporates in his plays. "He who sings says more than he who speaks," he asserts.[40] In some of his plays—in *Si les Sausoucis . . .* for example—songs are used in the Brechtian style: characters stop what they are doing, face the audience, and sing words that comment on the play's plot or characters. In others—for instance in *Les Nuits de l'Indiva*—songs are the characters' principal means of expressing their own hopes, dreams, deceptions. Songs and instrumental music lend a festive air to many of Germain's productions, and are part of an effort to create an all-encompassing spectacle, "situated halfway between the church and the cabaret,"[41] or, as one critic joked, "half mass, half ass."[42]

The Church is, in fact, as important a pole of attraction in Germain's theater as the cabaret. Not that he is in any way a Catholic writer; like most contemporary Quebec artists and intellectuals, he sees religion as an element in his country's past that did more harm than good. But the historic social function of the Church intrigues him, and he often compares the sacred feeling one has on entering a church with the way one feels on entering a theater. Significantly, he traces the birth of modern Quebec drama to a "happening" which took place in Montreal's Eglise Notre-Dame on 8 December 1968. A group of eight young people burst into the church during the ceremony of consecration of the Order of the Holy Sepulcre. They entered the chancel and, in front of the altar, turned to face the parishioners. They then proceded to cry out, in turn, a number of slogans such as "death to the establishment," "death to dogmatism," "death to the commandments of the Church," "make way for madness," "make way for hope"—echoing the *Refus global* which the painter Paul-Emile Borduas had issued in 1948 and which was the battle cry for an entire generation of nonconformist Quebec artists and authors. Finally, as the organ began to play, the eight "actors" walked together down the aisle, chanting "make way for orgasm" as they left the church. For Germain, this spectacle was "the birth of revolutionary Quebec theater and . . . its first act of liberation"[43] because it used those very symbols that had stifled creativity to proclaim the freedom of the imagination. As theater, it had some of the shock value of Artaud's proposed theater of cruelty and used ritual and ceremony to convey a sense of the battle of will taking place in Quebec between the old order and the new. "Place à l'orgasme," as the manifestation was called, coming four months after Michel Tremblay's *Les Belles-soeurs,* provided Germain with a symbolic jumping-off point, a crude but effective provocation that would influence the beginnings of his own theater.

The plays that Germain has produced and written since 1969 can be divided into three categories. The first of these are generally satirical works, attacks upon tradition in art and society. In his very first play, *Les Enfants de Chénier dans un autre grand spectacle d'adieu*

(Chénier's children in another grand farewell show),[44] Germain pokes fun at the French classic dramatists, Racine, Corneille, and Molière, and at other greats (Shakespeare, Aeschylus, Musset) via a simulated boxing match in which the Enfants de Chénier (coached by Germain) defeat the masters of the past.[45] It was a facile and somewhat immature attempt to cock a snook at the theatrical establishment but it strongly affirmed the unique direction Germain wanted his theater to take, for it boldly and publicly took up the problem of cultural identity and, through it, of national identity. Germain's next play, *Diguidi, Diguidi, ha! ha! ha!,* presented a month after the first had finished, is more complex and more ambitious. It implicitly puts into question middle-class assumptions regarding the family and society by turning the theater inside out. Two of the actors, the father and mother, are an "audience" on stage, and speak to the third actor, the son, seated in the middle of the real audience. The actors at first seem to be representatives of the traditional French theater; they claim that "there is no greater joy in the house of Molière than to play before an audience ignorant of the mysteries of our art" and see their "mission" as "initiating, as much as possible, into OUR CULTURE . . . the disinherited, the dispossessed."[46] But the reality these actors are called upon to present is, in its sordidness and cruelty, light years away from the world of belles-lettres. In a kind of distillation of Tremblay's scenes of family life, a mother and father bicker over their failed marriage and sexual problems ("she always rolled herself up in the sheets so I wouldn't touch her," says the father [73–74]) and ignore their unloved son, a situation which provokes the latter to kill his father. But Germain's play has none of the psychological realism we see in Tremblay. Germain's family is avowedly a fictitious exaggeration—the characters turn into dogs and answer accusations by barking—because it is the theatrical quality of daily life that is exposed here. The father believes in Santa Claus, the mother in the Star Fairy, and both parents try to instill a belief in the bogeyman *(le bonhomme sept-heures)* in their son. All three of them spend their time symbolically and really attached to their chairs with safety belts while a television blares away in English. The family here is a gullible audience that propagates the faith it absorbs from the media (conservatism) and transmits the values of the past (reliance on the Church, superstitition, ignorance of sex).

The wife, at the end of the play, achieves a kind of liberation when she breaks out of the mold of motherhood designed by the Church and society and cries: "I know that I don't know how to do anything . . . I know that I'm too old . . . I know but I don't give a damn . . . I just want to be free . . ." (91). But Germain never lets the audience feel sorry for the mother or any of the other characters; indeed, he never lets the audience feel sure of its own function and provokes it into asking some fundamental questions about theater itself. The title of the play (a tickle, followed by a laugh) points, in its irony, to one of these questions: can or should theater tickle and titillate its audience with plays about family life when the reality is so depressing as to stifle all laughter? But the family here is the pretext for a larger issue. The mother's cries at the end, in the context of the political tension of 1969, must be seen as a call for the independence of Quebec culture and society from the chains of the past. Moreover, the actors, whom we see very clearly and who are never confused with the characters they play, pose some other important questions: should theater give the public "a little bit of dream for its money" (82) or should it present reality? Should there be self-censorship so that nothing offensive to established religious beliefs is presented? Should the audience be passive in its seats—"poured into 'em" (34)—and let itself be "made, unmade, and remade" by the actors (35)? *Diguidi* asks these questions, answers some of them (it rejects censorship and passive audiences) but leaves others unanswered (should theater be reality or dream?). As one astute student remarked to Germain, "in *Diguidi* you sum up in an hour all the classic situations in traditional Quebec theater and you reject them."[47] The play leaves us with the impression of something unfinished. It is, like Borduas's document, a global refusal of theater's content and structure and, as such, its message is too diffused to strike any specific target.

The subsequent plays in Germain's satirical cycle pinpoint targets more clearly. Religious education and the myths it propagates are the subjects of *Si Aurore m'était contée deux fois* (If Aurora were told to me twice) presented in 1970. The play, whose title refers to a very popular melodrama of the 1950s recreated (and republished) in 1984, points to the absurd persistence of religious superstition and suggests its exploitation by the political machinery of the province, a suggestion made explicit in a follow-up play, *La Mise à mort de la Miss des Miss* [The putting to death of the Miss of the Misses].

But by the time *La Mise à mort* was presented, in October 1970, the political situation in Quebec had heated up beyond the boiling point, and the War Measures Act had been proclaimed. Germain's next play, *Les Tourtereaux, ou la vieillesse frappe à l'aube* [The turtle-doves, or old age strikes at dawn] was intended as a parody of radio talk shows, but inevitably, given the situation in which it was written, politics got in the way, and the play became a bitter indictment of the mass culture being propagated by Radio Canada and the cultural establishment.

In his early plays Germain appears to be an angry young man, using the stage to denounce institutions and what they represent. There are no sympathetic characters here; the characters exist only to reveal to the audience the difference between the images that society has of itself and the reality behind them. But in 1971 Germain presented a new kind of play, one which put on stage an average Quebecer who would strike a responsive chord in the audience.

Si les Sansoucis s'en soucient, ces Sansoucis-ci s'en soucieraient-ils? Bien parler, c'est se respecter! is the longest title in Quebec dramaturgy and is a real tongue twister (it is untranslatable, but roughly means "if the Careless care about it, would these Careless care about it? Speak well and respect yourself!"). The title, as Laurent Mailhot notes, is a spectacle in itself;[48] layers of meaning peel off it like an onion. It is an exercise in diction (the first sentence) followed by an advertising slogan from Quebec's Office de la Langue Française, whose job it is to promote "correct" French. The Enfants Sans-Souci was a Parisian dramatic corporation during the fifteenth century; their leader was called the *prince des sots,* a player of *soties,* satirical allegories of society. The first sentence of Germain's title, taken for its meaning, conveys the idea of indifference inherent in the name, but it is also a challenge, an accusatory question asked of the actors themselves.

In fact, the play is a trial. A musician is accused of a crime that is never defined and of which he is never convicted. He roams over the stage not as an actor but as himself (he is supposed to use his real name) playing the guitar (or any other instrument), in stark contrast to the play's other figures who, true to their medieval French namesakes, are *sots,* clowns or buffoons.

These clowns who play on a stage decorated with caricatures of judges are three members of the Sansouci family. Two sisters, Tharaise (intelligent and domineering) and Chlinne (a floozy), wear judges wigs and white, transparent robes; their brother, Farnand, is distinguished by the propeller beanie he always keeps on his head. All three are members of the lesser branch of a political family whose service to the country dates back to the British conquest when "the first of the name, the Chevalier de Sansouci, was sent to Wolfe to give him the keys to Quebec."[49] Since that time the family's upper branch (here called the branch of the Grand Table, for reasons which will be apparent later) never ceased to do the bidding of Canada's English power structure, and in their rise to political power they have acquired, besides English forenames (Fred, Rod, Tony, Frank), the dislike of Quebec's middle class, represented here by Madame Sansfaçon (unceremonious), the perennial speaker at ladies' club luncheons, in a dress reminiscent of kitchen curtains. The powerful members of the Sansouci family are absent from the play, and the lesser branch is singularly unprepared for its task. "We Sansouci are made for kitchen tables, maybe, but our asses aren't the right shape for the judge's bench," says Chlinne (135). Justice, represented by an empty bench, should be under the control of Farnand, Chlinne, and Tharaise, standing in for those other family members (like Red the police chief, Tony the minister without portfolio, or Frank the archbishop) in real control. But the lesser branch of the family finds itself caught up in events it cannot control, and the trial is aborted before it can even begin.

In this play within a play or trial within a trial it is Farnand who, called upon as a witness, ends up implicitly (if not explicitly) accused of a crime against his family and his background. It all starts when he refuses to identify the primary exhibit at the trial: the table of the Sansouci. This is a small table, symbolic not of the power of the great branch but of the inheritance (social, political, cultural) which, to be a Sansouci, Farnand should accept. "Maybe you're not made for the table, Farnand, but the table is made for you!" says Chlinne, "like it or not, you're going to inherit the table" (129).

But Farnand will not accept the imposition of the past that the table represents. Chlinne and Tharaise are comfortable living with the table, living on it (Chlinne dreams of all the men she could have sex with on it), but Farnand finds the table oppressive: "DAMNED TABLE! I came into the world on it, I lived around it, and if I don't succeed in getting rid of it I think I'll be buried with it. . . . DAMNED TABLE! . . . I THINK I'LL NEVER GET A HARD-ON AGAIN!" (127) His impotence is not only sexual, it is political and economic as well; all that his powerful relatives can tell him is that his situation is unchangeable because "the country is made that way" (177). Farnand is, in fact, powerless in every sense of the word—powerless even not to inherit the table—yet his sisters want him not merely to accept the inheritance, but to desire it.

Chlinne and Tharaise thus think of a ruse to get their brother to want the table. Adding yet another layer to this play within a play, Chlinne impersonates an English Canadian who wants to take the table from Farnand. There is, at first, a slight problem of comprehension ("I speak two langauges," says Farnand, "I'm perfectly bilingual in joual and French" [181]), but with Tharaise as an interpreter Farnand understands the words which come out of Chlinne's mouth but which express more than a century of English dominance in Canada: "This table is ours to do as we please!" (183). Farnand doesn't really see the menace here. He believes that the English want to purchase the table, and so when they magnanimously propose that he be the table's custodian for a while, he declares: "IF I HAVE TO TAKE CARE OF IT FOR SOMEONE ELSE . . . I'D RATHER KEEP IT FOR ME! (184) The ruse has worked; Farnand has been caught in Chlinne's trap and will voluntarily accept the table.

It is clearly Farnand who is at the center of the play and who is the first of Germain's characters to have an autonomous existence. He is not only, or even principally, a Sansouci—although the fact of his birth does predetermine his inheritance. He is, despite all the constraints put on him, a man struggling to create his own life by putting distance between his family (in the largest sense) and himself. He is characterized by what one critic calls "active indifference,"[50] that is, a voluntary neglect of that over which he has no control, a defensive reflex that gives him the illusion of control. Yet when finally he accepts the table, it is not with indifference but with the will to exert some influence over his destiny. "Have you understood, TABLE? You're going to have to change. . . . We're going to change you, TABLE . . . Yeah, 'cause Farnand here, HE CAN'T STAND YOU NO MORE LIKE YOU ARE!" (187). This transformation of Farnand's attitude is important because it accompanies his increasing solitude. Once he has taken on his inheritance he is left alone on the stage (accompanied only by the musician), and the entire performance is revealed as a pretext for the game his sisters have played on him. "I knew," he says, "that it wouldn't end up being a trial, and that it'd finish up like a THEATER PLAY . . . and that I'd find myself all alone in front of everybody with the TABLE!" (186).

The key to our understanding of Farnand comes from a song sung by the musician and entitled "La chanson du pays dans l'pays" (the song of the country within the country):

> Every word has a double bottom
> Every lake has a double bed
> Each word we say, as it should
> Comes from the country which is within the country
> (164)

The specific duality of Quebec (a country within another), evoked here, implies a duality of language: nothing one says can be taken at face value, and there is a hidden side to even the most innocuous of words. The audience is called upon to judge Farnand not on the basis of what he says but on the basis of what he cannot or will not say. For despite his indifference toward the table and all it represents, Farnand is anything but independent. He has, without being aware of it, already accepted that part of his past which is potentially the most harmful to his freedom, subservience to the values of the English Canadian establishment and what Germain would have called (until the Parti Québécois victory in 1976) its henchmen in Quebec. The way he succumbs to Chlinne's ruse reveals his belief that the worth of something is proportional to the value it has for English Canada. "I REFUSE! . . . I DISINHERIT MYSELF!" he cries (130), but once having made this resolution he finds himself obliged to keep the table for just a little while longer.

Farnand is thus a victim, a "sympathetic loser,"[51] and, like so many other protagonists in Quebec drama, a dupe of language. The power of those in power (and here we see the irony of the second part of the play's title) derives partly from their ability to use "good French" to create ambiguity and deception. The family honor and name are smokescreens to hide what the Sansouci really want from Farnand, which is to manipulate him politically. Farnand, because he speaks joual, uses language not so much for the effect it has on others but for the way in which it makes the world understandable to himself. His language, as Germain says, is his "principal weapon"[52] and he talks excessively in an attempt to get himself out of tight situations, to avoid admitting the inevitability of his fate. But

Farnand's words are powerless to change anything, and this is why his desire at the end of the play to change the table reveals the opposite of what he intends, simply reinforces his impotence.

Farnand Sansouci's saga continues in Germain's next play, *Le Roi des mises à bas prix* (The king of low bids). The circuslike atmosphere of *Si les Sansoucis* becomes here oppressive, almost absurdist, as we follow Farnand on his daily routine between tavern and apartment. The table, his inheritance, has shrunk in size; it is a stool, a chair, and, in the final analysis, himself. As the play progresses, as Farnand sits in front of his table loaded with beer bottles, society begins to move in on him. At first it is the voice of the train dispatcher which announces the departures of trains he will never take, the voice of the taxi driver, policeman, and other authority figures, even God. He has become the epitome of a loser, seeing organized society as both alien and hostile, regretting the loss of his "personal waiter," Speedy, the only person to whom he could talk.

Farnand's inheritance has become less personal, more universal. God has given him "a source of consolation, a *planche de salut*, . . . a last hope . . . TELEVISION!"[53] In his apartment Farnand finds the Television Man, alias the *chanteux de pomme* (sweet talker). All the authority figures in society coalesce in this one character; as Germain explains, the *chanteux de pomme* is a "living anthology . . . of the blackmail to which a typical Quebecer is subjected from birth to death" (45). The battle lines are drawn; Farnand, to save his individuality, must fight all the elements in his life that want to control him. But the threat is more Huxleyan than Orwellian. The Television Man is a faithful companion ("we're here with you twenty-four hours a day" [56]), inoffensive ("that's what television is, a game to pass the time" [64]), and reassuring ("to think like everyone else is to feel so much better" [78]). When Farnand insults him, he implores his pity; when Farnand catches on to his game, he changes the rules. In the end, Farnand succeeds in getting rid of him, but it is a pyrrhic victory, for Farnand exchanges one interlocutor (the power structure) for another, Speedy, who is nothing but the illusion of friendship and belonging. In this play, as in *Si les Sansouci,* Farnand is a completely alienated individual, afraid even to leave his apartment, resigned to spending his time drinking beer alone.

But *Le Roi des mises* takes the significance of Farnand as a Quebecer one step further than *Si les Sansouci.* If in the earlier play Farnand still thought it might be possible to change his inheritance, in this play he has, as he says, "UNDERSTOOD, GODDAMIT!" (96). In particular, he has understood that the past will always be with him, and that as he goes through life he will continue to acquire more "furniture," the word he uses to describe the various elements of the collective past of French Canada. And so his problem is not to accept or reject his past but to find a place, a context, in which to put it. His apartment, symbolic here of his country, is hard for him to find, and the directions to it exist only in English; it is owned by a company in Cleveland, Ohio, and, to open the door, one must recite into a microphone the password "meek as a lamb" (42). Moreover, the apartment's dimensions are too small; "I'm going to need a depot to put everything in," says Farnand, quickly adding "I'm going to need a country" (96). What he has dimly realized here is that his problem is very literally one of *espace vital* (living space), room for him to put the inheritance in. Farnand, as one critic has commented, "is the *king* of a 'country' *that is dying.*"[54] It is a country that needs to be found, not in the physical sense but as a mental space. And this notion, clearly expressed in *Le Roi des mises,* points the way to the plays that follow.

Since 1972, Germain has been writing plays whose decors are the theater itself and whose subjects concern the ways in which performers relate their own problems and preoccupations to the plays they perform. The first of these plays to be published was *Les Hauts et les bas dla vie d'une diva: Sarah Ménard par eux-mêmes* (The ups and downs of the life of a diva: Sarah Ménard by themselves), first performed in 1974. The title of the play is a reference to the famous French actress Sarah Bernhardt, who toured Quebec six times between 1880 and 1916, but Germain's direct inspiration was the French-Canadian diva named Emma Albani, intimate friend of Queen Victoria, who returned to a triumphal welcome in Montreal in 1883 where she sang the very-English "Home Sweet Home." Like the diva Albani, Sarah Ménard returns (from New York's Metropolitan Opera) to her home town in Quebec to receive the accolades of family and friends. But the Sarah Ménard Cultural Center which the town builds in her honor turns out to be a swimming pool, and, when we see Sarah, she has given up her operatic career to be a cabaret singer. The play itself is a kind of one-woman show where Sarah, accompanied by her pianist, reveals to the audience her strengths and weaknesses as a woman and as an artist.

In contrast to Farnand Sansouci, who was only dimly aware of his own dilemma (and never really aware of its causes), Sarah Ménard is keenly lucid. She knows her own failings and relates them to her role in society. She is, as she says, "wide-open . . . and game."[55] This natural generosity can hardly be said to be a moral flaw, but it is what gets Sarah into trouble in a society where role playing is more common than honesty and sincerity. The best example Sarah gives of this dilemma is the story of the night she lost her virginity. "I couldn't understand," she says, "everything was rollin' along nicely until we got to the bedroom . . . but there . . . well . . . well I was too game . . . so game that the poor guys didn't know what to do . . . I frightened them" (69). She soon learned, as she puts it, "the etiquette of sexual relations" (69) and, finally, by acting like the perfect naive teenager ("I saw that they liked them that way, timid, fragile, dependent, and a little bit scared." [70]), manages to seduce the type of married man who "deflowered girls all year long in every hotel on the coast" [71]) and fed each one the same hypocritical declaration of love. What bothers Sarah is not really the man's dishonesty but the role he is forcing her to play: "he didn't believe a word of what he said, but the craziest thing is that I had to believe all of it" (70). Her revenge will be in proportion to the crime perpetrated on her; she will threaten to reveal him to everyone else in the hotel unless he makes love to her again in all honesty, "just for the fun of doing it" (72).

Sarah's problem as a woman is not without comparison to her problems as an actress. To be effective with her audience, as with men, she has to become the personage they want her to be; as she puts it, "every time something good happens to a woman, she has to forget herself, she has to disappear, turn the same color as the sheets . . . it's as if men are happy only when they're looking at an empty plate" (63). But just as Sarah can't accept the role of the submissive woman, she can't accept the role of the famous diva who sings Mozart and Schubert in European opera halls. One way out of her dilemma would, of course, be for Sarah to assert her individuality in the face of men and of theater, and to abandon both until they can accept her as she is. But ironically she needs audiences and men more than they do her. "I need to bathe myself in a crowd every day," she says, "it's my secret, my magic cure, my treatment, my dope" (28). The eyes of the audience upon the actress are likened by her to hands caressing her body: "two eyes which jump on you

. . . and which rape you completely . . . it's an ORGASM . . . for
. . . a . . . second" (31). It is important that these hands be
anonymous—"I need to be recognized by unknown eyes" (29)—
because as soon as the looker is identified and becomes another
human being with a personality of his own, the pleasure is spoiled.

Because she is a Quebec actress, Sarah's existential problems are
even more complex. Just as she does not know how to act when
she is not acting, she does not quite know what to sing, what roles
to play so that her own identity pierces through the costume. "My
Antigone is all messed up," she sings, "and my Eurydice's all tuck-
ered out" (57). She has died so many times on the stage that even
a striptease seems an appealing role, anything but to continue to
play classical parts. Her instincts tell her to be herself, to create her
own roles with her own words, as Tremblay's Sainte-Carmen tried
to do. But Germain's diva is neither tragic nor saintly; she is, rather,
keenly aware of the failure her career has been to her and of the
uncertainty of her own identity. She is also aware of what she would
have been had she sublimated her desire for self-fulfillment and
played the role of the prudent, reasonable young woman. "Linda"
is a mannequin, a figure whom Sarah dresses up and upon whom
she confers the identity that she always refused to accept: "While
crazy me ran around like a wild devil, . . . you had the good
part. . . . You waited for the curtain to fall and then you picked
up the bouquets and the first prizes . . . simple and timid like all
great artists," Sarah tells the plaster figure (112). The reference to
herself as a devil is not without importance, for Sarah sees herself
and is seen by society as suspect; old attitudes likening actors to
instruments of the devil reinforce Sarah's personal reputation as an
outsider, a nonconformist.

Having refused to accept her role as a submissive woman (yet
needing men), having refused to be "Linda" (yet needing public
recognition), having refused to play any more classic roles (yet needing something more than a public swimming pool as representative
of culture), Sarah is in a dilemma that she cannot completely resolve.
In the image of her country, she is trying to be herself in the face
of "260 million Americans and English [Canadians] who are looking
over our shoulder" (130). The ideal would be to disregard the eyes
and judgments of other cultures, to "go hide in the woods and talk
only among ourselves" (130). But such a solution is impossible
because even within Quebec the national identity is confused: "The

only place it's difficult to be [a Quebecer] is here! . . . Even now, to be something now . . . you've got to be either exotic or else a memory" (134). Being one's self implies first assuming the identity one has as part of a group, and, for Sarah, this first step has yet to be taken.

Sarah's way out of her dilemma is to take the first step, to begin to define herself as a *québécoise.* She turns to "memory," that is, to folk music, to the "gigue à monocle Simon," a bit of folklore that is part of her immediate as well as extended family. Here, at the end of the play, the atmosphere changes, becomes dreamlike; in the dance and music Sarah sees "the forest in motion . . . the country . . . the country on its feet, dancing" (141), a phenomenon that Germain calls "the secret country of everyone" (142). The implications of this last part of the play are obvious: the identity for which Sarah is looking, which would allow her to play classical roles without the feeling that these were being imposed on her, can only come through memory, through a renewed contact with that popular culture in which Germain finds the true soul of Quebec.

The most important of the plays in Germain's most recent cycle is *Un Pays dont la devise est je m'oublie,* first performed in 1976, and whose title (A country whose motto is I forget myself) is a pun on the official motto of Quebec *(je me souviens,* I remember). The purpose of the play is avowedly didactic; "a people who gives itself 'I remember' as a motto ought to beware of its memory," says Germain,[56] and he undertakes to rewrite some of the important episodes in Quebec history. He is certainly not the first Quebec author to do this—Léandre Bergeron did it from a pop-Marxist point of view in 1971 *(Petit manuel de l'histoire du Québec);* in the theater Réjean Ducharme's *Le Marquis qui perdit* is a masterpiece of the genre. But Germain's parody is unique because its purpose is not merely, or not even principally, to criticize the way historians have seen the past but rather, as one critic put it, to create a "complex game . . . through which is revealed a search for an authentic legend, . . . a mythical truth."[57]

Like the other plays in this cycle, *Un Pays* is a play within a play. Two traveling comedians, Episode Surprenant (the meaning of the name should be obvious) and Berthelot Petitboire (he drinks not too little but too much) stand before us and impersonate various episodes in Quebec's history, from its foundation as New France to the event that Germain characterizes as marking the "modern era of our history," the revolt in the streets of Montreal, in 1955, following the suspension of the hockey star Maurice Richard.[58]

What especially interests Germain in this play is the reverse side of history, the side that cannot be written by historians, but that can be imagined by the playwright. For Germain, as we have seen in *Si les Sansouci,* society is divided into two groups: those in power, the establishment who formulate ideas and laws but who are essentially clowns and actors, and the working class, the common people, the habitants for whom life isn't at all theatrical but rather a struggle to survive. The problem is that the educated classes use the others not only as labor but as a symbol of a country whose image the elite has created but in which the other classes have only a limited role to play.

In the first half of the play—frescoes of the discovery of Canada, the French regime, the British conquest—the authentic Quebecer, the coureur de bois, is a strong character who resists being used by his rulers. He can laugh at the French discoverers, thumb his nose at their inefficient governors, even look philosphically at their disinterested generals. When the English win, he will, he believes, merely replace one governor with another, but he soon learns that the efficiency of the English is potentially more dangerous than was French bungling. "The English, without our even knowing it, were remaking us in their own image," he says,[59] and his fears are realized when it becomes obvious that the English will want not simply to rule over the Quebecois, but to make a new country complete with its own myths and images.

No English Canadian appears in the second half of the play, which takes us from the conquest to the present, because other Quebecers, like the Sansouci, will do the bidding of the English in North America. The essential structure of Canadian society, established just after the conquest, continues as one elite replaces another: political families, the Church, the C.B.C., the owners of the hockey teams are still on top while, on the bottom, the habitant, now a member of the urban working class, still gets the short end. The desire of the oppressed classes for freedom and independence is the only constant in Quebec history, according to Germain; from the time of New France when, as the French intendant complained, "obedience . . . here . . . isn't in the air we breathe" (41), the French-Canadians have never lost their heritage of individualism or forgotten their desire for self-determination; "once you've been free in your head and in your bones . . . you can't forget it!" says the habitant (34). We see here on a political level the same paradigm we saw on a psychological level in *Les Hauts et les bas:* a sincere longing for freedom must of necessity be hidden behind the roles that society forces French Canadians to play. So the average French Canadian continues to let himself be used by the political families (even if, as in this play, he has no political ambition), or by the Church (even if, to attract parishioners, religious fervor has to be replaced with American-type hard-sell). More interesting than the scenes concerning politics and religion are those in which Suprenant and Petitboire show how folk heroes cannot live up to the images others have created for them. Legendary strong man Louis Cyr recognizes that his success was due to showmanship, not brute force, and that, rather than push his force to the limit, "I earned my life making *tours de force,* . . . circus shows" (121) and ended up "part of the folklore . . . half alive, half in a dream" (121). The famous Rocket Richard is less lucid than Louis Cyr. "I don't understand," he says, "for everyone else, when I'm on the ice, I'm almost a god . . . but in life, most often, people take me for a mental midget! I DON'T UNDERSTAND!" (131–2). Richard's problem is that he hasn't internalized the showmanship, the disguise, that is so much a part of Cyr. Like Sarah Ménard, he still wants to be himself, but his image has become totally independent of him, not only in a negative sense (his being exploited by hockey club owners) but in a positive one as well, for he is the symbol of the riot that "gets people talking about Quebec in all the papers in the entire world for the first time in its history" (133).

For all his naïveté and lack of understanding, Maurice Richard is as close to a hero as any of Germain's characters. He incarnates the irresistible urge of people to disbelieve, to realize that what they are seeing is only a show, whether it be hockey or politics or the mass. Because Maurice Richard sees only the reality behind the game ("I never think about playing," he says, "I think about scoring" [132]), because he is literally blind to illusion, he can represent in this play some elemental purity, unsullied by forces that dominate him.

History, for Germain, is what the pageant of life appears to be in retrospect. What one remembers defines what one is; if the past doesn't actually determine the present, what we think of the past does influence who we are in the present and what we will do in the future. Some of the memories of the past in Quebec are frankly dangerous to the present. Such is the case, for example, of a certain image of the habitant projected into the present (with *tuque* and *ceinture fléchée*), used to adorn restaurants and cocktail lounges; the once free, once individualistic peasant in New France has become a relic of the past, devoid of meaning for the present, a bit of folklore, as Surprenant (in the role of the habitant) says: "When you've got nothing more of your own . . . you get together once a year . . . you put on your costume, and you make a bit of folklore!" (65). Similar characteristics could be found for other memories, such as that of the militantly reactionary Church, opposed to lay schools and to sex, especially to the latter. Should our memories of the past be selective? "Why," as the *curé* questions, "should we be ashamed of what we have been?" (96). The answer to this question seems to lie in the use one makes of memories rather than in the memories themselves. The habitant, Germain implies, can be a useful symbol if one remembers his individualism; even the Church of the past can be remembered for the generations of Quebecois that disobeyed it, that thought for themselves, and that tried to enjoy sex despite the abysmal ignorance perpetrated by the ecclesiastic authorities (this subject will be at the heart of a later play, *Mamours et conjugat*). What is above all dangerous to the future of a people is collective forgetfulness, the kind that, in Quebec, erased the memory of independence and substituted that of submissiveness. The hopeful message of *Un pays dont la devise est je m'oublie* is that memory can provide the basis for a new culture, based not on some superimposed image of a quaint folklore but on a clear vision of the constancy of the desire for independence, both personal and political.

Un Pays has a kind of sequel, created a year later (1977), called *L'Ecole des rêves* (The School of Dreams, a variation of Molière's title, *School of Women*). Once again Surprenant and Petitboire appear on stage, but this time they are accompanied by *"l'enfant dla balle,"* a young woman who is not exactly (as her name would indicate) born into the theatrical profession, but who would like to be adopted into it. Through a series of sketches the traveling actors teach her (and us) what theater is all about. Much of what they show has already been demonstrated by Germain: that the origins of theater are with the common people, that it is an integral part of daily life, that it creates and perpetuates myths. But where in *Un pays* Surprenant and Petitboire played out scenes from Quebec's history, in

L'Ecole des rêves it is dreams that are the stuff from which they make their drama, the collective dreams of the people of Quebec. The ultimate dream, at least in the eyes of l'Enfant dla balle, would be to act in the theater. In a very significant line she answers Petitboire's query of her motives for wanting to be an actress: "I want to be myself," she says.[60] She has intuitively understood the answer that Sarah Ménard was searching for: that playacting is the only way to externalize feelings, hence to be oneself. "Life is nothing more than the opacity of the dream," Germain says in his introduction to this play (8), and Petitboire and Surprenant proceed to demonstrate how "dream and reality always get confused because actors are characters who always dream of being something other than what they are at the time they are being it."[61] In the end they get so caught up in their game that Surprenant's staged death fools both his fellow actor and the girl. The actor is here a metaphor for all humans; to live in society is to constantly want to be what one isn't. The solution to the human dilemma is, in the end, attending Petitboire and Surprenant's "school" and learning that playacting is the only possible mode of existence.

Here lies the essential difference between Antonine Maillet and Germain. While Maillet attempts, through the presentation of strong characters, true heroes and heroines, to revive pride in the folk culture of Acadia, in its oral traditions, and in its language, Germain tries to show how the falseness of all human conduct and the ambiguity of all of Quebec's traditions pose serious problems for the development of a new culture. In this sense, Germain's theater is much more complex than Maillet's, and it coincides with the generalized questioning, since the 1960s, of the image Quebec has of itself. Writers like Peirre Vadeboncoeur or Hubert Aquin (who, in his "Essai crucimorphe," showed how the face Montreal presents to its citizens and the world is a false, superimposed invention of the anglophone business community)[62] argue that the ambiguity of Quebec's political position prevents any kind of authentic self-image. As Jean Bouthillette writes, "The Canadian identity is a mirror which reflects the image of the Other when we look at ourselves in it."[63]

Germain's theater can be seen as a dramatization of Bouthillette's statement, because it shows how the mirror image has become the only image French Canadians have of themselves. At the same time, and through an understanding of the way in which the mirror distorts reality, Germain's theater shows how new myths and a new identity can begin to be created, an identity based on the aspiration for freedom rather than on the subservience of a people.

Chapter Five
The Theater of Politics /
The Politics of Theater

"Quand les mots sont mûrs, ils s'ouvrent comme
des grenades."
(Robert Gurik, *A coeur ouvert*, 35)

("When words are ripe, they open like grenades.")

It may seem somewhat artificial to devote a distinct chapter to political theater, since much of what has been written by Tremblay, Barbeau, and especially Germain has political overtones and is rooted in a vision of Quebec that has political implications. Moreover, there was a wave of political theater throughout Western Europe and North America in the 1960s and early 1970s; much of what was written in Quebec at this time can be linked to a general climate of questioning of middle-class values along with the adoption of various modes of Marxist or neo-Marxist analysis. As the 1970s came to a close, and even as the Canadian political debate between Ottawa and a newly elected Parti Québécois government was heating up, political theater became less and lesss important and it is unlikely that many of the political plays of this period will survive.

On the other hand, political theater, if it has produced few memorable texts, has played an important role in redefining the concept of theater in Quebec. In the pages that follow we shall explore the ideas behind three types of political theater: the participatory, agressive theater of Françoise Loranger, the Brechtian theater of Robert Gurik, and the complex theater of opposing archetypes written by Jacques Ferron.

The *théâtre-choc* of Françoise Loranger

Françoise Loranger, born in 1913, came to political theater relatively late in her career and after having written novels (*Mathieu,*

1949) and especially radio and television plays (*Jour après jour,* 1956, *Une maison, un jour,* 1965). In 1969, in the shadow of Charles De Gaulle's visit to Quebec, she teamed up with Claude Levac to write *Le Chemin du Roy,* and, a year later, she wrote, in response to Bill 63 on the French language, her best effort, *Médium saignant.*

Le Chemin du Roy, like her other political plays, is a drama of circumstance, "a sort of *happening* where the audience feels it is directly involved," said one critic.[1] Like Barbara Garson's *MacBird* in the United States, which, on the model of *Macbeth,* accused President Johnson of the murder of John F. Kennedy, or like Robert Gurik's *Hamlet, Prince du Québec,* which refers to the political situation in Quebec in 1968, the play by Loranger and Levac depends for its success on an audience that not only understands the political situation and the public figures involved, but is sympathetic to the political messsage; it does not try to preach but rather assumes complicity. This is a basic difference with the political theater of a Bertolt Brecht, for example, which requires of its audience a critical response to a situation presented in such a way as to make the familiar unfamiliar.[2]

The cultural specificity of *Le Chemin du Roy* is accentuated by its staging: the stage is turned into a hockey rink (more precisely the Montreal Forum, stylized) and the actors wear costumes identifying them as members of the "Ottawa" or "Quebec" teams. Laurent Mailhot has shown[3] how, in fact, the hockey game hides another structure of the play, the confrontation between two languages, two modes of discourse that render mutual understanding between the teams impossible. In fact, mutual misunderstanding and political (or even ethnic) polarization are necessary ingredients in Loranger's theater. The audience is called upon to think of the play not so much as the representation of a reality but as the reality itself. The play becomes "the symbol of our humiliated collective life,"[4] and the experience of seeing it a collective exorcism of the fears and complexes that, for Loranger, have prevented Quebec from becoming "self-governing, evolving toward the best of itself."[5] But the Quebec that Loranger puts on the stage in *Le Chemin du Roy* is black and white; no anglophone Quebecer is to be trusted and, perhaps more important, immigrant groups are presented as aggressively unilingual in English. In response to a recorded voice which says, in English, "Quebec is mine as well as yours! I was born here!" (125)

the francophone Quebecers, actors and audience, join in singing (to the tune of "We Shall Overcome") a song whose words are, in part,

> We shall be ourselves
> Quebec is still to be made, we are making it
> We shall always be ourselves.
>
> (127)

There is no room for reason in this play, no attempt even to look at the issues surrounding De Gaulle's visit and the Canadian government's reaction to it. An emotional response is called for that effectively replaces political analysis with group and ethnic identification.

Médium saignant, first performed in 1970 and then reperformed under the title *Médium saignant revisited* in 1976, is Loranger's most successful attempt at audience involvement and political exorcism and, in many ways, her most disturbing. The political situation for the first version was Bill 63 of the Jean-Jacques Bertrand Union Nationale government of 1969, a bill whose purpose it was to allow free choice of parents regarding the school, anglophone or francophone, to which they sent their children. The law was in response to the actions of the school commission of Saint-Léonard, a Montreal suburb, which, two years earlier, had tried to force the children of nonanglophone immigrants to attend French public schools. Bill 63 became somewhat of a cause célèbre for independentists and the opposition Liberals who were afraid that, as new immigrants to Quebec sent their children to English-language schools in increasing numbers, the francophone population of the province would decline and, just as important, the French langauge would lose prestige in the business and cultural spheres.

The second version of *Médium saignant* had as a backdrop Bill 22 passed by the Liberal government of Robert Bourassa in 1974. Like its predecessor, this piece of language legislation did little to please Quebec's independentists who were arguing that French should be the *only* official language of the province. Bill 22 required that all children of nonanglophone parents attend French schools, but a loophole in the form of an English test administered to preschoolers, a passing grade on which would allow them to attend an English school regardless of the language spoken at home, was large (and cruel) enough to anger many segments of the population, both

English- and French-speaking. The Parti Québécois government attempted to resolve the problem once and for all with Bill 101 (1977) which satisifed most of the independentists' demands. Despite the hostility of the anglophone community, this law remains one of the most popular pieces of legislation passed by the Parti Québécois.

The very real problem that led a succession of Quebec governments to pass langauge legislation is represented in Loranger's text. At the meeting of a city council of a Montreal suburb not unlike Saint-Léonard, the councillors are acutely aware, for example, that (in 1961) 78 percent of new immigrants to Quebec knew English as opposed to 10 percent who learned French,[6] and they propose that French be the only official language of business for their council. Reason alone, in this circumstance, would (and did) argue for some sort of legislative remedy, but reason is not what Loranger is interested in here. "The real subject of *Médium saignant*," she says, "is not language but rather fear in front of the decisions we must take to affirm the necessity to be French and Québécois."[7] The director of the play, Yvan Canuel, is even more specific: "The most important lesson that comes from *Médium saignant* is that of an exorcism. . . . It is a play that stigmatizes our collective fear."[8]

Loranger's purpose in citing statistics is not to bolster the case for a measure of French unilingualism but to topple the believers in statistics in favor of a young generation who lets its emotions rather than logic dictate its actions. For, in truth, statistics alone (for example, the fact that, in Quebec, French-Canadian salaries were, in 1961, twelfth lowest out of fourteen ethnic groups) could argue not for a unilingual French Quebec but for a movement toward more English education for francophone Quebecers. This is the sentiment of the play's *bête noire,* the very middle-class Ouellette (played in both versions by veteran actor Jean Duceppe). It is the violent reaction of a group of young Quebecers that provides both the dramatic tension of the play and its message. Typical is the following exchange: the young Louis and Claude are reflecting aloud on the repeated request from an anglophone Quebecer (Pinkerton) for a translation of the proceedings into English:

LOUIS: Is there a law that requires them to translate?
CLAUDE: It's because they don't have balls!

In fact there was (before Bill 101) a law that required translation, but Claude's answer to Louis's question makes reasonable debate over its merits impossible; the question becomes not what to do but rather whether or not the older generation will have the "balls" to do what the younger generation instinctively feels must be done.

A thumbnail sketch of Quebec history presented by the younger players leads to one inevitable and preconceived conclusion: that Quebec has been the constant (and too willing) victim of English Canada, the latest step in this victimization being "progressive suffocation of Quebecers by immigration" (68). Here is where the play begins to be frankly disturbing because the audience's hostility toward immigrant groups (especially Italians) is progressively exploited. An Italian woman is the scapegoat. Even though she clearly explains the extent of her victimization (to succeed financially she, and her family, must learn English) and claims that immigration officials never informed her that French was the usual langauge of Quebec, neither the young players nor the audience wants to hear her. The former mock her and the latter often hiss and boo her presence. As the play draws to an emotional close, anglophone and some other spectators are left with the very uneasy feeling of being where they are not wanted. Loranger's method is to exorcise fear and hate by stating them openly—hence a litany of *Je les z'haïs* (I hate them) directed at English Canadians, immigrants, politicians, and even at Quebecois themselves, a litany joined by the Italians and English Canadians on stage as they declare their hate of the francophone Quebecois.

Clearly Loranger's purpose is less political than psychological; as in a previous play entitled *Double jeu* (Double game), where spectators were invited to participate on stage in the sociodrama, in *Médium saignant* "the audience cannot remain indifferent. Insults are hurled at the stage. Spectators get into the act and try to silence the actors who are debating a point of view different from theirs."[9] For an Anglophone critic the play was nothing more than "a dramatized, unilingualist pamphlet"; a Francophone critic responded: "Françoise Loranger is now putting forward a theater incarnated in the social and cultural reality that is ours."[10] But the wisest comment on this popular and widely discussed political play, and on Loranger in general, was made by Jean-Claude Germain whose nationalist credentials, in matters of culture, are impeccable. Germain compares the play to a poster of Che Guevara and goes on to say: "Buy a poster, see [the play]: it's nice, it brightens things up, and it gets old as quickly as the philosophy of newspaper columns."[11] Loranger's experiments have aged rapidly, and no one in the Quebec of the 1980s, where dialogue has replaced screams, seems ready to repeat them.

Brecht in Quebec: The Theater of Robert Gurik

In one important way the political theater of Robert Gurik differs from that of Françoise Loranger: it appeals to reason rather than to emotion; it tries to get audiences to analyze problems rather than to scream their feelings.

There are other important differences, too. Loranger's theater was the product of a long experience of psychological drama; the political situation of the 1970s turned her psychodrama into political drama. Gurik's theater is political right from the start. It is less of a reaction to a situation than a well-planned, theoreticaly based political statement whose origins, like those of the playwright himself, are European.[12]

"My theater is, for me, a tool to build a society that appeals to me," wrote Gurik in 1976, "a socialist society. Each play is a gesture, the most efficient possible, to expose the cogs in certain problems or the obstacles in the way of a solution."[13] We can trace the role of theater as a tool for socialist revolution back to the comments of Leon Trotsky and of A. V. Lunacharsky (Soviet Russia's first minister of culture). More recently, the theater of Bertolt Brecht in Germany before and after World War II has spawned a number of experiments in left-wing theater: the Bread and Puppet Theater in the U. S., in France the theater of Roger Planchon, Armand Gatti, Ariane Mnouchkine, to name a few. It is especially the influence of Brecht, and of his French counterparts, that Gurik has tried to bring to Quebec.

Brecht's theories are well known, as are his principal plays (*The Caucasian Chalk Circle, The Good Woman of Setzuan, Mother Courage*). We can separate essential Brechtian theory into two areas: audience reaction and acting technique. Brecht early in his career developed the theory of "watching and smoking," an attitude that contrasted sharply with the kind of empathy or identification with characters that most theater of the time expected of its audience. This idea soon developed into what is known as the *Verfremdungseffekt*, or alienation effect; the audience is expected to keep itself at a critical distance from what is happening on stage, so that questions may be asked which would be impossible were the audience to empathize with the characters. As Brecht said, "A representation that alienates is one which allows us to recognize its subject, but at the same time makes it seem unfamiliar."[14]

So too should the actors, Brecht says, keep a distance between themselves and the roles they are playing. In opposition to Stanislavsky's acting theory where the actor becomes the character, Brecht wants his actors to develop what he calls the "social gest" of the character, "the realm of attitudes adopted by the characters towards one another."[15] Thus the actor, in Brecht's theater, has a didactic role to play, for it is he who allows the audience to question whether or not what is seen on stage is normal or strange, whether it reflects an immutable human condition or whether it is a situation that can be changed.

Like Brecht, Gurik requires the audience to refuse to accept an absurd situation. In his 1970 play *Le Pendu* (The hanged man) a man tries to earn his living by tying a rope around his neck and selling bits of the rope as good luck charms to the wealthy and superstitious. "To contemplate other choices is utopia," he says in one of his plays,[16] and this sentence aptly describes the dramatic purpose of his theater, a purpose which can be realized once the play is over and the audience has thought about it. Unlike some politically oriented efforts in Quebec that work on the basis of collective creation, usually without texts (the Théâtre Parminou, for example), Gurik prefers a more traditional, hierarchical structure in which the text of the play passes from author to director to actors. "In [politically] involved theater . . . there is a kind of distancing which perhaps doesn't exist in the theater of collective creation," he asserts.[17]

One of the founders of the Centre d'Essai des Auteurs Dramatiques, Gurik was, during the 1960s and 1970s, one of the most widely played of Quebec dramatists. His play *Api 2967* has been seen in Paris, at the 1969 Vienna Biennial (with decor by the French artist Folon), on Dutch television, and in Edmonton, Alberta. *Le Pendu* won the first prize in the 1967 Dominion Drama Festival in St. John's, Newfoundland. The relatively wide dissemination of this theater may seem odd, given the fact that Loranger, for example, is rarely performed outside the province of Quebec, but Gurik's theater is less a theater of nationalism than of internationalism, more a criticism of capitalism as a world phenomenon than an attack on the specifically Quebecois example of capitalism, with its attendant French-English conflict.

Much of Gurik's theater remains, however, rooted in the reality of Quebec. His successful "prophetic political fiction"[18] of 1968, *Hamlet, Prince du Québec,* uses Shakespeare's plot to hypothesize what was to be the political situation ten years later as René Lévesque, become premier of Quebec (Horatio in the play), duels with Pierre-Elliott Trudeau, prime minister of Canada (Laertes in the play). But unlike Loranger's *Le Chemin du Roy,* Gurik's play does not exploit the language question nor, indeed, does Gurik give great weight to De Gaulle's visit to Quebec, though the general does appear (as the ghost). Gurik's play, though based in political reality, really exists outside it, for as Hamlet (Quebec) dies he calls into existence a new Quebec for whom the phantoms of the past (English Canada, the Church, the ghost of De Gaulle) have disappeared. Other plays by Gurik were written in response to political events like the Kennedy assassinations and the October crisis of 1970 *(A coeur ouvert, Les Tas de sièges),* but the playwright's anger over these events prevents real dramatic tension; these plays are best characterized as dramas of circumstance.

As with Brecht, Gurik is at his best when his plays transcend politics to touch upon universal human emotions and problems. Two of his plays do this quite successfully. One of them is *Api 2967,* originally written and performed in 1966 under the title *Api or not api* (a takeoff on Hamlet's soliloquy). It is one of Gurik's most widely performed plays, undoubtedly because, like the apple from which it takes its title (a *pomme d'api* in French), it has a core of meaning that speaks to everyone regardless of nationality or political view.

The play, with all the trappings of a plastic, futuristic civilization, is actually a reenactment a thousand years from now of the biblical story of the Fall, although the fatal fruit is that of wisdom, of what the society of the future does not want people (here, numbers) to know. In an effort to stave off inevitable death and the ravages of time on the human body, the society of the future neither speaks too often nor walks too much; each extra word, each extra footstep costs a predetermined number of years off one's life. The apple that is suddenly introduced into an anonymous professor's life is more than the forbidden fruit; it is time itself, more specifically the past, "one of the cornerstones on which was founded the edifice of a forgotten civilization."[19] The apple is also the will to disobey authority, to have unauthorized movements, especially sex. And, of course, the apple hastens the moment of death or, in the euphemistic language of the future, "the cessation of life" (76).

The play is also, even principally, about language, and its message is not so much about the future as about the present. The dilemma dramatized by the play is the uncertainty, the ambiguity of our own language which leads some people to prefer quantification, statistics, to poetry or metaphor. "Former civilizations have been destroyed by words," says the professor (47), "many beings . . . accepted giving their lives for words" (49). The ambiguity of words as tools of communication befuddles A and E who, having tasted the apple, search for absolutes. "Humans of this era believed in finality," says A of the past. "This finality had many forms, since its enunciation depended on the word whose fragility I have just demonstrated" (49). To accept the language of the past is to accept this fragility, one element of human weakness that the society of 2967 is attempting to abolish. E understands the dilemma better than does A, and she tries to communicate her feelings to the professor, but his obsession with finding the absolute, the truth, prevents him from hearing her.

The professor's tragedy is a very human one: he cannot accept the inevitable. Whatever the means by which human experience is recorded, the expression and understanding of that experience depends on mortal, error-prone individuals. Words die on the professor's lips as he ages, as his memory fails him. He has glimpsed the beauty of ambiguity, of language, but frustration and death are the prices he must pay for having eaten the apple. As the play ends, the television screen repeats over his immobile body, "Life is everything." There is no solution to the dilemma in this play, just a question that the audience must contemplate. Going well beyond politics, Gurik puts us, at the end of *Api 2967,* in front of our own basic weaknesses as human beings.

A more classically Brechtian play is *Le Procès de Jean-Baptiste M. (The Trial of Jean-Baptiste M.),* first presented in 1972. It is based on a real event: in September 1971 an employee of a large Montreal company, Jean-Baptiste Meloche, shot three of his supervisors because he had just been fired from his job. Gurik's play tries to understand this murderous act not from a psychological point of view but as a symbolic gesture of a human's frustration in an inhuman situation. "Jean-Baptiste M. has killed authority," says Gurik, "but he has not killed those responsible, for in a company there isn't anyone really responsible—just those higher up in the hierarchy."[20] But rather than dramatizing the anonymous structure of the organization in a straightforward fashion, Gurik has created a play-within-a-play where the employees of the multinational company are called upon to "try" J-B (Jean-Baptiste), while at the same time they are "trying" themselves before the audience because they are both jurors and participants in the event.

It is of some importance that J-B is French-Canadian and that his bosses are anglophone (Roy Marshall, Doug McPherson, and Dave Lalonde, the latter an anglicized francophone), but Gurik has defused the language issue by makaing J-B into a bilingual French Canadian from Ottawa. In fact, J-B's problem is that he is too exemplary a Canadian; as those in attendance at his birth say, "he is going to be a real Canadian . . . a fireman . . . or a policeman . . . or an M.P."[21] He tries very hard, too hard, to do what his superiors expect of him. And yet he loses, commits murder, and, once having been the victim of those in power, finds himself accused as their oppressor.

The irony is that J-B is anything but a rebel; if he was fired from the Dutronc company it was not, as the company pretends, for insubordination but because he saw waste and inefficiency and tried to correct them. But clearly Gurik is not interested in giving us an apology for a whistle-blower. The bosses he kills are too dull, too faceless for their death to be anything but pathetic; the Dutronc company is too exaggerated for us to take it as a serious threat to the values of humanism. And unlike Arthur Miller's Willie Loman, Gurik's J-B does not internalize his defeat and kill himself; there is no tragedy here, just an (almost) everyday trial.

The notion of the trial is the key to understanding the play because, as in Brecht, the audience must make its own judgment. So while it is easy to take J-B's side against his callous and bumbling bosses, it is less easy for the audience to empathize with his reaction to Robillard, ex-convict and executive director of Reinstallation, Inc., whose seemingly laudable purpose is to bring convicts back into society by providing them with useful (but to whom?) work. Robillard's language is full of clichés, but his message is clear:

Your duty is to spread love around you, to have the satisfaction of a duty accomplished, to make your family and friends happy. Happiness is a lot of little things, I'm sure you can do it, J-B. (69)

Robillard's advice contrasts sharply with J-B's instinctual reaction to the society that oppresses him. In a highly symbolic scene Robillard grabs J-B's gun from him as the latter grabs at his crotch "as if he'd been castrated" (70). Significantly it is the secretaries of the company that give J-B back his gun, his manhood, thus enabling him to commit the crime. But J-B's revolt is not so much against the company or society as it is against Robillard and what he represents. To take J-B's side against Robillard is to put into question a fundamental tenet of our society: the inherent value of work, of "duty accomplished," and the notion that satisfaction can be derived from the approval of one's superiors.

The jury of the play reaches no conclusions in the case of Jean-Baptiste M.; indeed, the play ends with the three judges (who are also the three bosses and three victims) reciting in crescendo a litany of product names that, by their very volume, drown out J-B's action, absorb it into the world of consumerism and big business. This is one of the play's stronger messages: the power of society to render meaningless the actions of a single person. And yet, like Ionesco's Béranger in *Rhinocéros,* J-B is important here because he is alone.

As Gurik's theater evolved into the 1970s it became less successful and more narrowly Marxist. Such is the case with *Le Champion* (about Muhammad Ali) published in 1977 or *La Baie des Jacques* (about the hydroelectric dam at James Bay). Typical was the play *Lénine* (1975) which, although it has the political ambitions of Brecht's theater, lacks the epic sense of humanity and movement. "Robert Gurik: the author who has nothing to teach," wrote Jean-Claude Germain in 1968.[22] It is perhaps an unfair, summary judgment, especially because, in matters of theatrical theory, Gurik was an active voice. But the political climate in Quebec has changed considerably since the 1960s and 1970s, and what is likely to endure in Gurik's theater is its humanitarian, rather than political lesson.

The Politics of Antithesis in the Theater of Jacques Ferron

Jacques Ferron was, until his death in the spring of 1985, one of the most influential authors in Quebec, but most of his influence was in the area of prose writing (his short stories and novels such as *Le Ciel du Québec* or *L'Amélanchier*). His influence as a political thinker was also widespread, profoundly affecting some individuals (such as Victor-Lévy Beaulieu and Pierre Vallières) as well as Quebec politics in general (he founded the Rhinoceros Party that ran such notables as singer Robert Charlebois in provincial elections). Ferron, a medical doctor, wrote at length on politics, most often in magazines (especially in *L'Information médicale et paramédicale*).[23] He wrote only two plays that could be called political, but these are the best of his dramatic works and, because of their subtlety and complexity, deserve an important place in the contemporary repertory.

The first of Ferron's political plays was entitled *Les Grands Soleils* (The great suns) and was written in 1958 although not put on stage until a decade later. It concerns the Patriots' revolt of 1837 and takes place within two time frames, 1837 and the present. It is basically the story of the legendary hero, Dr. Jean-Olivier Chénier who, prompted by his servant girl Elizabeth, decided to leave his medical practice and take up arms against the English. In the play Chénier is befriended by a drunkard named Mithridate and by an Indian named Sauvageau, and is somewhat hampered in his activities by Félix Poutré, a habitant who was the subject of an eighteenth-century play, and by the local parish priest. But Chénier's destiny is never in doubt, for throughout the play we see the statue erected in his honor in Montreal.

The complexity of this play is revealed in Ferron's use of images which are substantial, ambiguous, impenetrable; they envelop the characters and refer back to a central antithesis that underlies the entire play. At the center of this imagery we find the principal symbol of the play, the sunflower, the heliotrope, the *grand soleil* of the title.

The sunflower image contains in itself the antithetical structure of the play. When it is turned toward the sun, it reflects Elizabeth's face as, in the morning, she tells her dreams to Chénier; but because it symbolizes heat, this flower represents the flames that envelop the church where, in Elizabeth's dream and later in reality, Chénier will meet his death. As mere plants, the sunflowers are the "wide eyes of autumn"[24] which "will bend down their blind flowers" (41) before the battle of Saint-Eustache; as setting suns, the evening before the confrontation, these *grands soleils* will "explode at sunrise," gorged with blood (56). The sunflowers are at once the fires burning at the Patriot's bivouacs and the stars in the sky; but they are also the ostensory of the church to which the English have set fire and the burning napalm dropped by military forces in the twentieth century. Finally, these sunflowers signify life growing in Chénier's garden "where children drink the milk of flowers" (67); but, after the battle of Saint-Eustache is lost, they "have turned to seed and are bent to the ground" (76).

This essential ambiguity of the sunflower image—life and death, flowers and napalm—sets the tone for the play's political message. Ferron's political view does not allow for compromise. French Canadians and English, like Quebecers and English Canadians today, are for him so fundamentally opposite to each other that they seem to belong to two different species of human beings. The French Canadians are "poachers, amazed and astonished" when faced with war, and Chénier, their captain, "knows only the blood shed by women in childbirth" (74). The English, on the other hand, are born warriors; they wear a red uniform (color of blood) and they come from "that continent of death called Europe" (74). One must be careful not to take these images as illustrations; on the contrary, we are faced here with essences that are revealed inescapably in the behavior and mentality of the characters. The French Canadians never seem to be more perfect poachers than when they point their hunting rifles at men, and the English (who never appear in the play) are never more perfect warriors than when they are polite.

The opposition of essences that Ferron sees in the French-Canadian / English conflict is not, however, racial in origin. Elizabeth is, after all, an English girl who has decided to live with and like her French-Canadian employer. She is a foreigner, but at the same time, as the priest tells her, "I fear . . . that you are more of a Canadienne than you should be" (45). Just like Mirthridate and Sauvageau, Elizabeth incarnates the essence of Quebec, but this essence has not been passed on to her by heredity. It is the result of her having been in contact with the land of Quebec, with the mysterious forces of nature that, as Sauvageau tells her, recognize her true identity as a French Canadian: "The country sees you and admires you" (42).

Ferron's political vision, in this world of antithetical essences, is of a historical destiny incarnated in the personnage of Chénier whose future existence as a national myth (though, it must be pointed

out, not an official myth) is implicit in his taking up arms against
the English in 1837. The monument erected in the twentieth century to Chénier is the materialization of his life, of his destiny. But
Chénier the man does not see this destiny until the middle of the
second act; he then realizes the extent to which his freedom is
limited:

I hadn't seen this monument at the end of my life. Everything is decided.
I have nothing more to ask . . . I could have been a doctor, a mere
doctor, gone through life with my bag in my hand and disappeared silently
like a respectable man. (66)

But Chénier is not completely impotent in the face of his future,
for he does, in the course of the play, choose to follow his destiny.
The choice is really one of head or heart, of reason and reasonableness
or love of country. As a man, Chénier does not rise above events,
he is not a superhero, not even an ordinary hero. But he is so deeply
rooted in "a country which is ours, which envelops us with its
sympathy" (74) that he is incapable of doubting that the French
Canadians can triumph over the English. The outcome of his life
is thus not determined by the future course of history but by his
patriotism, in the strictest and purest sense of the word.

Chénier, like the other characters in this play, reaches a sort of
perfection in his essence as an imperfect man. Everything in him
is human; everything in him is French-Canadian. And the French-
Canadianness of his character is all the clearer because he is involved
in a fight against an enemy whose essentially European character is
incompatible with his. The French Canadians belong to their country, Ferron suggests, even if their country does not yet belong to
them; the English, on the other hand, come from an old continent
and introduce war and servitude in the New World. Chénier's moral
victory is thus generalized by Ferron to be the victory of all oppressed
peoples against their masters. Ferron takes us out of the realm of
practical politics and introduces us to what he sees as the permanent
impossible political situation of Canada, indeed of the world. Yet
the play is not altogether pessimistic because Chénier, by meeting
his fate of death in a burning church and by becoming a legend,
has shown that one man's sacrifice can at least incite future generations to awaken to their own consciousness.

Ferron's second political play, *La Tête du roi* (The king's head) first appeared in 1963 and was inspired by the tearing down of a statue of General Wolfe by independentists in Quebec City the same year. Like *Les Grands Soleils,* this play brings together several moments in history: the Riel rebellions of 1870 and 1885, the period following World War I and the conscription crisis, and the period of political unrest and even of violence in the Quebec of the 1960s.

The play concerns the fictional decapitation of the statue of Edward VII in Philips Square in Montreal by Simon, son of a French-Canadian prosecutor. The latter is about to be named to replace a judge who has just died; his career would obviously be ruined were the king's head to be discovered in his house. But the head, important as an image, is merely the pretext for what amounts to a great theatrical debate on the attitude to take when one is faced with an intolerable situation, here that of Quebec's dilemma within Canadian confederation. Simon's brother Pierre has invited an old friend, an English Canadian, to visit, and it is the confrontation that develops between this anglophone Canadian and the prosecutor's family (Simon, Pierre, and Elizabeth, their sister) that forms the substance of the drama.

Like *Les Grands Soleils, La Tête du roi* is built around an antithesis, represented by two all-encompassing symbols: that of the king's head and that of the beaver-skin hat supposedly worn by Louis Riel. The hat is above all the symbol of exile, of the weak crushed by the strong, and it confers on him who wears it a purity of intention that is reminiscent of Chénier. The hat is worn throughout the play by a self-styled *canadien errant* (wandering Canadian) named Taque. The king's head, on the other hand, is the incarnation of brute force, of pitiless domination. Surrounded by its royal halo, it permits Queen Victoria to have a "clean conscience" while sanctioning the hanging of Riel.[25] It incarnates a historic force, "a great machine which functioned on its own" (105) existing beyond the will of man, for "even if the Windsors had been apes nothing would have changed" (105).

But *La Tête du Roi* does not contain the rich imagery of *Les Grands Soleils.* It is by far the characters that are important, and the central antithesis of the play revolves, even more than in *Les Grands Soleils,* around the characters.

On one side of the antithesis are found the English and their Canadian descendants. No longer are we concerned with "bad"

Englishmen like Coleborne and others who fought the *Patriotes*. The Englishman who dominates *La Tête du Roi* and who is defined as the archetype of his group is a liberal Canadian, a partisan of negotiation with separatists, of comprehension and accommodation; he is an English Canadian who "speaks French too well" (148). Scott Ewen (really Scott Symons, to whom the play is dedicated) has given himself the mission of bridging Hugh MacLennan's "two solitudes"; he is a friend of Pierre and yet he is an English Canadian who cannot, no matter what he does, escape his English essence. Scott Ewen invokes the whole litany of progressive English-Canadian ideas: the recent evolution of Quebec toward a more responsible society, tolerance, compromise. But try as he may, he cannot separate himself from his colonialist forebears. Simon will never pardon him for having replaced London with Ottawa: "You no longer have any feeling for us except condescendence," Simon tells him, "We no longer have any feeling for you but resentment. Your domination is more odious to us than that of England ever was" (142). Hearing such a statement, Scott has to accept the facts. He tries to escape the inevitable conclusion of the conversation by claiming that he cannot be held responsible for English imperialism: "I am alone here, I only speak for myself," he says. "Would you like me to feel guilty for the death of Joan of Arc?" (142). But these very statements prove that Scott, despite his claims to the contrary, speaks in the plural, for English Canadians as a group:

SCOTT: What are you really getting at?

SIMON: I want Québec to be my country, and I want to feel at home in my own land.

SCOTT: Go ahead, feel at home, and let's not talk about it any more.

SIMON: Only, of course, if I don't disturb you. But what if we had to disturb you a little?

SCOTT: I'll answer you frankly: disturb us as little as possible. (142)

Taque, the prosecutor, and his two sons incarnate the essence of Quebecness in all its complexity. The prosecutor's situation is particularly interesting: he seems to epitomize the moral dilemma that is at the heart of the play. In this context his two sons simply reflect the crisis of conscience that he himself feels: Simon, like his biblical namesake so avid for miracles, wants to confer on the king's head the magical power to change everything in Quebec by its being toppled; Pierre, the poet who believes he can rise above reality, changes his ideas depending upon how the wind blows, for he is the perfect actor, "linked as I am to both sides" (122). Just as the prosecutor was able to bring up such different sons, he was able to accommodate himself to his contradictions, and "to be a rebel and a loyalist, to combine the function of servant of the Crown and of an eminent nationalist" (149). The prosecutor's problem is quite literally an incapacity to come to a decision. When called upon to replace the deceased judge, he suddenly sees his career compromised by the presence of the king's head in his house. What will he do? Will he denounce those who have decapitated the statue, that is, his own son Simon? Will he side with the independentists?

La Tête du Roi, like *Les Grands Soleils*, ends in ambiguity. Until Scott Ewen arrives, the prosecutor seems to lean further and further toward an attitude of open sympathy with the nationalists. He willingly accepts being treated as guilty and assumes upon himself the symbolism of Riel's gallows. He calls to the English Canadians (though there is none around at the time): "Boss, we're not saying anything to you, you bug the hell out of us and I'm telling you to piss off!" (114). When Simon questions the sincerity of this anger, the prosecutor replies, "I've become aware of a new consciousness" (128). But Scott Ewen's presence changes everything. His English eyes, gazing at the prosecutor, put the latter very obviously ill at ease and remind him that he is inferior, colonized. And here is where a question mark hangs over the play. By the time Scott has left, the prosecutor has still not told him how he feels about the English and their domination. Did he, as it appears to everyone else, get drunk in order to avoid saying "what had to be said and what we all expected to be said" (136)? Has he humiliated his people? Or is he telling the truth when he asserts that he feigned drunkenness in order not to spoil "this [Englishman's] long conquest by some inconsiderate behavior" (151)? Can we believe him when he says "I will no longer hesitate between black and white" (151)? Ferron deliberately leaves us hanging. In any case, the prosecutor has been faithful to his character, his essence; his drunkenness, real or feigned, has allowed him to put off once more the decision that he must make in front of an English Canadian and on which he will never be able to go back. The nationalists, by the end of the play, are in a similarly ambiguous position. True enough, the king's head remains theirs and finds its final resting place upside down with flowers in it. But even this small victory is tenuous because the authorities, ready for just such an eventuality, keep numerous spare parts for statues and will soon provide the king with a new head. If, thus, the play ends with the dream of a future in which Quebec will finally be independent, with the English living there as guests rather than as masters, this future is indeed very hypothetical.

Ferron's political theater has as its purpose then not political action (the avowed purpose of Loranger's and Gurik's theaters) but the portrayal of a national dilemma. Ferron confronts us with a fixed, immutable situation; he asks us to take sides, to become conscious of ourselves. But at the final moment, when we ask him to help us find the certainty we are looking for, he disappears, leaving us with these words spoken by Simon: "What we are seeing is one of two things: either the last confusion of a beaten people, or the beginning of its liberation" (143).

Ferron's political theater is disquieting to English Canadians because he leaves no room for compromise. Indeed, Ferron tried, in his lifetime, to seek a compromise of the Quebec situation with such progressive people as Scott Symons; he espoused the theory of pan-Canadian social democracy for a while. But to no avail; Ferron's political testament can be summed up in these bitter words, written just after he left the Social Democratic party (P.S.D.):

The socialism of our English compatriots is only a mask to pursue the only policy they have ever had in Canada: to impose their domination, catchup on steak coast to coast. On that point, they never give an inch. [26]

But despite its pessimistic political message, Ferron's theater will probably live on in Quebec, for it expresses the author's uncompromising love for his country, for its people, and his devotion to (and mastery of) its language.

Chapter Six
The End of an Era
of Quebec Theater[1]

What has happened to Quebec theater since the 1970s? Something has obviously changed. Compared with that of a few years ago, the 1982–1983 season was a disaster: out of thirty productions in Montreal only thirteen were written by Quebec playwrights; in 1982–83 there were only six Quebecois productions of which four were reprises of plays previously presented. When one realizes that in 1977 the then minister of culture Louis O'Neill demanded that every theater financially aided by the province produce at least one new Quebec work each season,[2] one sees just how much has changed. And this under a nationalist PQ government!

Actually, the apparent contradiction between a stalled theater in Quebec and the continuing reign of the Parti Québécois may hold the explanation for the dilemma. Of all forms of artistic expression, theater is the most closely linked to society, and in Quebec the links between theater and government itself are, of necessity, strong. The necessity arises from the very real financial dilemma faced by producers and directors who incur substantial costs but have relatively small audiences; governments, since the liberals came to power in the 1960s, have felt it their responsibility to aid theater. This aid became part of a vast cultural enterprise sponsored by the state and federal governments to help the development of a uniquely Quebec culture. Whatever the differences between the Quebec and federal Liberal parties, both supported the notion that culturally, at least, Quebec could be autonomous. To this end, the big effort in theater became the encouragement of "serious" playwrights and directors, those who eschewed both the commercialism of American, Broadway-type theater and what was regarded as the cultural imperialism of French classical drama. When, in 1976, Jean-Claude Germain spoke out against the "Mid-Atlantic Seven Arts Club Band" (the community of critics and others who establish cultural legitimacy in North America), he was asking for the kind of commitment to native culture to which the Canada Council and the Quebec Ministry of Culture were already moving, although not with the speed he would have wished.[3]

The danger in promoting antiestablishment culture is that a new establishment is created, and this is what happened in Quebec in the 1970s. The types of culture that the government supported tended to be either professional (created by established artists such as Jean-Pierre Ronfard) or national (promoted through state institutions; in theater this would include the Conservatoire d'Art Dramatique and the Ecole Nationale du Théâtre as well as university theater), although a great deal of aid also did go to what might be called nontraditional activities (counterculture or experimental forms of theater which range from Germain's Théâtre d'Aujourd'hui to groups like the Parminou, the Eskabel, or the Théâtre de Carton). A kind of fusion took place between professional and national cultures, thereby creating a new establishment whose clientele was the new professional elite created by the expansion, in political, social, and economic spheres, of the state of Quebec. "Popular" culture, on the other hand, appealed to students, professors, and progressive professionals, and became a kind of semiofficial opposition to the establishment, not dangerous enough to see its funding cut off completely, but not safe enough to enjoy the same benefits as the new establishment. During this period the former establishment culture, that of the 1940s and '50s, benefited little if at all from government aid. Clerical or religious culture virtually disappeared in the 1970s when the feminist playwright Denise Boucher's play Les Fées ont soif (which contained a virulent attack on the cult of the Virgin Mary) went on despite vocal opposition from the Church (1978). Mass culture, however, strongly influenced by commercial U.S. culture, continued to exist (the Théâtre des Variétés in Montreal's east end is still a commercial success) and to be far more popular with the working class than "popular" culture.

The relationship between the state and culture in the 1970s favored the dynamism of a new Quebec theater for two reasons. The first is a practical one: the state saw the image it had of itself reflected in the new culture, and used that culture to represent it both at home and abroad. The festivities organized for the Fête Nationale (ex-St-Jean Baptiste day) included a liberal dose of musical and theatrical artists and became, in part, a festival of the creative Quebec spirit; similarly, playwrights like Michel Garneau, Michel Tremblay, and Antonine Maillet took their plays abroad with the blessing, and often the financial aid, of the Quebec and federal governments. The advantages of that kind of support are numerous and obvious. The second reason for theater's blossoming in the 1970s is an ideological one. As the Quebec government expanded in the 1960s and early '70s, as it became more autonomous in a number of political areas, its prevailing ideology became, to diverse degrees, receptive to the messages expressed by the new Quebec culture. It was not even necessary to be actively independentist to applaud the nonpolitical plays of Tremblay, Garneau, or Ducharme; hence the good reception this theater got in Ottawa, at the National Arts Centre and among numerous federal bureaucrats. One notable hold-out remained, of course; Pierre-Elliott Trudeau warned that "for men of intellect the talk about energy set in motion by national independence means nothing."[4] But Trudeau here was wrong: tremendous creative energy had been released in Quebec because of the inspirational power of the idea of independence. Even when, as is often the case, plays (or other theatrical manifestations) are not overtly political, the independence of Quebec from Canada is there as a given, as a necessary point in the future, as the condition without which creation becomes impossible. Tremblay, for example, and despite all his popularity in English Canada, remains convinced that "the only way for Canada and Quebec to be friends is to be two countries."[5] Michel Garneau, another seemingly nonpolitical playwright, also claims solidarity with the independentist movement: "Theater is political action," he says. "They gave me thirteen days to think about it in Parthenais prison [during the October crisis of 1970], and I clearly saw the weapon I should choose."[6]

Within this context the electoral victory of the Parti Québécois and the subsequent defeat of the referendum on sovereignty-association are very important for the development of Quebec culture, and especially of theater. The PQ came to power just as creativity in Quebec theater was reaching its highest point; there was a coincidence, in 1976 at least, between the ideology of the PQ and the ideas conveyed by the new Quebec theater. Probably the best example of this is *Un pays dont la devise est je m'oublie* by Germain, first performed 25 March 1976 and throughout the 1976–77 season. It is indicative of Germain's viewpoint—and of the ideology of the new PQ government—that the Maurice Richard riots of 1955 are seen as a turning point in Quebec history. Throughout the play the emphasis is on the individualism of the people of Quebec and on their desire to be free of those who rule them from outside; so the hockey club owners and NHL represent English-Canadian and American power, against which Quebec is asserting itself for the first time.

Both Louis Cyr and Maurice Richard were exploited by Quebec's monied interests, and in the play they know it, but their successes are the only way in which their desire for freedom can be expressed . . . until the riots of 1955. This is where the game between the power structure and the people ended; Maurice Richard became irrelevant, Germain suggests, when the people of Quebec expressed spontaneously their frustration with powerlessness. By refusing to be what the rest of Canada (and the world) thought they should be, by refusing to be submissive and to accept that others control their lives, the people of Quebec, beginning in 1955, started on the route that would, Germain implies, ultimately lead them to their destiny of independence.

Germain's interpretation of history corresponds in an elementary way with the ideology promoted by the PQ, especially during the period leading up to the referendum. The white paper on sovereignty-association makes mention, in its preamble, of the "great laws which have presided, throughout the ages, over the accession of peoples to national sovereignty,"[7] and as the art historian Raymond Montpetit has pointed out, the ideology of the PQ tends to see culture as the projection "not of what we are [but as] what we ought to become to remain faithful to what it is said we have been."[8] The campaign for the *oui* in the referendum of May 1980 can be seen partly as an attempt at popular confirmation of this new ideology of a Quebec destined to be independent. Among intellectuals, at least, the goal of political autonomy was inextricably tied to the development of a new culture and each was impossible without the other. As Marcel Rioux wrote, just before the referendum:

So we believe that it must be said that if we desire sovereignty for Quebec, it is not only to repair the wrongs which have been done to Quebec during this long period of dependence but especially to secure the prospering of culture in the decades to come . . . As one might expect, we are not talking about some vague cultural sovereignty but about a full and entire sovereignty through which a distinct culture can and must become embodied in political and economic institutions.[9]

What is remarkable about Rioux's statement is the role he gives to culture in the independence process; culture has become the vanguard of the movement, powerful enough as a force to permeate the economic and political structure of the country. In fact, the dilemma facing the PQ and other proponents of the *oui* was that the cultural sphere remained well outside the economic and social spheres. Jacques Godbout was certainly right to declare in a postmortem on the referendum that "the independentists had won the oratory contest [and had] once more won independence through discourse."[10] The problem was, as Godbout pointed out, that "our ideas come from France, but our myths, our credit cards, our comfort, come from the United States."[11]

The result of the 1980 referendum was an enormous cultural shock for Quebec precisely because of the inability of many of its intellectuals to separate the discourse of independence from practical concerns regarding sovereignty-association. Even if there remains hope in some quarters that a future referendum might be approved, the rejection of the *oui* was seen as the rejection of the new mythology of Quebec, of the sense of historical destiny. The entire question of Quebec's past and future has become suspended; as the novelist and critic François Hébert points out, "We are falling into the abyss of introspection."[12] Parallel with this postreferendum depression came a disappointment with the Parti Québécois. Hébert calls it "a sort of arteriosclerosis of the spirit" which gradually set in after 1976 and caused the abandonment of the profound raison d'être of the movement in favor of what had been acquired, stabilized, and of the State, too often reduced to its showy manifestations (words and songs, carpets and flags).[13] Confronted with the reality of power, the future seemed to become less important to the PQ than the present, and the creators of the new Quebec culture who had so fervently supported the party began to see themselves abandoned. "It's been six years since they [the PQ] came to power," says the actor/director Jean Duceppe. "If at least they had told us: play! You've got to play! But no, they plague us with forms, and it's the same bureaucrats who keep asking for full accounting before we play, it's worse than before. . . . We've been swindled by the PQ."[14]

Duceppe's and Hébert's bitterness is reflected in a noticeable diminishing of activity since 1980, especially in the realm of theater. Michel Tremblay's cycle of the *Belles-soeurs* ended in 1977 and, with some exceptions, he has turned to prose as a medium of expression. Other "greats" of the 1970s—Robert Gurik, Jean Barbeau, Michel Garneau—have written little or no drama since the referendum.

Because, five years after the referendum, Quebec is divided in its national purpose, theater is no longer part of a nationalist struggle toward self-determination. Governments, federal and provincial, continue to fund productions, but the conjunction of post-referendum blues and a change in Quebec's political leadership (the Parti Québécois has broken up and René Lévesque has resigned) marks the end of the new Quebec theater that began in 1968.

But what has taken its place? Fewer new Quebec plays are being presented in the 1980s, but there still are some, as the increasingly interesting theater review *Jeu* will attest. We can, I believe, divide new dramatic production into three areas. The first of these is experimental and avant-garde drama. A constant in Quebec theater since the 1970s has been the desire, on the part of a substantial number of (usually) young directors and actors to achieve collective production, that is, production in which no single person dominates, in which every participant has an equal hand in creation. Despite the lack of success that Michel Garneau and Jean-Claude Germain had with this type of production in the 1970s, groups like the Eskabel, the Organisation ô, the Théâtre de la Grande Réplique, the Théâtre de Carton, and others continue to create productions that range in form from mime and statuesque poses to politically involved theater with Brechtian overtones. One of the most interesting and original of these experiments has been the Ligue Nationale d'Improvisation of Montreal. Composed of actors, playwrights, and directors, this group performs twice weekly during the season, which is organized (like the Ligue Nationale de Hockey from which it gets its name) into a series of matches topped off by a final play-off. The LNI is a school for both actors and audience, a meeting place for spontaneous creation (on themes proposed by the audience) and honest judgments. It has toured in Europe and is the direct inspiration of similar Ligues in France, Belgium, and Switzerland.

The nature of improvisational, experimental theater is that its creations cannot be reproduced. Some of the productions have been captured on videotape (available at the library of the Université de Montréal) and a few have even been published, but physical presence is such an essential part of this theater that it is inaccessible to those who cannot attend and participate in the productions. "Allowing people to talk after the spectacle is part of the demystification of theater," says the group Théâtre de Carton.[15]

The continued existence of this type of theater attests not only to the constant desire to reinvent forms of theater but also to the persistence of a counterculture movement in Quebec. Experimental theater did not suffer the same kind of depression that more established theater suffered after the referendum precisely because, even in the 1970s, the avant-garde considered itself to be in opposition (from the left) to official or semiofficial ideology. Hence, for example, one finds today in Quebec such groups as Carbone 14 which, in *Marat-Sade* and especially in *Le Rail* (both 1984), present a fusion of video effects and body movement in which the message is more physical than verbal.[16]

One experimental group that is particularly active is called the Théâtre Expérimental des Femmes, and it is the spearhead of another major current in Quebec theater today, women's theater. The movement began with the 1976 collective production entitled *La Nef des sorcières,* a series of monologues by women "each one isolated in her monologue, as she is in her house, with her husband or lover, incapable of communicating her project to other women."[17] Since 1976 women have broken out of their isolation and women's theater in Quebec is now at its most vigorous.

Groups like the Théâtre des Cuisines and the Théâtre Expérimental des Femmes show that there is a strong link between collective creation and feminist theater, but the latter does include some playwrights, the most noticeable recently being Marie Laberge and Jovette Marchessault. The latter has published two plays in a series of three[18] whose purpose it is to bring to public attention the personalities of women writers (from Quebec and elsewhere) seen not through the eyes of literary history (for Marchessault male-dominated and therefore distorting) but through women's eyes. Her purpose is avowedly didactic—"I believe one can change the world through words" she says in *La Saga des poules mouillées*[19] *(The Saga of the Wet Hens)*—and is part of a general feminist searching for a new langauge that allows women to express their thoughts in their own way. There is a sense in which this search for a new type of discourse has links to the questioning of language that took place in Quebec culture in the 1970s—whether or not joual expressed the Quebecois reality better than standard French, whether or not one could write in a uniquely Quebecois style of French. These are questions largely solved today (in theater joual is commonplace; in poetry Miron, Francoeur, Lapointe have found their individual and collective languages). But for feminists the question of language is far from being solved, and this is undoubtedly why Marchessault chooses, in her first play, to represent four Quebec women authors (Laure Conan, Germaine Guèvremont, Gabrielle Roy, and Anne Hébert) each of whom has to come to terms with langauge as a woman and as a *Québécoise*. Actually it is Marchessault who gives these women words; their own discourse (in the form of direct quotes) is surrounded with that which the author provides them in an attempt to end the "night of anonymity, of pseudonyms" (133) from which these authors suffer. The play itself—an extended conversation across time and space—is a kind of rebirth ("perhaps we're bringing ourselves into the world" says Guèvremont [97]) for authors for whom convention prevented the expression, in their own words, of innermost thoughts. In this sense the play is antirealist, in opposition to what the author calls "this realism which only serves to chase us away by denying us words and imagination" (35). A more realist play is *C'était avant la guerre à l'Anse à Gilles* (It was before the war, in Gilles' Cove) by Marie Laberge, a prolific playwright who owes much to Quebec's oral tradition of storytelling and whose heroine in *L'Anse à Gilles*, Marianna, is a strong feminine counterpart to Maria Chapdelaine. It is not only the submissiveness of women in traditional French-Canadian society that Laberge tries to combat in her theater; it is also the past, tradition, the fear of building a new identity in the Quebec of the future. "We wear our past like a fur stole," says Marianna, "our face is buried in it, and we see nothing."[20]

Despite the quality of their plays, neither Marchessault nor Laberge break new ground theatrically. More experimental are productions such as *E* (by the troupe Organisation ô, 1978), *De force je déchire ma camisole* (by the same group, 1980), or *A ma mère, à ma mère, à ma voisine,* (by the Théâtre Expérimental des Femmes, 1978, and published by Editions du Remue-Ménage). These collective creations tend to be more concerned with presenting, often through mime and dancelike movements, the problems involved in the lives of women from youth to marriage and beyond.

The third type of theater that has emerged in Quebec in recent years is less easily categorized than experimental or women's theaters. It has been created by dramatists such as Jean-Pierre Ronfard, René-

Daniel Dubois, and Normand Chaurette. Of these, Chaurette seems to me the most interesting and promising. He has written three plays to date, with the first one, *Rêve d'une nuit d'hôpital* (A hospital night's dream), serving as a model for the two others.[21] What interests Chaurette in all his plays is the writer who goes silent (either through death or madness) at an early age, and in *Rêve d'une nuit d'hôpital* he chooses the ultimate Quebecois example of this phenomenon, Emile Nelligan.

The title of Chaurette's first play is that of one of Nelligan's poems, where he imagines that angels will bring him out of the hospital where he was interned from age twenty until his death. But the title has a more universal meaning for Chaurette; it becomes a metaphor for a prison (the prison of the mind), the final destination of those whose imaginations take them a bit too far; as the dramatist says in his preface, "at the end of the dream there's always the risk of a hospital."[22]

Two theatrical techniques enable Chaurette to make us feel the inevitability of the hospital: a false, theatrical time which contradicts the chronological sequence of events in Nelligan's life and shows how an understanding of his poetry can be accomplished only when the imagination dictates which events preceded others, and the emphasis of a single moment in time (high noon), the summit of the day (and the play), the moment of truth toward which the play inexorably progresses. What makes Chaurette's play particularly interesting is the way in which it exploits the possibilities of the theater to present us with a vision of a poet. Chaurette knows that words are only a part of theatrical language and that total effect is obtained when space and time become part of the dramatist's means of expression. The reality Chaurette presents in this nonrealistic play is of the *poète maudit,* certainly, but it is more than that: it is of the power of the imagination to transform reality into dream, and of the tenuous boundary between the poet's imagination and insanity.

Chaurette's plays, while they show a great measure of dramatic maturity and literary sensitivity, are essentially different in nature from those of the most prominent dramatists of the 1970s. The latter attempted to present, in various ways, a reality of Quebec life which, with some notable exceptions (Gélinas, Dubé) had been absent from the scene; the locus of the plays was often the kitchen (Tremblay, Barbeau), the bedroom (Garneau), the hockey rink (Gurik, Loranger), all recognizably Quebecois decors, implying the familiarity and complicity of an audience that was seen as part of the *grande famille* of Quebec. In contrast to this consciously national theater, Chaurette's plays are not really set in Quebec (*Provincetown Playhouse . . .* takes place in the head of an American author just as *Rêve* takes place in Nelligan's head), and the playwright's desire is to impress a dream world upon his public rather than to ask for their complicity. Other new playwrights show similar differences from their counterparts of the 1970s. Jean-Pierre Ronfard's epic cycle of six plays, *Vie et mort du Roi Boiteux* (1981), takes its audience on an imaginary voyage that spans centuries, continents, and literary cultures; it is the epitome of self-conscious theater. René-Daniel Dubois's *Panique à Longueil* (1980) and his one-man show *Ne Blâmez jamais les Bédouins* (1984) take place in the darkest recesses of the mind where logic and continuity are suspended and where reality and phantasm are intertwined.[23]

These changes in the decors of the plays of the 1980s reveal a change of emphasis that corresponds to the general mood in Quebec. "A theater of interrogation," the critic of *Le Devoir* calls it,[24] and in general this title is correct. Interrogation on the subject of language and identity in women's theater, interrogation on the theme of madness in Chaurette's drama, on the subconscious in Dubois's theater, the theater of the eighties asks questions but provides few answers. Even experimental theater, which seems to have inherited some of the themes and subject matters of the 1970s, is by its very nature a constant interrogation, not only of society but of theater itself.

What we see in Quebec theater in recent years is at once a breakdown of the certainty of national purpose that existed in the seventies and a breaking up of interests and themes into separate, often autonomous areas (especially in the case of feminism). How permanent is this state? One does not know. But it seems likely that, in the absence of consensus about fundamental issues such as nationalism, Quebec theatre will be increasingly interesting in its variety and will continue to give evidence that, whatever the political situation, the spark of creativity that was born in the late 1960s will not soon be snuffed out.

Notes and References

Chapter One

1. See in particular Anne Ubersfeld, *Lire le théâtre* (Paris: Editions Sociales, 1978), 43–46.
2. Jean-Guy Pilon, "Le Québec et le fait français," *Europe* nos. 478–79 (February-March 1969), 15.
3. Jean Bouthillette, *Le Canadien français et son double* (Montreal: L'Hexagone, 1972), 15.
4. Max Dorsinville, "The Changing Landscape of Drama in Quebec," in *Dramatists in Canada*, ed. W. H. New (Vancouver: University of British Columbia Press, 1972), 180.
5. *Mandements, lettres pastorales et circulaires des Evêques de Québec* (Quebec: Côté, 1887), 1:305–6, quoted by Baudoin Burger, "Les spectacles dramatiques en Nouvelle-France (1606–1760)," in *Le Théâtre canadien-français* (Montreal, 1976), 51. Burger gives a complete account of the "Tartuffe affair."
6. Tartuffe was not to be presented in Quebec for some 220 years, not until 1893.
7. Jean Béraud, *350 ans de théâtre au Canada français* (Montreal: Le Cercle du Livre de France, 1968), 13.
8. John Hare, "Panorama des spectacles au Québec: de la Conquête au XXe siècle," in *Le Théâtre canadien-français*, 63. Hare gives a complete history of theater in Quebec from 1790 to 1900.
9. C. P. Lucas, ed., *Lord Durham's Report on the Affairs of British North America* (Oxford, 1912), 2:294–95, quoted by Hare, 79.
10. Antoine Gérin-Lajoie, *Le Jeune Latour* (excerpt), in *Anthologie de la littérature québécoise* (Montréal: La Presse, 1978), 2:166–68.
11. See Jacques Cotnam, *Le Théâtre québécois, instrument de contestation sociale et politique* (Montreal: Fides, 1976), 23–25.
12. Louis Fréchette, *Félix Poutré* (Montreal: Leméac, 1974).
13. Jean-Claude Germain, *Les Faux-brillants de Félix-Gabriel Marchand* (Montreal: VLB Editeur, 1977), 171.
14. Cited by Hare, "Panorama. . . ," 83.
15. Cited by Cotnam, *Le Théâtre québécois*, 106.
16. Anonymous letter published in *La Presse*, 20 April 1901, quoted by Cotnam, 42.
17. Elzéar Roy's address of 30 September 1898, cited by Cotnam, p. 41.

158 FRENCH-CANADIAN THEATER

18. John Hare, "Le Théâtre professionnel à Montréal de 1898 à 1917" in *Le Théâtre canadien-français*, 239.
19. Ibid., 243.
20. Ibid., 245.
21. Béraud, *350 ans de théâtre*, 156.
22. Hare, "Le Théâtre professionnel", p. 246.
23. Jean-Cléo Godin, "Les Gaietés montréalaises: sketches, revues," *Etudes françaises*, 15:1–2, 145.
24. Ibid., 146.
25. Ibid., 147–48. See Chantal Hébert, "Sur le burlesque, un théâtre 'fait dans notre langue,' " *Jeu* 18 (1981):19–31.
26. The name Fridolin, in this French-Canadian context, does not, as it would in France, connote someone of German nationality.
27. Laurent Mailhot, introduction to Gratien Gélinas, *Les Fridolinades 1945 et 1946* (Montreal: Quinze, 1980), 11.
28. Ibid., 13.
29. Gélinas, *Les Fridolinades*, 143.
30. Ibid., 17.
31. Ibid., 155.
32. Ibid., 155–56.
33. Jacques Larue-Langlois, "Tit-Coq porte très bien ses 30 ans," *Le Devoir*, 9 October 1981, 13.
34. Gélinas, *Les Fridolinades*, 265.
35. "This play . . . is . . . the image of our bastardness, our solitude, our 'alienation.' " Normand Leroux, "Tit-Coq," *Livres et auteurs canadiens*, 1968, 73.
36. Jean-Cléo Godin in Jean-Cléo Godin and Laurent Mailhot, *Le Théâtre québécois* (Montreal, 1973), 37. Godin's chapter on Gélinas contains a particularly illuminating analysis of *Tit-Coq*.
37. Gratien Gélinas, *Tit-Coq* (Montreal: Editions de l'Homme, 1968), 44.
38. Ibid., 117.
39. Godin, *Le Théâtre québécois*, 36.
40. See Michel Vaïs, "L'auteur dramatique et la production théâtrale au Québec depuis 1948" in *Aspects du théâtre québécois* (Trois-Rivières: Université du Québec à Trois-Rivières, 1978), 120–22.
41. See *Cité Libre*, no. 23 (May 1959):34–48.
42. Gratien Gélinas, *Bousille et les justes* (Montreal: Editions de l'Homme, 1960), 108.
43. Gélinas, *Tit-Coq*, 197.
44. Marcel Dubé, *Zone* (Montreal: Leméac, 1968), 138.
45. Paul-Emile Racicot, s.j., in *Relations* (March 1953), reprinted in Dubé, *Zone*, 181.

46. Anonymous article in *Métropole* (1 March 1953), 9, reprinted in Dubé, *Zone*, 181.

47. Godin, *Le Théâtre québécois*, 90.

48. Dubé, *Zone*, 35.

49. Godin, *Le Théâtre québécois*, 92.

50. Marcel Dubé, "Problèmes du langage pour le dramaturge canadien-français," *Textes et documents* (Montreal: Leméac, 1968), p. 46.

51. Marcel Dubé, interviewed by Godin in *Le Théâtre québécois*, 83.

52. Marcel Dubé, *Au retour des oies blanches* (Montreal: Leméac, 1969), 144.

53. See Anne Caron, *Le Père Emile Legault et le théâtre au Québec* (Montreal: Fides, 1978), 43–61.

54. Emile Legault, "Quelques notes sur les Compagnons de Saint Laurent (1937–1956)" in *Le Théâtre canadien-français*, 252.

55. Ibid., 251.

56. Ibid., 252.

57. Ibid., 255.

58. Ibid., 257.

59. Ibid., 248.

60. See Caron, *Legault*, 168–180.

61. Quoted, ibid., 76.

62. Gilles Marsolais, quoted in *Centre d'essai des auteurs dramatiques 1965–1975* (Montreal: C.E.A.D., 1975), 11.

63. See André-G. Bourassa, *Surréalisme et littérature au Québec* (Montreal: L'Etincelle, 1977).

64. Paul-Emile Borduas, "Refus global" in *Anthologie de la littérature québécoise*, vol. 4 (Montreal: La Presse, 1980), 415.

65. Ibid., 416.

66. Claude Gauvreau, *Les Oranges sont vertes*, in *Oeuvres créatrices complètes* (Montreal: Editions Parti-Pris, 1977), 1378.

67. Jean-Pierre Ronfard, "Monter Gauvreau, Ducharme, Vézina," *Jeu 21* (1981), 88–89.

68. Gauvreau, *Les Oranges sont vertes*, 1377.

69. Ibid., 1463.

70. Ibid., 1475.

71. Laurent Mailhot, "Orientations récentes du théâtre québécois," in *Le Théâtre canadien-français*, 337 n.64.

72. Gauvreau, *Les Oranges sont vertes*, 1487.

73. Pierre Gobin, *Le Fou et ses doubles* (Montreal: Presses de l'Université de Montréal, 1978), 193.

74. Gavreau, *Les Oranges sont vertes*, 1481.

75. Gauvreau, *Le Coureur de marathon* in *Ecrits du Canada français*, vol. 4 (1958):210.

76. Ibid., 201.
77. Ibid., 219.
78. See Jacques Languirand, *Les Insolites et Les Violons de l'automne* (Montreal: C.L.F., 1962).
79. See, for example, Guy Beaulne's article in *Hebdo-Revue*, 28 April 1956, 18.
80. See Jacques Languirand, *Klondyke* (Montreal: C.L.F., 1971).
81. Yves Thériault, *Le Marcheur* (Montreal: Leméac, 1968), 54.
82. Ibid., 48.
83. Laurent Mailhot, *Le Théâtre québécois*, 71.
84. In Thériault, *Le Marcheur*, 79.
85. The play received a public reading on 4 March 1968 and was performed for the first time on 14 August of the same year.
86. Jean-Louis Roux, "Le Théâtre québécois," *Europe*, nos. 478–79, 228.
87. See Laurent Mailhot and Benoît Melançon, *Le Conseil des Arts du Canada* (Montreal: Leméac, 1982), 185.
88. For more details on this aspect of theater history, see Hélène Beauchamp-Rank, "La Vie théâtrale à Montréal de 1950 à 1970," in *Le Théâtre canadien-français*, 267–90.
89. Hélène Dumas, "c.e.a.d.: un mode d'emploi," *Jeu 21*, 11.

Chapter Two

1. At the Théâtre du Rideau Vert.
2. Zelda Heller in *The Montreal Star*, 25 May 1971; reprinted in Michel Tremblay, *Les Belles-soeurs* (Montreal: 1972), 155.
3. Cf. Tremblay's novel, *La Grosse femme d'à côté est enceinte* (Montreal: Leméac, 1978).
4. Rachel Cloutier et al, "Entrevue avec Michel Tremblay," *Nord* 1 (1971):53.
5. Most of his plays have been translated into English and have been performed in Canada from Ontario to British Columbia; four plays have been performed in the United States (including New York, Washington, Boston); others have been performed in Paris, Rome, and London.
6. For example, in 1972 Quebec's ministry of cultural affairs refused to support a production of the play at the Paris Théâtre de Nations; the Canadian federal government came to the rescue the next year and the play was performed in Paris at the Espace Pierre Cardin.
7. Lise Gauvin, "Littérature et langue parlée au Québec," *Etudes françaises* 10, no. 1 (February 1974):81.
8. Martial Dassylva in *La Presse*, 29 September 1968.
9. Jean Ethier-Blais in *Le Devoir*, 3 April 1971, 11.

10. Cf. the poem by Michèle Lalonde, "Speak White" (Montreal: L'Hexagone, 1974), and her *Defense et illustration de la langue Québécoyse* (Paris: Seghers, 1980). For a point of view opposing that of Tremblay or Lalonde, see Jean Marcel, *Le Joual de Troie* (Montreal: Editions du Jour, 1973).

11. "*Les Belles-soeurs* are in *joual* in the same way that *Andromaque* is in Alexandrine verse," wrote a critic in *Le Monde* (quoted by Donat Valois, "Paris, séduit, redemande *Les Belles-soeurs,*" *Le Devoir,* 21 November 1973, 14). Jacques Poulet praised the "spicey French" of *A toi, pour toujours, ta Marie-Lou* presented for the first time in Paris ("C't'à toé de te débrouiller," *L'Humanité,* 17 October 1979, 10).

12. For an excellent summary of the controversy over joual see Betty Bednarski, "The Humiliation of Canadian French," *Times Literary Supplement,* 26 October 1973, 5.

13. Interview in *Le Magazine Maclean* 9, no. 6 (June 1969):60.

14. Cloutier, "Entrevue," 63.

15. See Maximilien Laroche, "Le Langage théâtral," *Voix et images du pays,* no. 3, 1970, 168–70.

16. Cloutier, "Entrevue," 63.

17. "It's as if I wrote music," says Tremblay (Ibid., 61).

18. Laurent Mailhot in Godin and Mailhot, *Le Théâtre québécois,* 198.

19. Paul-André Bourque, "Masculin-féminin: le rêve triste et la triste réalité," *Nord,* no. 1 (1971), 43.

20. Michel Tremblay, *Les Belles-soeurs,* 94; hereafter page references cited in the text in parentheses.

21. Cloutier, "Entrevue," 56.

22. Tremblay, *La Grosse femme,* 259.

23. Mailhot, *Le Théâtre Québécois,* 195.

24. The popular pronunciation of the word *fermé* in Quebec is *farmé;* hence the pun.

25. Cloutier, "Entrevue," 73.

26. Cf. André Turcotte, "Les 'Belles-soeurs' en révolte," *Voix et images du pays,* no. 3 (1970), 188–89.

27. For Tremblay, Beckett is "the greatest theatrical author of all time" (Cloutier, "Entrevue," 69).

28. The "cycle" includes the following, all edited by Leméac in Montreal: *En pièces détachées* and *La duchesse de Langeais* (1970), *A toi pour toujours ta Marie-Lou* (1971), *Trois petits tours* (1971), *Demain matin Montréal m'attend* (1972), *Hosanna* (1973), *Bonjour, là, bonjour* (1974), *Sainte Carmen de la Main* (1976), *Damnée Manon Sacrée Sandra* (1977). Other recent plays include *L'Impromptu d'Outremont* (1980), *Les Anciennes odeurs* (1981), and *Albertine en cinq temps* (1984).

29. Thérèse is called Hélène in the first version of this play. All quotes will be taken from the second (televised) version.

30. Tremblay's own, this play being the most personal in the cycle.

31. For a detailed analysis of Marcel (called Claude in the first version of the play) see Pierre Gobin, *Le Fou et ses doubles* (Montreal, 1978), 72–76.

32. Cf. André Brassard, interviewed in *L'Envers du décor* 10, no. 7, for whom Serge, along with Carmen (in *Sainte-Carmen de la Main*) is one of the few positive figures in Tremblay's dramaturgy.

33. Cloutier, "Entrevue," 58. Serge would seem to be an exception to this statement, but he is a successful character only because he abandons the traditional male role; his relationship with his sister can be interpreted as a disguise for homosexual tendencies, as members of his family realize (cf. *Bonjour, là, bonjour*, 88).

34. Cloutier, "Entrevue," 73. See also an interview in *Canada Today / Aujourd'hui* 8, no. 6 (1977):12: "The only men I knew, before I was three or four, were children or older men. I didn't know what a grown-up man looked like."

35. Cf. Gobin, *Le Fou*, 219–26.

36. Cf. Ibid., 221. According to Gobin, Bernhardt never did play *L'Aiglon* after having lost her leg.

37. "*A toi, pour toujours, ta Marie-Lou* is really a political play, almost in the first degree. You've got the Quebec of the past, the father and the mother who are submissive, but who at least had enough intelligence to commit suicide." (Tremblay, in Cloutier, "Entrevue," 60).

38. For Tremblay, Carmen represents "the Quebec of the future" (ibid.).

39. Cf. Yves Dubé's introduction to *Sainte-Carmen de la Main*.

40. Cf. Bernard Andrès, "Le Cycle inachevé de Michel Tremblay," *Le Jour* 1, no. 5 (4–10 March 1977):36–37.

41. Adrien Gruslin, "Michel Tremblay achève un premier cycle," *Le Devoir*, 26 February 1977, 15.

42. First produced by La Compagnie Jean Duceppe in the summer of 1976, the play closed after three performances; it had a more successful run, in a modified version, two years later at the Théâtre du Nouveau Monde.

43. Brassard in *L'Envers du décor*, n.p.

44. Yolande Villemaire, "Damnée Manon, Sacrée Sandra," *Jeu*, no. 5, 1977, 105.

45. The Thérèse of *La Grosse femme* is obviously the Hélène/Thérèse of *En pièces détachées;* moreover, Tremblay has dedicated the novel to "Hélène, who rebelled twenty years before everyone else, and who had to bear the consequences" (8).

46. Cf. Michel Vaïs in *Livres et auteurs québécois,* 1977, 188.

47. Tremblay, quoted by Martial Dassylva in *La Presse,* 26 February 1977, D4.

48. Andrès, "Le Cycle inachevé," 37.

49. Cf. Bernard Dort, interviewed by Thérèse Arbic and Robert Chartrand in *Chroniques* 1, no. 4 (April, 1975):17.

50. Cloutier, "Entrevue," 64.

51. With the performance of *Le Chemin de Lacroix* on 26 March in Quebec City.

52. Quoted by Martial Dassylva, "Jean Barbeau et les valeurs oppressantes," *La Presse,* 12 June 1971, C4.

53. Quoted by Martial Dassylva, "Jean Barbeau, sa plomberie et celle des autres," *La Presse,* 17 March 1973, D4.

54. Jean Barbeau interviewed by Aurélien Boivin and André Gaulin, *Québec français,* no. 35, October 1979, 35.

55. Jean Barbeau, *Cahiers de la Nouvelle Compagnie Théâtrale* 13, no. 3, March 1979:3.

56. Jean Barbeau interviewed by Donald Smith, *Lettres québécoises,* no. 5, February 1977, 34.

57. Barbeau, *Cahiers,* 6.

58. Ibid.

59. Barbeau, *Québec françaois,* 33.

60. *Québec français,* 35.

61. As we shall see, Barbeau's titles are often plays on words. "All dressed" is the term used in Quebec, in French and in English, to order a sandwich complete with all the mustard and relishes available.

62. *Cahiers,* 33.

63. Quoted by Murray Maltais in *Le Droit,* 3 April 1971, 23.

64. Cf. John Willet, ed. *Brecht on Theater* (New York: Hill and Wang, 1957), 94–96.

65. Jean Barbeau, *Ben-Ur* (Montreal, 1971), 9; hereafter page references cited in the text in parentheses.

66. Quoted by Dassylva, "Jean Barbeau et les valeurs oppressantes," C4.

67. Quoted by Maltais, *Le Droit,* 23.

68. The term is borrowed from Margaret Atwood's *Survival* (Toronto: Anasi, 1972).

69. Gaston Miron, "Notes sur le non-poème et le poème," in *L'Homme rapaillé* (Montreal: P.U.M., 1970), 127.

70. "Speak White" is an expression used by some English Canadians to shame Quebecois into speaking English; it provides the title for a well-known poem by Michèle Lalonde.

71. Quoted by Michel Beaulieu, "Québec a son auteur à succès," *La Presse* (*Perspectives* magazine), 17 April 1971, 17.

72. Jean Barbeau, *Le Théâtre de la maintenance* (Montreal, 1979), 80; hereafter pages references cited in the text in parentheses.

73. Or, without the religious connotations, Father Emile Legault in Quebec.

74. Cf. Jacques Copeau, *Souvenirs du Vieux Colombier* (Paris: Nouvelles Editions Latines, 1931).

75. *La cour* is stage right, *le jardin* stage left. As for *les frises*, they are the short backdrops used for the sky; the pun here is on *fraises* (strawberries).

76. Quoted by Dassylva, "Jean Barbeau et les valeurs oppressantes," C5.

77. See Laurent Mailhot, "Un certain réalisme poétique: Michel Garneau," in Godin et Mailhot, *Théâtre québécois II* (Montreal, 1980), 189ff.

78. Michel Garneau in *Le Théâtre sur commande* [interview with Roland Lepage] (Montreal: Centre d'Essai des Auteurs Dramatiques, 1975), 40.

79. Quoted by Victor-Lévy Beaulieu, "Les libres propos (et propos libres) de Michel Garneau, *Le Devoir*, 9 February 1974, 16.

80. François Ricard, "Michel Garneau poète et dramaturge," *Liberté*, no. 97–98, January-April 1975, 304, 307.

81. Quoted by Adrien Gruslin, "Michel Garneau et son théâtre public au Festival d'Avignon," *Le Devoir*, 30 June 1978, 29.

82. Garneau quoted by Adrien Gruslin, "La Manufacture ouvre sa troisième saison avec une pièce de Michel Garneau," *Le Devoir*, 15 October 1977, 39.

83. Quoted by Jean Royer, "Michel Garneau et le plaisir du langage," *Le Devoir*, 8 February 1978, 46.

84. Garneau quoted by Martial Dassylva, "Quand un Taureau, ascendant Taureau, s'appelle Garneau," *La Presse*, 14 September 1974, D4.

85. Michel Garneau, *Les Célébrations* (Montreal: V.L.B. Editeur, 1977), 8.

86. Garneau quoted by Rudel-Tessier, "Au théâtre, 1976–1977 aura été l'année de Michel Garneau," *La Presse*, 30 October 1976, C6.

87. Garneau, *Le Théâtre sur commande*, 12.

88. Michel Garneau, *Pour travailler ensemble* (Montreal: La Fondation du Théâtre Public, 1978), n.p.

89. Garneau, *Le Théâtre sur commande*, 14.

90. André Smith, "Michel Garneau," *Livres et auteurs québécois*, 1974, 156.

91. Laurent Mailhot, "Un certain réalisme poétique," 192.

92. Garneau, *La Chanson d'amour du cul* (Montreal: L'Aurore, 1974), 24; hereafter page references cited in the text in parentheses.

93. Garneau, *Les Célébrations*, 58.

94. Garneau, *Sur le matelas* (Montreal: L'Aurore, 1974), 25; hereafter page references cited in the text in parentheses.

95. The play was presented at the Théâtre de la Commune d'Aubervilliers by Gabriel Garran, and later at Paris's Palais de Chaillot and in Bordeaux. It got excellent reviews by both Jean-Jacques Gauthier in *Le Figaro* and Michel Cournot in *Le Monde*. See Adrien Gruslin, "Une plume dépareillée tant au Québec qu'à Paris," *Le Devoir*, 6 November 1976, 15.

96. Garneau, *Quatre à quatre* (Montreal: L'Aurore, 1974), 31; hereafter page references cited in the text in parentheses.

97. Garneau, *Strauss et Pesant (et Rosa)* (Montreal: L'Aurore, 1974), 17 and 23. All further quotes will refer to this edition, the definitive published version of a play Garneau began in 1966 and which went through some seven or eight versions.

98. Mailhot, "Un certain réalisme poétique," 198.

99. Garneau, quoted by Dassylva, "Quand un taureau," D4.

100. André Pagé, introduction to Garneau, *Strauss et Pesant (et Rosa)*, 16.

101. Garneau quoted in "Lecture publique de la dernière pièce de Michel Garneau, 'Le Ravi,' " *Le Droit*, 25 April 1969, 11.

Chapter Three

1. See "Paris semble vouloir clore 'L'affaire Réjean Ducharme,' " in *Le Droit*, 9 February 1967, 12. *Lettres françaises* editorialized: "this little literary scandal won't materialize."

2. Réjean Ducharme, *L'Avalée des avalés* (Paris: Gallimard, 1966); *Le Nez qui voque* (Paris: Gallimard, 1968); *L'Océantume* (Paris: Gallimard, 1968); *La Fille de Christophe Colomb* (Paris: Gallimard, 1969); *L'Hiver de force* (Paris: Gallimard, 1973); *Les Enfantômes* (Paris: Gallimard, 1977).

3. "Ducharme nous écrit," in *Cahiers de la Nouvelle Compagnie Théâtrale* 11, no. 1 (October 1976):22.

4. See Manuel Maître, "Réjean Ducharme va choquer avec 'Le Marquis qui perdit,' " in *La Patrie*, 18 January 1970, 2.

5. See Gilles Marcotte, "Réjean Ducharme contre Blasey Blasey," *Etudes françaises* 11, no. 3–4 (October 1975):249.

6. Ducharme, *L'Océantume*, 112.

7. Ibid., 183.

8. Marcotte, "Réjean Ducharme," 255.

9. Ducharme, *L'Avalée des avalés*, 1.

10. Ibid., 160.

11. See André Major, "La postérité: une nouvelle sensibilité?" in *Le Devoir*, 11 November 1969, 12.

12. Ducharme, *Inès Pérée et Inat Tendu* (1st version), typewritten text, 22–23; hereafter references to this version cited in the text as 1st followed by page number.

13. Ducharme, *Inès Pérée et Inat Tendu* (2d version), (Montreal: Lemeac, 1976), 76. All subsequent quotations will refer to this edition, unless otherwise indicated.

14. This name refers to Paul-Emile, Cardinal Léger, former archbishop of Montréal.

15. In the first version she was called Sister Saint-New-York-de-Russie. Ducharme subsequently rejected this political connotation.

16. The ocean constitutes a key image in Ducharme's works (note that Inès and Inat are born from *water*) and, in part, confirms his affinity to Lautréamont.

17. Laurent Mailhot in *Le Théâtre québécois*, 209.

18. See, for example, Michel Lebel, *"Inès Pérée et Inat Tendu,"* in *Livres et auteurs québécois*, 1967, 190.

19. Michel Dumas (decorator of the 1976 production of *Inès Pérée*), quoted by Bernard Andrès, *"Inès Pérée et Inat Tendu," Jeu 4* (winter 1977), 83.

20. "Le Mot de Rejéan Ducharme," in *Le Devoir*, 25 May 1968, p. 17.

21. Quoted in *Le Théâtre québécois*, 213. Yvan Canuel, the director of the play, suggests that the following incident was at its origin: Ducharme saw a young couple walking by a building in front of which two adolescent boys were loitering. One of the boys whistled at the girl; the girl's male companion promptly walked over and slapped the whistler in the face. "It was the slap on Don Diègue's face," says Canuel (see Martine Corrivault, "Yvan Canuel et la folie du Cid'maghané.' " *Le Soleil*, 19 February 1977, D2).

22. Ducharme, *Le Cid maghané*, typewritten manuscript, p. 1. All subsequent quotations from this play will refer to this edition.

23. Corneille, *Le Cid*, in *Théâtre complet*, vol. 1, (Paris: Garnier, n.d.), 601. All quotations from this play will refer to this edition.

24. For those unfamiliar with Montreal's architecture, it may be helpful to know that many houses have outdoor, wrought-iron curving stairways to the second and third floors.

25. See, for example, " 'Le Cid maghané' au Capitol" in *Le Droit*, 21 September 1968, 15.

26. See Renald Bérubé, "Le Cid et Hamlet: Corneille et Shakespeare lus par Ducharme et Gurik," *Voix et images* 1, no. 1:40.

27. Ibid., 41.

28. Godin and Mailhot, *Le Théâtre québécois*, 210.

29. Corneille, "Avertissement" preceding *Le Cid, Théâtre complet,* vol. 1, 579.

30. Ducharme, *Ah! Ah!,* typewritten manuscript without page numbers. All quotes from this play will be from this version, with act and scene numbers identified. The text was published in 1982 (see bibliography).

31. "If you're a man, if you can't defend me: phone, hurry, find me another job" (1:4) evokes at once Corneille's *Cid* and Ducharme's parody.

32. "Un Party drôle et cruel," press communiqué of the Théâtre du Nouveau Monde issued prior to the play's performance, n.p.

33. Michelle Talbot in *Dimanche-matin,* 19 March 1978, B15.

34. See Jean-Pierre Ronfard (director of the play) in *L'Envers du décor* 10, no. 5, n.p.

35. Godin and Mailhot, *Le Théâtre québécois,* 220.

Chapter Four

1. Antonine Maillet, quoted in "Trois auteurs, trois lettres," *Le Droit,* 25 August 1969, 15.

2. Antonine Maillet, "Ce pays de vaches et de morues," *La Presse,* 13 May 1972, C3.

3. Antonine Maillet, *Rabelais et les traditions populaires en Acadie* (Quebec: Les Presses de l'Université Laval, 1971), 8.

4. Ibid., 8–9.

5. See Laurent Mailhot and Doris-Michel Montpetit, *Monologues québécois 1890–1980* (Montreal: Leméac, 1980).

6. Antonine Maillet, quoted by Paul-André Bourque, "Entretien avec Antonine Maillet," *Nord* 4–5 (1972–1973):126.

7. Mailhot and Montpetit, *Monologues,* 27.

8. Antonine Maillet and Rita Scalabrini, *L'Acadie pour quasiment rien* (Montréal: Leméac, 1973), p. 15.

9. See Jean-Cléo Godin, "L'Evangéline selon Antonine," *Si que* 4 (Autumn 1979):34–35.

10. Maillet, quoted by Bourque, "Entretien," 112, 118.

11. Antonine Maillet, *Les Crasseux* (Montreal: Holt, Rinehart, & Winston, 1968), 68.

12. Antonine Maillet, *La Sagouine* (Montreal, 1974), 90; hereafter page references cited in the text in parentheses.

13. Maillet, *Rabelais,* 15.

14. Antonine Maillet, quoted by André Major, "Entretien avec Antonine Maillet," *Ecrits du Canada français* 36 (1972):15.

15. Antonine Maillet, *Evangéline Deusse* (Montreal, 1975), 27; hereafter page references cited in the text in parentheses.

16. Antonine Maillet in *Revue Théâtre* (Magazine-program of the Théâtre du Rideau Vert) 16, no. 4 (February 1977):n.p.

17. Henry Wadsworth Longfellow, *Evangeline, a Tale of Acadie* (Boston: William D. Ticknor & Co., 1848), 159–60.

18. *Gapi* (1976) is a retelling of a novel, *Gapi et Sullivan*, published in 1974; *Le Bourgeois gentleman* (1978) is a less than successful remake of the Molière play, set in the Montreal of the 1940s, with a Quebecois parvenu, predictably, playing the *bourgeois*.

19. Antonine Maillet, *La Veuve enragée* (Montreal: Leméac, 1977), 168.

20. Ibid.

21. Antonine Maillet, "Interview," *Actualité,* May 1978, 12.

22. See Laurent Mailhot, "Jean-Claude Germain, critique," *Jeu* 13 (Autumn 1979):92–100.

23. "Jean-Claude Germain: au Théâtre d'Aujourd'hui," interview in *Voix et images* 6, 2 (Winter 1981):183.

24. Jean-Claude Germain, "Le théâtre québécois contemporain et son langage," *Canadian Drama* 1, 2 (Fall 1975):25.

25. Jean-Claude Germain, "Entretien(s),"*Jeu* 13 (Autumn 1979):21.

26. Quoted by Mason Wade, *The French Canadians 1760–1967,* vol. 1, (Toronto: The Laurentian Library, 1968), 198, 212.

27. Germain, "Le théâtre québécois contemporain," 24.

28. Jean-Claude Germain, "Théâtre québécois or théâtre protestant," *Canadian Theatre Review* 2 (Summer 1976):9.

29. Jean-Claude Germain, "Un pays c'est avant tout un rêve commun," *Le Pays théâtral* I, 2 (1977–78):n.p.

30. Germain, "Entretien(s)", 62.

31. Ibid., 58.

32. Jean-Claude Germain, in *Bulletin du Théâtre Populaire de Québec* 2, 3 (Winter 1976):n.p.

33. Ibid.

34. Germain, "Entretien(s)," 58.

35. See Robert Claing, "Le Visage à deux faces de Jean-Claude Germain," *Voix et images du pays* 9 (1975):208.

36. Germain, "Entretien(s)," 36.

37. Ibid., 13.

38. See Laurent Mailhot, *Théâtre québécois II,* 132.

39. Jean-Claude Germain, quoted by Micheline Lachance-Handfield, "Ça sera pas un gros show mais un show de gros," *Québec-Presse,* 18 July 1971, n.p.

40. Ibid.

41. Jean-Claude Germain, "C'est pas Mozart, c'est le Shakespeare québécois qu'on assassine," *L'Illettré* 1, 1 (January 1970):2.

42. André-G. Bourassa, "L'Ecole des rêves," *Jeu* 14 (1980):176.

43. Jean-Claude Germain, "Le théâtre québécois libre au pouvoir," *Digeste-Eclair*, February 1969, 9.

44. The "Enfants de Chénier" was the first name of Germain's troupe, which then became "Les P'tits Enfants Laliberté" and finally the company of the Théâtre d'Aujourd'hui. Dr. Jean-Olivier Chénier was a *patriote* hero of the 1837 uprising in Quebec (see Jacques Ferron's play, *Les Grands Soleils*) and *Les Enfants de la Liberté* were what the rebels were called in the same revolt.

45. See Michel Bélair's detailed description in his *Le Nouveau théâtre québécois*, 69–71.

46. Jean-Claude Germain, *Diguidi, diguidi, ha! ha! ha!* (Montreal: Leméac, 1972), 61, 63; hereafter page references cited in parentheses in the text.

47. "Jugements critiques sur *Diguidi*," in Germain, *Diguidi*, 192.

48. See Mailhot, *Théâtre québécois II*, 133, 137.

49. Jean-Claude Germain, *Si les Sansouci s'en soucient, ces Sansouci-ci s'en soucieraient-ils? Bien parler c'est se respecter* (Montreal, 1972), 149; hereafter page references cited in parentheses in the text.

50. Robert Spickler, introduction to *Diguidi* and *Si les Sansouci*, 20.

51. Jean-Claude Germain, interview with André Dionne, *Les Lettres québécoises* 8 (November 1977):18.

52. Germain, "Entretien(s)," 38.

53. Jean-Claude Germain, *Le Roi des mises à bas prix* (Montreal: Leméac, 1972), 33; hereafter page references cited in parentheses in the text.

54. Pierre Gobin, "*Le Roi des mises à bas prix* de Jean-Claude Germain," in *Le Théâtre canadien-français*, 688.

55. Jean-Claude Germain, *Les Hauts et les bas dla vie d'une diva: Sarah Ménard par eux-mêmes*" (Montreal: VLB Editeur, 1976), 69; hereafter page references cited in parentheses in the text.

56. Jean-Claude Germain, interview with Rudel Tessier, "Jean-Claude Germain raconte l'histoire des Québécois," *La Presse*, 27 March 1976, D7.

57. Jean-Cléo Godin, "Un Pays dont la devise est je m'oublie," *Jeu* 4 (Winter 1977):80.

58. Interview with Tessier, D7.

59. Jean-Claude Germain, *Un Pays dont la devise est je m'oublie* (Montreal: VLB Editeur, 1976), 59; hereafter page references cited in parentheses in the text.

60. Jean-Claude Germain, *L'Ecole des rêves* (Montreal: VLB Editeur, 1979), 42; hereafter page references cited in parentheses in the text.

61. Interview with Adrien Gruslin, "Jean-Claude Germain: le rire contre la bêtise," *Le Devoir*, 8 April 1978, 49.

62. Hubert Aquin, "Essai crucimorphe," in *Blocs erratiques* (Montreal: Quinze, 1977), 179.

63. Bouthillette, *Le Canadian français et son double*, 47.

Chapter Five

1. André Major, "Le Chemin du Roy et du rire," *Le Devoir*, 1 May 1968, 15.

2. See Bertolt Brecht, "A Short Organum for the Theater," in *Brecht on Theater* (New York: Hill & Wang, 1964), 190.

3. In *Théâtre québécois II*, 65.

4. Françoise Loranger, *Le Chemin du Roy* (Montreal, 1969), 9; hereafter page references cited in parentheses in the text.

5. Françoise Loranger quoted by Henriette Major, "Que pensez-vous du sentiment nationaliste?" *La Presse* (*Perspectives* magazine), 28 August 1971, 8.

6. Françoise Loranger, *Médium saignant* (Montreal, 1970), 59; hereafter page references cited in parentheses in the text.

7. Quoted by Martial Dassylva, "Françoise Loranger et la peur québécoise," *La Presse*, 6 November 1976, D10.

8. Yvan Canuel, quoted by Michel Bélair, "Yvan Canuel, Médium saignant et le théâtre engagé," *La Presse*, 14 February 1970, 14.

9. Raymond Bernatchez, "Médium saignant, du théâtre servichaud," *Montréal-Matin*, 6 November 1975, 25.

10. Zelda Heller and Michel Bélair, respectively, quoted in appendix to *Médium saignant*, 134, 136.

11. Jean-Claude Germain, "Le Chemin du Roy: un théâtre d'épinal, *Le Petit Journal*, 19 May 1968, 50.

12. Robert Gurik was born in 1932 in Paris and immigrated to Canada in 1950.

13. Robert Gurik interviewed by Marie-Françoise Hébert in *Théâtre et engagement* (Montréal: Centre d'Essai des Auteurs Dramatiques, 1976), 2.

14. *Brecht on Theater*, 192.

15. Ibid., 198.

16. Robert Gurik, *A Coeur ouvert* (Montréal: Leméac, 1969), 39.

17. Hébert, *Théâtre et engagement*, 40.

18. Laurent Mailhot, in his introduction to Gurik's *Hamlet, Prince du Québec* (Montréal: Leméac, 1977), 12.

19. Robert Gurik, *Api 2967* (Montréal: Leméac, 1971), 51; hereafter page references cited in parentheses in the text.
20. Quoted by Gisèlel Tremblay, "Condamneriez-vous Jean-Baptiste M.?" *Le Devoir*, 14 October 1972, 13.
21. Robert Gurik, *Le Procès de Jean-Baptiste M.* (Montreal, 1972), 17; hereafter page references cited in parentheses in the text.
22. Jean-Claude Germain in *Digeste Eclair*, November 1968.
23. His collected political writings can be found in two volumes entitled *Escarmouches* (Montreal: Leméac, 1975).
24. Jacques Ferron, *Les Grands Soleils* in *Théâtre I* (Montreal, 1969), 40; hereafter page references cited in parentheses in the text.
25. Jacques Ferron, *La Tête du Roi* in *Théâtre II*, (Montreal, 1975), 102; hereafter page references cited in parentheses in the text.
26. Jacques Ferron, "Adieu au P.S.D." in *La Revue socialiste*, Summer 1960, article reproduced by Jacques de Roussan, *Jacques Ferron, quatre itinéraires* (Montreal: Presses de l'Université du Québec, 1971), 35.

Chapter Six

1. This chapter appeared in different form in *The American Review of Canadian Studies* vol. 13, no. 2 (Summer 1983):64–73.
2. See Robert Lévesque, "Le théâtre québécois en panne," *Le Devoir*, 11 June 1983, 17.
3. Germain, "Théâtre québécois or théâtre protestant," 9.
4. Pierre Elliot Trudeau, "The New Treason of the Intellectuals," in *Federalism and the French Canadians* (Toronto: MacMillan, 1968), 174–75.
5. Quoted by Lawrence Sabbath in *The Montreal Star*, 11 March 1978, D7.
6. Interview with Roland Lepage in *Le Théâtre sur commande* (Montreal: Centre d'Essai des Auteurs Dramatiques, 1975), 17.
7. *La nouvelle entente Québec-Canada* (Québec: Editeur Officiel, 1979), 3.
8. Raymond Montpetit, "L'Autre culture québécoise," *Critère* 35 (Spring 1983):141.
9. Marcel Rioux, "Le besoin et le désir d'un pays," *Possibles* 4, 2 (Winter 1980):12.
10. Jacques Godbout, "Les bons sauvages," *Liberté* 131 (September-October 1980):7.
11. Ibid., 11.
12. François Hébert, "Québé . . . quoi?," *Critère* 35 (Spring 1983):278.
13. Ibid., 275.

14. Quoted by Robert Lévesque, "Les dix ans la Compagnie Jean Duceppe," *Le Devoir,* 20 November 1982, 17. Duceppe's Company received $308,000 from the Quebec government in 1981–82, the third highest amount accorded a theater in the province. Nevertheless this grant, which has not increased in six years, is grossly insufficient. See Adrien Gruslin, "Subventions 1981–1982," *Jeu* 24 (1982):21–31.

15. Adrien Gruslin, "Le théâtre de Carton veut toucher une nouveau public," *Le Devoir,* January 13, 1979, 17.

16. See *Jeu* 32 (1984):147–51.

17. *La Nef des sorcières* (Montreal: Quinze, 1976), 7.

18. *La Saga des poules mouillées* (1981), and *La Terre est trop courte, Violette Leduc* (1982).

19. Jovette Marchessault, *La Saga des poules mouillées* (Montreal, 1981), 15; hereafter page references cited in parentheses in the text.

20. Marie Laberge, *C'était avant la guerre à l'Anse à Gilles* (Montreal: Leméac, 1981), 116.

21. These are *Provincetown Playhouse, juillet 1919, j'avais 19 ans* (1981) and *Fêtes d'automne* (1982); all his plays are published in Montreal by Leméac.

22. Normand Chaurette, *Rêve d'une nuit d'hôpital* (Montreal, 1980), 21.

23. On Ronfard's play (Montréal: Leméac, 1981) see *Jeu* 21 (1981):105–114; Dubois's *Panique à Longueil* was published by Leméac in Montréal in 1980; on his *Ne Blâmez jamais les Bédouins,* as yet unpublished, see *Jeu* 32 (1984):87–97.

24. Robert Lévesque, "Le théâtre québécois en panne," 17.

Selected Bibliography

The following selection of books is intended for the reader who understands French and wishes to pursue the subject of Quebec theater. Some English translations of plays exist, and these are listed in section 2 of Primary Sources. Unless otherwise specified, place of publication is Montreal.

PRIMARY SOURCES

1. Principal Dramatic Works

JEAN BARBEAU
Ben-Ur. Leméac, 1971.
Le Théâtre de la maintenance. Leméac, 1975.

NORMAND CHAURETTE
Rêve d'une nuit d'hôpital. Leméac, 1981.

RENÉ-DANIEL DUBOIS
Panique à Longueil. Leméac, 1980.

RÉJEAN DUCHARME
Inès Pérée et Inat Tendu. Leméac et Parti Pris, 1976.
Ah! Ah!, Lacombe/Gallimard, 1982.

JACQUES FERRON
Théâtre I (contains *Les Grands Soleils*). Déom, 1969.
Théâtre II (contains *La Tête du Roi*). Déom, 1975.

MICHEL GARNEAU
Quatre à quatre. VLB Editeur, 1979.
Strauss et Pesant (et Rosa). VLB Editeur, 1979.

JEAN-CLAUDE GERMAIN
Si les Sansoucis s'en soucient, ces sansoucis-ci s'en soucieront-ils? Bien parler c'est se respecter! Leméac, 1972.

Un Pays dont la devise est je m'oublie. VLB Editeur, 1976.

ROBERT GURIK
Le Procès de Jean-Baptiste M. Leméac, 1972.

MARIE LABERGE
C'était avant la guerre à l'Anse à Gilles. Leméac, 1981.

FRANÇOISE LORANGER
Le Chemin du Roy. Leméac, 1969.
Médium saignant. Leméac, 1970.

ANTONINE MAILLET
La Sagouine. Leméac, 1974.
Evangéline Deusse. Leméac, 1975.

JOVETTE MARCHESSAULT
La Saga des poules mouillées. Editions de la Pleine Lune, 1981.

MICHEL TREMBLAY
Les Belles-soeurs. Leméac, 1972.
A toi pour toujours ta Marie-Lou. Leméac, 1975.
Sainte Carmen de la Main. Leméac, 1976.
Damnée Manon sacrée Sandra. Leméac, 1977.

2. Selected Works in English

MICHEL GARNEAU
Four to Four. Toronto: Simon and Pierre, 1978.

ROBERT GURIK
Api 2967. Vancouver: Talonbooks, 1974.
The Champion. Toronto: Playwrights Canada, 1974.

ANTONINE MAILLET
La Sangouine. Toronto: Simon and Pierre, 1979.

JOVETTE MARCHESSAULT
The Saga of the Wet Hens. Vancouver: Talonbooks, 1983.

MICHEL TREMBLAY
Les Belles-soeurs. Vancouver: Talonbooks, 1974.
Forever Yours, Marie Lou. Vancouver: Talonbooks, 1974.

Sainte Carmen of the Main. Vancouver: Talonbooks, 1981.
Damnée Manon, sacrée Sandra. Vancouver: Talonbooks, 1981.
On Tremblay: Renate Usmiani, *Michel Tremblay.* Vancouver: Douclas and
   McIntyre, 1982.

SECONDARY SOURCES

1. Books on Quebec theater
Bélair, Michel. *Le Nouveau théâtre québécois.* Leméac, 1973.
Hébert, Chantal. *Le Burlesque au Québec. Un divertissement populaire.* Hur-
   tubise H M H. 1981.
Dassylva, Martial. *Un Théâtre en effervescence.* La Presse, 1975.
Godin, Jean-Cléo, and Laurent Mailhot. *Le Théâtre québécois.* H M H,
   1970. *Théâtre québécois II,* H M H, 1980. Essential reading, excellent
   bibliographies.
Gobin, Pierre. *Le Fou et ses doubles.* Presses de l'Université de Montréal,
   1978.
Lavoie, Pierre. *Pour suivre le théâtre au Québec. Les ressources documentaires.*
   Québec: Institut Québécois de Recherche sur la Culture, 1985.
Le Théâtre canadien-français. Volume 5 of the *Archives des lettres canadiennes.*
   Fides, 1976. A variety of articles.

2. Theatrical Journals
Jeu, the primary theatrical journal in Québec, began publication in 1976
   (4 issues yearly). See particularly volumes 12 (theater production
   1976–1980), 16 (women's theater), 21 ("un théâtre qui s'écrit"), 25
   (on production techniques), 33 (on acting). Other theater journals
   include *En bref* (published by the Centre d'Essai des Auteurs Dramatiques) and *La Grande Réplique* (published by the theater of the
   same name).
Spirale, founded in 1979, appears ten times a year; it contains articles on
   all literary genres.
Lettres québécoises (founded in 1976) appears quarterly and contains articles
   on texts and productions.
Etudes françaises (published by the Université de Montréal), *Etudes littéraires*
   (published by the Université Laval), and *Voix et images* (published by
   the Université du Québec à Montréal) also contain valuable articles,
   as does *Livres et auteurs québécois* (published yearly).
Two theater reviews published in English Canada often contain articles
   on French-Canadian theater: *Canadian Drama / Art dramatique canadien*
   and *Canadian Theatre Review.*

Index